Praise for *Fair Food*

A *Boston Globe* Bestseller

"The author displays a wide-ranging knowledge of production, consumption, natural resources and public policy. He also writes about reform efforts with contagious energy and palpable authority. . . . An important, accessible book on a crucial subject. Food for thought and action."

—*New York Times*

"Hesterman has written a book that just might wake you up and get you to care about what's going on with the food you eat and how it gets to your table. I've got to admit, this reporter covering food news cracked open his book a tad wary. Would this highly educated and well-meaning agronomist-activist guy really offer anything new to the sustainable food conversation, I wondered, and more importantly, would he speak to regular people trying to feed their families in a tough economy and who might not understand the difference between grass and grain-fed (or why it matters)? Boy was I wrong and thrilled to stand corrected. Hesterman breaks free from a tradition of densely written, muddled prose intended for inside baseball players and instead speaks to us all, loud and clear."

—Civil Eats

"Over many years, Oran Hesterman has fought to make access to good food a reality and right for all Americans. *Fair Food* . . . illuminates a clear path toward a more sustainable, fair, and delicious future."

—ALICE WATERS

"Hesterman's upbeat outlook and gentle push toward activism inspired me to further my own engagement. His book is one of the best I've read on how we as individuals can be involved in the future of America's food system."

—Serious Eats

"This focus on the things that are working makes *Fair Food* an inspiring and enjoyable read. There are numerous books setting out 'what's wrong' with global food production, but Hesterman—while offering a powerful summary of such issues from a north American perspective—describes initiatives across the country that are putting things right. They may be isolated cases but, in offering a model both to policymakers and to grassroots consumers, they deserve attention in the US and beyond."

—*The New Agriculturalist*

"Hesterman . . . aims to change the landscape of who gets to eat what and how it gets to us. He has outlined what's gone awry and how it might be repaired in his new book, *Fair Food: Growing a Healthy, Sustainable Food System for All.* . . . Hesterman's work follows a library's worth of books and movies that have questioned the wisdom of enormous corn and soybean farms, the morals of food advertising, the dangers of fast food diets, the health of confined animal feeding operations and more. But while Hesterman argues that the status quo is not working, he hopes to inspire readers to do more than plant tomatoes in their yards. He wants a food system that values "equity, diversity, ecological integrity and economic viability," and much of the book is taken up with examples of people and institutions working toward a just food system."

—*Los Angeles Times*

"Hesterman's message represents an important evolution in the increasingly popular trend of growing and consuming healthier food. He takes nothing away from the backyard garden or the organic restaurant—change has to start somewhere. [But] real political engagement is key. It's the only way to realign the billions of dollars in public monies spent to prop up a food network that produces lots of cheap eats at low cost, but to damaging consequence to our diets, farmland, environment and safety."

—*The Jewish Daily Forward*

"Oran Hesterman convincingly argues that reinventing our food system is crucial for improving the health of our cities and our economy—policy makers are wise to spend time considering the ideas he lays out in this book."

—RICK SNYDER,
Governor, State of Michigan

"In recent years, there have been dozens of books and films documenting the dangers and problems in our current food system but *Fair Food* is one of the ones that is truly exceptional. This excellent book is an enlightening and inspiring plan to change not only what we eat but how our food is grown, packaged, delivered, and sold."

—*The Tucson Citizen*

"In a very comprehensive and insightful way, *Fair Food* examines the problems of a broken food system, and puts forth bold—and doable—strategies to redesign a system that is healthy for people, communities, and the environment."

—PolicyLink Equity Blog

"Intended as a practical guide for community food activists who want to take the locavore movement across race, class, and city lines, this book illuminate ways in which consumers can become "engaged citizens." Especially important (and rare) is Hesterman's willingness to work constructively with corporate giants like Costco and the Kellogg Foundation. The dedication to social justice is clear, genuine, and logically argued as a food issue. A helpful and hefty final chapter of "Resources" provides readers with a comprehensive national listing of organizations to join, support, or replicate."

—*Publishers Weekly*

"Superb, important, and tremendously readable. From eating healthily to understanding the Farm Bill, this is a great book."

—NIGEL SAVAGE,
Executive Director, Hazon

"The author's deft explanation of our current cultivation and consumption of food should have families moving away from their supermarket aisles and into farmers' markets and community-supported agriculture programs. A thorough, inspiring guide on how to restructure the food system for a long and healthy future, for consumers and legislators alike."

—*Kirkus Reviews*

"Oran Hesterman has been both a longtime pioneer in the movement and, at the same time, a pragmatic visionary about food systems change. *Fair Food* is a book that many of us have been waiting for."

—JOSH VIERTEL,
President, SlowFoodUSA

"Hesterman's *Fair Food* is an encyclopedia of interesting projects being done around the nation to try to fix our broken food system, and not just for the rich and powerful. Hesterman's book is a call to action—a practical guide for what to do if you care about good food for all, not just for those who can afford it."

—*The Chicago Reporter*

"Timely and inspiringly optimistic, *Fair Food* challenges and guides readers toward sustainability and health, for themselves and their communities."

—*Ode Magazine*

"Dr. Oran Hesterman has illustrated a long-standing commitment to increasing the access to healthy foods for inner city residents, while also doing what he can to support our local farmers."

—BARBARA LEE,
Congresswoman and former chair,
Congressional Black Caucus

"*Fair Food* is a serious book about a serious subject. It offers ideas for local communities, as well as suggestions for local, state and national policy makers (I hope members of the Legislature read this book!) It should add immeasurably to the national conversation about fixing our food—and world!—for the better."

—*The Clarion-Ledger*

"Truly a 'How-to Guide' for changing the way our food is grown and distributed, *Fair Food* sheds light on the often hidden food disparities in America, while also giving solutions to recreating the system."

—*New York House*

"The body of work that Oran's leadership and support enabled has set the stage for the possibility of seeing our food system change within our lifetime. While there are plenty of trend-followers scrambling to lay claim, Oran is more than the real deal—as is this book."

—MICHEL NISCHAN,
Chef and President/CEO, Wholesome Wave

"With an emphasis on community, Hesterman puts into writing what our celebrity chef culture commonly puts on television but breaks it down for the everyman. Ordinary people, who are not farmers or foodies, will feel empowered after reading this book."

—*Edible Buffalo*

"Our food chain is broken. And never in the history of mankind has there been such a need to get back to basics—plain food, grown in a logical manner and delivered to everyone—rural and urban. In *Fair Food*, Oran Hesterman makes the case that this move is imperative and sustainable."

—NANCY L. SNYDERMAN, MD, FACS,
NBC News chief medical editor

FAIR FOOD

Growing a Healthy, Sustainable Food System for All

ORAN B. HESTERMAN, PhD

Founder, Fair Food Network

PUBLICAFFAIRS
New York

Hardcover edition first published in 2011 in the United States
by PublicAffairs™, a Member of the Perseus Books Group
Paperback edition first published in 2012 by PublicAffairs

PublicAffairs books are available at special discounts for bulk purchases
in the U.S. by corporations, institutions, and other organizations. For
more information, please contact the Special Markets Department at the
Perseus Books Group, 2300 Chestnut Street, Suite 200, Philadelphia, PA
19103, call (800) 810–4145, ext. 5000, or e-mail
special.markets@perseusbooks.com.

Book Design by Brent Wilcox

The Library of Congress has cataloged the printed edition as follows:
Hesterman, Oran B.
    Fair food : growing a healthy, sustainable food system for all /
Oran B. Hesterman.—1st ed.
        p.   cm.
    Includes bibliographical references and index.
    ISBN 978–1–61039–006–4 (hardcover)
    ISBN 978–1–61039–007–1 (electronic book)
    1. Food supply—United States.   2. Sustainable agriculture—United
States.   3. Food industry and trade—United States.   I. Title.
HD9005.H47 2011
338.1'973—dc22

                                                                2010053129

ISBN 978-1-61039-102-3 (paperback)
ISBN 978-1-61039-204-4 (paperback e-book)

10 9 8 7 6 5 4 3 2 1

This book is dedicated to the many people who are focusing their lives and their work on creating a fair food future. These thousands of fair food "solutionaries" are not content to leave the work to others: in their homes, in their communities, and across the nation, they are working to ensure that current and future generations will enjoy a food system that is healthy and sustainable for us all.

CONTENTS

PREFACE TO THE REVISED
PAPERBACK EDITION

The movement to create a healthy, sustainable food system for all has grown quickly and become strong—even in the year since *Fair Food* was first published. Some call it the Fair Food Movement, the Good Food Movement, or the Slow Food Movement, but no matter what you call it, more people are buying and eating locally grown, sustainable/organic food, and more farmers are on the land producing for this expanding market. Since the initial publication of *Fair Food*, the number of farmers' markets in the United States has increased by 17 percent, the USDA says that local food is now a $5 billion market, and congressional leaders introduced a Farm Bill framework that eliminated direct payments to commodity farmers and introduced the idea of a federally funded healthy food incentive similar to Fair Food Network's Double Up Food Bucks program in Michigan (described on pp. 59). Change in the food system is happening—not yet deeply enough for me and others who are committed to a healthy, sustainable food system to declare victory and go home, but sufficient to give me hope that our collective work over many decades is starting to pay off and that now is the time for many more conscious consumers to engage as fair food citizens.

When *Fair Food* was first published, I decided to promote the book in an unconventional fashion: to contact the vast network of leaders and activists with whom I have worked throughout my career and ask them to help host events in their cities. These events would not be book readings, but rather opportunities for the food system activists and advocates in their locale to gather for a real-time networking event, a chance to introduce new people (especially young ones) to the movement, and to introduce *Fair Food* as a new resource for the field. I often have called it a "tool book"—like a toolbox—for the movement. I had no idea how this concept would work, but as a first-time author with the greatest resource at hand being the network of relationships I have been fortunate to build over my career in many and varied aspects of food systems change, I thought this was the most logical way to proceed.

Did we succeed? Some indicators: close to 5,000 people attended these events in more than twenty-five locations, from Brooklyn to Berkeley and at many stops in between, including Ann Arbor, Chicago, Boston, Philadelphia, Washington, D.C., and Los Angeles; at least half of the audience members at each of these events were in their twenties and thirties; we know of ten colleges and universities that started using the book as a classroom text during the first semester after publication; and connections were made in real time and are moving the movement forward. What excited me most about these events were the interactions I had with the young people there. On many occasions, after I would conclude my short presentation and offer shout-outs to organizations and leaders doing great food systems work locally, I would sit down to sign books and personally meet many of those attending the event. And I would find that many of those standing in line were students (some were even in high school) or recent college graduates absolutely on fire about the issues of food access and food justice. These young people could not wait to introduce themselves to me, to get their books signed, and to share with me in excited tones the work they were doing (from rooftop gardening in Brooklyn to incubator kitchens in San Francisco to moviemaking in Hollywood). They were eager to ask me such questions as where they might consider applying to graduate school to prepare themselves for a significant career in this field. What hope and inspiration I have gained from those conversations!

I set many long-term goals and intentions for *Fair Food*, but an experience in the Seattle area illustrates the best of what I am trying to achieve.

On the evening of October 17, 2011, I spoke at Village Books in Bellingham, Washington. Attendance was not overwhelming—about twenty-five people overall, with very modest book sales. During the Q & A session that followed, a young woman sitting with two young men asked me my thoughts on how to get better food into the dining service at Western Washington University, where all three were freshmen. She said that students living on campus are required to purchase a meal plan and that she would much prefer to spend her money on a plan that includes more fair food.

I used this opportunity to describe the Real Food Challenge, an organization founded by college students working to transition 20 percent of all university food service purchasing to local and sustainable sources by 2020—a $1 billion shift. I told these three students that I describe the program in my book and provide contact information.

Then, when I said that every state has a regional coordinator for the Real Food Challenge, another young woman sitting in the front row jumped up and said, "I am the Real Food Challenge coordinator for the Pacific Northwest." Her name was Emma, and by the time we left that bookstore, the Western Washington University chapter of Real Food Challenge was on its way to being organized—right there in the store.

Before I left, Emma and I exchanged business cards, and I told her that on Thursday evening I was due to speak at the University of Puget Sound in Tacoma, Washington, about three hours south of Bellingham. I also told her that if she could make it, I would introduce her to the students. She attended the talk, and when I described the Real Food Challenge as one way college students can become fair food "solutionaries," I invited Emma on stage to explain the program and her role in it. Later, when I was finding my way to the back of the auditorium to sign books, I noticed Emma huddling with a group of students. By the end of the evening, the University of Puget Sound chapter of the Real Food Challenge had been birthed.

Selling and signing books is great fun, and I love giving public lectures. And certainly the media attention is an important part of the mix. But the progress we made toward a fair food system that week with the students at Western Washington University and the University of Puget Sound is really why I wrote the book.

Sharing the concepts and ideas of *Fair Food* has provided a great education for me. The staff at Fair Food Network and I have learned a lot about social media and how to use the power of Facebook, Twitter, and YouTube to connect people with ideas for changing the food system and to join together more of the activists in this movement. In fact, in several places of this paperback edition we have included QR codes so that you can use your smart phone to directly connect to important websites (such as the Fair Food List) as you read the book.

I have learned a lot about my own connections to hardworking and committed leaders all across the country who are trying to make our food system healthy for our families, our communities, our economy, and our environment. In the coming years, I look forward to many more opportunities to meet with other movement leaders to share ideas about how to work together to shift our food system, and to continue recruiting an "army of solutionaries," so that our children and grandchildren have a chance to grow and thrive amid a food system that supports their health and well-being.

Oran Hesterman
January 2012

INTRODUCTION

Many of our country's systems are in need of repair. We have an education system that is failing some of our youth and ultimately compromising our future. We have a health care system whose costs are spiraling out of control, leaving many without insurance coverage and depriving more and more low-income and working families of adequate medical care. We rely on an energy system that will not sustain us in the future. And we have a financial system that has come close to melting down.

But there is another system that gets much less attention than it deserves, even though we all rely on it to keep us alive—if we are lucky, three times a day: our food system. When a system we depend on to meet essential needs isn't working, the consequences are enormous. The food system that evolved to bring us abundant food at low cost has grown out of control, nourishing us by destroying some of what we hold most precious: our environment, our health, and our future. The problems it has engendered—from agricultural chemical runoff in our rivers, streams, and oceans, to soaring rates of diet-related illness (such as diabetes) in our inner cities, to the loss of prime farmland due to urban and suburban sprawl, to corporate conglomeration that concentrates 80 percent of our meat supply in the hands of only four companies—are not isolated issues to be solved one by one. Rather, they are symptoms of a food system that is broken and needs to be redesigned.

With any broken system, the place where the dysfunction is most acute is in our inner cities. Take one city, Detroit, which stands out as the most troubled of them all. Detroit is enormous. At 138 square miles, it could encompass San Francisco, Boston, and Manhattan all at once, yet it has lost residents and jobs at an alarming rate. Designed to accommodate more than two million people, it houses fewer than 900,000, and its citizens live among almost 130,000 abandoned homes.

At around 24 percent, Detroit's official unemployment rate is one of the highest in the nation, but when we consider those who are not receiving unemployment benefits, the actual jobless rate is closer to 35 percent.[1] One in every three people lives below the poverty line. The federal government pumped more than $480 million worth of food stamps into the city in the past year,[2] but less than 10 percent of the stores where these benefits can be redeemed are considered grocery stores or supermarkets. Many of these benefits are spent at what are considered "fringe" retailers, such as gas stations, liquor stores, party stores, dollar stores, bakeries, pharmacies, and convenience stores.[3]

Good food has all but forsaken Detroit. The last two supermarket chains moved out in July 2007, making it the only big city (the eleventh-largest in the United States) without any major supermarkets. Most of the city's residents would have to travel more than twice as far to reach a grocery store as they would to get to a corner store. Many rely on gas stations, liquor stores, or convenience stores for their food. It's not uncommon to be asked in Detroit, "What gas station do you buy your groceries at?"

If we want to repair this broken food system and create a chance for a healthy generation of Americans, we need to start in cities like Detroit. The men and women of this city, like many others, want change. They recognize the gaps in their diet and enjoy cooking. They'd love to have access to the fresh produce available at suburban supermarkets, but transportation difficulties keep them away. "People would walk to their neighborhood store if it offered a selection of healthy, fresh produce and if it was clean and safe. . . . There's so much excess demand for that kind of thing in our local neighborhoods," one Detroiter told me recently. "You can't get any produce," fumed another. "And the children, they don't even know what produce is. I was picking a pea pod this morning, and none of the children knew what a pea pod was. Never heard of it."

These men and women feel overlooked. Ignored. Disrespected. While there is the beginning of a national conversation about our food system that sings the praises of backyard vegetable gardens and pricey organic produce, the people of Detroit don't even have a supermarket.

Along with my colleagues in the fair food movement, I am thrilled that the country has finally started talking about what we eat and where our food comes from. But conversations don't build grocery stores or make fresh food more affordable at inner-city farmers' markets. The advice to "eat food, mostly plants, not too much" doesn't help if, as Chicago Congressman Bobby Rush once pointed out, you can buy ketchup where you live, but not fresh tomatoes.

The food system is failing Detroiters and many other families who live in what the U.S. Department of Agriculture (USDA) has termed "food deserts," places where access to healthy food is severely limited. But actually the system is failing us all. Even those of us who live in "food oases" and have enough money to buy virtually any food product from any place in the world are living with the fallout of a broken system.

These symptoms all point to a system that is working poorly for us at this moment in history. But *Fair Food* is not a book primarily about how broken the system is. Rather, it is a book that aims to foster the creation of a redesigned system, one that is healthy for people, communities, and the environment. To redesign that system, we need to understand that the one we have was developed at a time when we needed lots of cheap food and needed to encourage farmers to produce it. Plentiful, affordable food for all is still a vital need and an essential objective for a redesigned system.

Good food means a lot to me. Because I suffer from ulcerative colitis, otherwise known as Crohn's disease, my efforts to find food that soothes my symptoms have led to numerous revelations about the healing power of a good diet. In addition, I've devoted my entire thirty-five-year career to making sure good food is available and affordable for everyone. In the 1970s, long before "organic" was a word in the national vocabulary, I started an organic alfalfa sprout farm; in the years since, I've worked as a farmer, food salesman, university professor, and president of a foundation focused on food issues.

As a scientifically trained agronomist, I know what it takes to grow good food, from the right climate conditions and soil pH levels to the best fertilizers and crop-rotation sequences. While I was a professor of agronomy at Michigan State University, I spent several years as a consultant to the W. K. Kellogg Foundation, one of the oldest and largest philanthropic institutions in the United States. In 1996, I left academia to work as a full-time program director at the foundation, first leading its Integrated Farming Systems and then its Food and Society Programs. For fifteen years, I co-directed the largest philanthropic program in sustainable food and agriculture that had ever been developed. During that time, the Kellogg Foundation granted more than $200 million to organizations attempting to shift food and agriculture systems in their communities and through public policy. In 2008, I left Kellogg to start Fair Food Network, a new institution committed to building a more just and sustainable food system. This national nonprofit organization has projects on the ground in Michigan focused on creating greater access to healthy, fresh, and sustainably grown food, especially in historically underserved communities. We also work to change public policy so that it facilitates greater access to healthy food while supporting local small and midsize farmers to produce it.

While many of our country's systems are in need of repair, if we do not fix the food system, efforts in all of the other areas will be for naught. We are, after all, living creatures, a species that, just like any other on this planet, needs to eat to survive. Our relationship to food is the most basic relationship we have with our environment—

whether we are environmentalists or not. The natural ecological systems of soil, water, and air are needed to produce every ingredient of every meal. If we do not feed ourselves in a way that sustains our environment, our agriculture, and our communities, then as a species we are not long for this world. So while we focus attention on education, health care, and energy, we also need to focus our attention on fixing the broken food system.

With most other large systems, we must rely primarily, if not solely, on our policy makers and industry leaders to act on our behalf. We can write letters, attend meetings, and try to make our voices heard on local and national levels. But in the long run, there is little that one individual, family, or neighborhood can do to fix the broken education or energy system.

With the food system we can have more impact. We can take responsibility for fixing it both through individual decisions *and* through collective action. As individuals we can make different choices about what we purchase and what we eat. We can choose to support a more local and sustainable agriculture and can decide to eat in a way that keeps us healthier. We can join with other concerned individuals to demand different food at our children's school cafeteria and at our college food service. We can plant backyard and community gardens. We can shop at farmers' markets. All of these individual actions can and will make a difference in our own lives and in the food system—now more than a $1 trillion economic engine in our national economy—but they alone will not produce the kind of change we need.

At the same time that we shift our own food habits, we also need our policy makers and industry leaders to work toward a redesigned food system—one that provides safe, healthy, and nutritious food to all our residents in a manner that protects our natural resource base for future generations. As is the case with the health care problem and the energy problem and the environmental problem, if we're going to solve the food problem we need to look at bigger, systems-level solutions and not get caught up in the small stuff.

Not sweating the small stuff is a principle that President Barack Obama understands. In the run-up to the 2008 election, *Newsweek* caught him in a great off-the-cuff moment. During a prep session for a debate among the Democratic candidates, he was riffing on what he'd say if moderator Brian Williams asked him a fluffy question, for example, what he did every day to make the world a greener place. "Well," he said, "the truth is, Brian, we can't solve global warming because I f—ing changed light bulbs in my house. It's because of something collective."[4]

He's right. Changing your incandescent lightbulbs isn't a bad thing, but if you really want to impact the course of climate change, other goals should be higher on your list of priorities, such as new laws and economic incentives that will create lasting change. You won't solve much by staying in your house. I know that the president and the First Lady care deeply about sustainable eating, and the lightbulb principle applies there, too. The vegetable garden on the south lawn of the White House is a wonderful symbol and an inspiring action, and the first family's focus on ending childhood hunger while also tackling the tricky issue of childhood obesity is admirable. But it will take more than symbolic gestures to truly change the food environment for kids and their parents. It will require redesigning our food system, which is the focus of this book.

Fair Food is divided into three parts. The first part discusses our current food system, how and why it evolved as it has, and the ways in which it is no longer serving us well. Part Two describes four key principles a redesigned food system should embody and offers examples of how various individuals and organizations have started to integrate these principles, providing inspiring new models for farmers and foodies, businesses and communities. Finally, Part Three offers a practical guide to how you can participate in precipitating big, collective changes in our food system, from your kitchen to your community to your statehouse and the White House. I'll give you questions to ask about community-supported agriculture and at farmers' markets; tools for starting Buy Fresh, Buy Local campaigns in your community; advice for forming buyers' clubs that purchase food directly from farmers and fishermen; and guidance about the legislation you should support at the local, state, and federal level so that your dollars and your votes encourage the development of an efficient, sustainable food economy. Throughout these pages, many of the examples I use to illustrate what a redesigned food system might look like focus on plants or crops rather than meat or livestock. This is a reflection of my orientation as an academically trained agronomist and not because I think animal agriculture is any less important.

This book, a product of my long career and ground-level experience, is intended to add needed perspective and pragmatism to a shelf dominated by journalists and chefs. Michael Pollan, Eric Schlosser, and their peers have compellingly documented and aroused public concern about the full extent of our food problem and have been passionate advocates for reform. But they haven't shown us exactly what we need to do to make sustainable farming and eating a reality. They write from interviews, reading, and observation. I write from experience, based on years of training in agricultural science, and my years of practice evaluating, funding, and assessing the results of sustainable food and agriculture projects nationwide.

I'm not saying that these writers' books aren't useful, or that they haven't contributed an enormous amount to the fair food movement. But you can't go to a journalist or a chef for advice about how to bring fresh, sustainable food to everyone. That would be like coming to me for advice on how to prepare a great tomato salad. I could give you my amateur opinion as a food lover who cooks, but my specialty is how to redesign the food system so that we all have access to tasty tomatoes grown in environmentally friendly ways. My concern isn't only about bringing back heirloom tomatoes to farmers' markets or demonstrating in my upscale restaurant how much more delicious my tomato salad is for using them. My concern is making sure that those living in inner-city neighborhoods have access to tomatoes in a form other than a ketchup packet at a fast food joint.

National change is not going to come from upscale restaurants and backyard gardens alone. It's going to come from the kinds of people you will meet in this book. Now that nearly everyone with the means to subscribe to the *New York Times*, shop at Whole Foods, or eat at expensive locally sourced restaurants is doing so, the time for systemic, practical, and widespread action is at hand. And I can't wait to show you how to do it.

PART I

Our Broken Food System

CHAPTER 1

The System and Its Dysfunctions

A system, according to Merriam-Webster, is "a regularly interacting or interdependent group of items forming a unified whole" or "an organization forming a network for distributing something or serving a common purpose." In a household security system, motion detectors, wires, alarms, and monitors interact to warn authorities of intruders and to keep the homeowner's property safe.

All parts of a system need to be in place and functioning for the system to carry out its purpose: if even a single wire shorts out in the car, the entire electrical system is at risk. The order in which the parts are arranged will affect the performance of the system, and every system, when working properly, creates something that is more than the sum of its parts. A car battery and a bunch of wires, lights, a starter motor, and windshield wipers won't do me much good just lying side by side on the garage floor. But when they are put together in the right order and location—voilà! My car starts, lights up the road at night, and keeps the windshield clear of raindrops.

Just like a car's electrical system, our food system has many components, from soil, water, and sunlight to inputs such as seeds and fertilizer, to equipment including tractors, planters, cultivators, and harvesters, to the knowledge of the farmers themselves, and these are all just in the realm of production. As we consider the food system in its entirety, from production, to processing, to distribution, to retail sales, to consumption, the number of components is staggering. While we can argue the fine points of the purpose of our food system, the major purpose, obviously, is to provide nutrition to keep us all alive.

One way to understand what I mean by "food system" is to follow a single crop from field to fork. In 2011 corn was harvested on 85 million acres of land in the United States (about 27 percent of the total cultivated farmland in the country).[1] Since this grain is grown on more acres of cultivated farmland than any other single crop in the United States, let's see what happens as it moves through the parts of our food system.

Food *production* occurs on farms and ranches. This involves everything from preparing fields, selecting crops and seeds, planting and cultivating, ensuring adequate soil fertility so the plants have all the nutrients they need to grow, managing pests (such as weeds, insects, and diseases), harvesting the crop, and then managing the crop residue in the field.

When you think about corn, the image that comes to mind likely is of a late summer picnic, a bowl or basket piled high with ears of roasted sweet corn, salted, dripping with butter, and ready to devour. Actually, in terms of acreage planted and harvested, this type of corn represents only about one-half of 1 percent of the total corn crop grown in the United States.[2] "Field" corn, or #2 dent corn in agricultural parlance, is the predominant kind of corn cultivated by farmers across the country. It is grown in virtually every state in the continental United States but is concentrated in the "corn belt," an area ranging roughly from Nebraska to Pennsylvania.

A farmer typically plants corn seeds at a rate of 30,000 to 35,000 seeds per acre, which is equivalent to 20 to 25 pounds per acre.[3] Since corn typically is measured in bushels, and each bushel of corn weighs 56 pounds, on average, a farmer plants about four-tenths of a bushel per acre in the spring, after some type of tillage or cultivation (mixing) of the soil to break up clods, kill any visible weeds, and prepare the seedbed, and after applying fertilizers (at least the three major fertilizer macronutrients: nitrogen, phosphorus, and potassium). From after WWII until the past decade or so, farmers would use what's known as a preemergent herbicide, which is sprayed on the field after planting but before the seeds germinate and the crop emerges above the soil surface, to prevent the growth of weeds early in the season. Additional herbicide and insecticide applications come later in the season, along with more nitrogen fertilizer. Increasingly, farmers are now planting a "Roundup-ready" seed, which has been genetically modified to tolerate a broad-spectrum herbicide, one that kills any green plant with which it comes into contact. This allows the farmer to plant the corn seeds, wait until the corn emerges, and then spray the entire field with an herbicide that kills every plant in the field except the herbicide-tolerant corn.[4]

In the fall, the corn crop matures quite uniformly, thanks to the fact that every plant in the field is genetically identical—one of the traits we get by using hybrid corn. The farmer then harvests the crop with a combine, which strips the cob off the plant and the kernels off the cob. The only plant part that the farmer harvests for sale or use is typically the kernel. The corn kernels are then dried out to reduce the chance of an insect infestation or mold developing during storage. The corn is stored either on the farm for later sale or is hauled to a local grain elevator for more immediate sale.

On average, the 0.4 bushel of corn planted in the spring has turned into about 150 bushels per acre by harvest time. For 2011, the estimated U.S. average corn yield per acre was 148 bushels,[5] for a total estimated harvest of 12.6 billion bushels.

Once the crop (or animal, in the case of meat production) is harvested, the next step is *processing*. Some food products are processed only minimally. Fresh fruits and vegetables, for example, may only get washed, sorted, and packaged for consumers. Milk gets cooled, separated into component parts, and bottled. Other crops, including much of the field corn and soybeans grown in the United States, become ingredients for a myriad of processed products. Of the total field corn crop harvested in 2010, about 43 percent was used to feed domestic livestock and 13 percent was exported, also primarily for animal feed. Thirty-four percent was processed into ethanol for fuel. The remaining 10 percent of the crop was processed and used in thousands of products.[6] Out of the more than 38,000 items found in a typical full-service grocery store—from breakfast cereal and cheese spread to mustard and beer, more than 25 percent contain corn in some form or another.[7] Field corn finds its way into industrial products as well, everything from adhesives and paint to shaving cream.

In our current food system, meat processing is a complex undertaking that is regulated and subject to federal inspection to maintain food safety. The Office of Food Safety oversees the Food Safety and Inspection Service (FSIS), the agency within the USDA responsible for ensuring the safety, wholesomeness, and correct labeling and packaging of meat, poultry, and egg products. FSIS operates under the authority of the Federal Meat Inspection Act, the Poultry Products Inspection Act, and the Egg Products Inspection Act. FSIS sets standards for food safety and inspects and regulates all raw and processed meat, poultry, and egg products sold in interstate commerce, including imported products.[8]

Over time, many authors, from Upton Sinclair to Eric Schlosser, have given us graphic, often quite disturbing descriptions of the meat processing industry. For example, Schlosser recounts his experience working a night shift in a slaughterhouse. He paints a vivid picture of sharp knives swinging as he wades through ankle-deep blood and dodges cattle carcasses traveling along conveyers hung from the ceiling. He writes about this "most dangerous job in the United States . . . with injury rates three times higher than the rate in a typical factory." One of the reasons the injury rate (mostly due to cuts with sharp knives) is so great is that the workers, who are paid a paltry wage, are being pushed to slaughter and process carcasses at rates of up to four hundred cattle per hour on a single line.[9] (I know a few folks who decided to switch to a vegetarian diet after reading his book.)

After processing, the next key step in the system is *distribution*. In the United States, the average distance that a food product travels from its point of production to a dinner plate is 1,500 miles.[10] Whether it moves by truck, train, or air, most of our food is involved in a complex and resource-intensive distribution system. One way to measure the energy intensiveness of a system is through an energy audit, which analyzes the total energy inputs in a system compared to total energy output. Both inputs and outputs can be expressed with a common energy unit, the calorie. According to an energy audit of the U.S. food system, our food system consumes 10.3 calories of fossil fuel energy to create 1.4 calories of food energy.[11] Much of this energy (more than 30 percent) is used in packaging, transportation, and retail/food service sales. And it is not only in terms of energy that we have a resource-intensive food system. To produce just one bushel of field corn takes nearly 4,000 gallons of water.[12] To put this in the simplest terms, it takes the equivalent of nearly eighteen flushes of an average toilet to produce a single pound of corn.

Ultimately our food finds its way to the next stop in our food system, *point of sale*. Whether you buy it at a grocery store, restaurant, or convenience store, your dinner has traveled through a vast system and many hands. Products that contain ingredients from corn plants grown on those corn-belt farms find their way into wholesale and retail outlets and are distributed far and wide. And while the system for sweet corn might be a bit simpler, it still can have many varied components, depending on the end product (fresh, canned, or frozen corn).

But wait—that's not the end of it: in any system, we need to follow the entire cycle of the product. So we might think of the last stop in our food system as *waste*. All those parts of our meal that we do not eat—including packaging, wastewater and chemicals from processing, and food that is prepared but not eaten—end up either in a landfill or a compost heap to be recycled back into soil. And, I suppose, we need to consider the waste products that come out of our own bodies, too. The part of the consumed food that is not incorporated into our bodies is excreted and ultimately becomes part of another system—our sewage system.

In generations past, the food system was much simpler. When a majority of our population lived in rural areas and engaged in agriculture, the system was much more localized. Farm families grew most of what they ate and long-distance distribution was a rarity. As our society became urbanized and fewer families were directly involved in producing or even aware of the source of their food, our system needed to evolve to serve those inhabitants of our growing cities. In 1810, 93 percent of the U.S. population lived in rural areas and only 7 percent were city dwellers. By 1900, an additional 33 percent of our population had migrated to the cities. In 1950, only 36 percent of our residents made their homes in rural communities, and our cities had swelled to hold 64 percent of the country's residents. In 1990, more than three-fourths of our population lived in urban areas.[13]

The Industrial Revolution affected the food system as well. Technological advances in machinery, crop genetics, and agricultural chemicals have all played a role in creating the most productive food system the world has ever seen in terms of the amount of food produced and the number of people being fed. Each U.S. farmer is estimated to be providing food for 155 people, including those in the United States and those outside the country who are eating food grown here.[14] Given that statistic, you might imagine that the average U.S. corn yield was not always in the range of the 160 bushels per acre that it is today. The year I was born, 1951, corn yields averaged only 37 bushels per acre. When I started graduate school in 1979, yields had increased to 109 bushels per acre.[15] This steady increase is due to a combination of better crop genetics (especially with corn hybrids) and advanced technology, including tillage, planting, and harvesting machinery, and the ability to apply synthetic fertilizers at specific rates to optimize plant growth. Many of these advances have been fueled by one of the best-funded and -supported public research systems for agriculture in history.

A food system that allows less than 2 percent of our population to feed the rest of us (yes, less than 2 out of every 100 people living in the United States are farmers or ranchers) is exactly the system you want to free the other 98 percent to develop other sectors of our economy, such as manufacturing, health care, social services, the arts and sciences, and education.

If the vast majority of our people power had still been engaged in farming, we would not have educated and trained generations of engineers and physicians and businesspeople; we might not yet have benefitted from phenomenal discoveries such as antibiotics or cures for devastating diseases; we would never have seen the information revolution that now connects us all through television, computers, the Internet, and smart phones. We would never have had the concentrated time and brain power to develop air transportation or sophisticated institutions of higher education. Advances in the food system enabled our society to rapidly develop in other areas. They also enabled many smart and motivated farm kids to pursue education in the science of farming and agriculture. Some of these well-educated farmers' sons and daughters became scientists and helped develop such areas as soil biology and chemistry, agricultural engineering, and plant and animal genetics. Scientific discovery and application in agriculture have fed information and new practices and technologies into our food system in ways that created even greater specialization and centralization. For example, advances in plant breeding and crop genetics enabled the development of new crop varieties and hybrids that have reduced the problem of endemic hunger in places such as Asia and South America.

Along the way, public policies were enacted to help the food system become so productive while at the same time keeping consumer prices relatively low. President Abraham Lincoln established the USDA in 1862, and over the past century, federal and state governments have implemented policies to support advances in agriculture through research and education. Perhaps the most significant example is the policies that created the land-grant university system.

Starting in the late 1800s, the federal government gave each state land that it could sell specifically to raise money to create public universities dedicated to research and education supporting agriculture and rural communities. In 1913, Congress also created the cooperative extension service, which has responsibility to extend scientific discoveries from university research to farmers, food processors, manufacturers, and distributors. These research and outreach institutions have trained generations of high-tech farmers and have developed the basis for most scientific advances in agriculture and food in the past century.

Policies have also been enacted to conserve soil and water resources. From creation of the Soil Conservation Service (now called the Natural Resources Conservation Service) at the USDA to local soil and water conservation districts in most rural counties, a small army of technicians has helped farmers create and implement plans to keep soil in place (such as contour plowing, a method that follows a field's topographical features to minimize the risk of soil erosion when it rains) and to keep sediment and agricultural chemicals from entering the water system (such as buffer strips, which are plantings of trees, shrubs, or other perennials along streams and rivers so that soil is less likely to run into the water). Without these technicians and without cost-sharing to help farmers implement conservation solutions—both funded with public money— our highly productive and specialized food system would have caused much greater environmental damage than it has.

During the Depression and Dust Bowl of the 1930s, several important pieces of legislation were passed to shield farmers from price volatility and provide them with a basic level of income security while protecting vital natural resources. The Agricultural Adjustment Acts of 1933, 1938, and 1940 and the Commodity Credit Corporation Act of 1948—now joined into what we refer to as the Farm Bill—created what we refer to today as the commodity programs. The basic goal of the original commodity programs was to maintain prices to farmers by controlling the supply of nonperishable crops (such as corn, soybeans, wheat, and cotton) in the marketplace. Over the years U.S. agriculture policy has, for the most part, moved away from attempting to control supply or establish price but has maintained a commitment to protecting the income of farmers who grow tradable, nonperishable crops. Sometimes these farm policies are referred to as crop subsidies, and sometimes they are called direct payments. No matter what they are called, these policies have been in place for more than seventy years, encouraging farmers to grow crops that are produced on large acreages and are now ingredients for many of the processed and prepared food products that we find on our grocery store shelves. While these policies were devised primarily as a way to maintain economic viability for farmers and rural communities, they were also created and have been continued partly to ensure an abundant food supply at low cost to the consumer.

These crop subsidies (now called direct payments) have become one of the most contentious issues in the agriculture policy arena. Many people believe that they no longer serve the purposes for which they were intended, no longer really benefit either rural communities or consumers, and are now largely about the politics of rural elections and maintaining revenue streams to those who have become used to them. These subsidies, currently provided to specific farmers as direct cash payments, have become, in essence, incentives for farmers to produce as much as they can per acre of a very limited number of crops. The good news is that when the Farm Bill is reauthorized in 2012 or 2013, these direct payments likely will be eliminated and replaced by an expanded crop insurance program. The economic incentive to produce more per acre has always been strong in the production part of the food system. After all, if a farmer has fixed costs in land, machinery, and irrigation, the additional cost for more seed and fertilizer to produce a greater yield per acre is minimal compared to the potential increase in revenue from the higher yield. To give you an idea of what it costs to farm "commodity" crops today, here are a few figures. A modern corn planter costs between $75,000 and $100,000, and a combine can run up to $200,000. Add in a tractor and tillage equipment, and the costs for equipment alone are more than half a million dollars.

With these kinds of policies and incentives in place, it made complete sense for farmers to become more specialized in their production. With larger and larger acreages to manage, larger machinery was called for—and not every machine can be used for every crop. So some farmers specialized in producing corn or soybeans, others in wheat or barley. Still others specialized in producing vegetables or fruit, and others specialized in producing livestock. Specialization in agriculture and the food system is really no different from specialization in any other sector of our economy. A company focused on producing automobiles rarely makes tennis shoes. And even automobile manufacturing has become more and more specialized, with one company making only windshields and another only floor mats.

Specialization in the manufacturing sector is often considered a natural outcome of economies of scale—the costs of production per unit become lower as the number of units produced increases—and comparative advantage, or the ability of one firm or group of firms to produce a product more economically than another due to the relative advantage of available resources, whether favorable climate or cheap labor. During the past century, a time of great expansion of manufacturing and industry, agriculture has often been viewed as just another sector of industry, with both economic and policy incentives in place that encouraged farmers to "get big or get out." Some of these incentives, such as farm commodity payments, have driven farmers to plant more and bigger acreages of a single crop.

Unlike other industries, however, farming—and ranching—are not just economic systems: they are also biological systems. Farmers need to make decisions about what they produce based on their particular climate and soil, and many of the inputs (rainfall, solar radiation, disease incidence) are largely out of their control. But despite this fundamental difference, advances in industrial, chemical, and information technology have allowed farmers to treat their fields more like controlled manufacturing plants than living biological organisms.

Back when we had many fewer people to feed and what seemed like an endless supply of soil and water, we could get away with this approach. Agricultural professionals, whether they worked in the Central and Salinas Valleys of California producing fruit and vegetables for the rest of the country or the Great Plains producing corn and soybeans, began to view the farm as a big factory floor. Their focus, as in any other manufacturing endeavor, was on the inputs and the yields. The system we have in place is still largely based on this outdated concept that agriculture is part of the manufacturing sector.

As specialization became a more common feature of our food system, so did centralization. If, due to the forces of specialization as well as their particular climate and soil, farmers in a particular area primarily produce corn and soybeans, then it also makes sense for the companies that purchase corn and soybeans to locate their grain elevators in that same area. Food wholesalers and distributors have also become more centralized as they have taken advantage of the same economies of scale as farmers. Even in the retail food sales part of the system, centralization has evolved as a key feature. As long as most people have ready access to a car or other form of transportation and can afford the gas, it makes sense to build 40,000- to 60,000-square-foot grocery stores and supermarkets to sell food to urban and suburban consumers. Busy shoppers can find everything they need under one roof, and retailers can spread their fixed costs over a much larger total sales amount.

This specialization and centralization has also led to a feature known as concentration: for some parts of the food system, only a few companies control the vast majority of commerce. Two examples: in the meat slaughtering and meatpacking industry, the USDA reports that 80 percent of all our beef, 70 percent of our lamb, and 65 percent of our pork in the United States is slaughtered, packed, and sold by only four companies. And in the retail sector, the four largest grocery firms—Wal-Mart, Kroger, Safeway, and Supervalu—account for 47 percent of all sales. (We can see similar patterns if we look at grain trading and coffee or cocoa processing.) According to one expert, one of the reasons for this kind of concentration in the meatpacking industry is that theories of antitrust changed in the 1980s to focus on consumer welfare, defined as the prices consumers pay, as the main test of whether consolidation was harmful. Since food prices were not going up as the meatpacking industry consolidated, the government stayed out of the way. This view of antitrust ignored the impact of consolidation on producers or workers. More recent consolidation (say, in the past ten years) in both the meatpacking and grocery sectors may have more to do with the exigencies of either serving or competing with Wal-Mart, now the largest single grocery retailer in the United States.[16]

The evolution of our food system has enabled our country's food and agricultural producers to become global players. In fact, our president and Congress tout agricultural exports as the primary means to balance our trade with other countries. We purchase cars, electronics, and clothes made elsewhere because other countries can produce these goods and get them to us for less money than domestic manufacturers can. Likewise, our capacity to produce huge amounts of low-cost agricultural products, fostered by policies that pay farmers to do so and by our very productive soils and farm technology, allows us to sell our agricultural products for less money than it costs to produce those same products in other countries. We are living in an era of globalization, and that extends to what we eat. Many of the food products you purchase at a grocery store could have been grown and processed literally anywhere in the world. The grapes at a grocery store in California could have been grown in Chile or within 100 miles, and unless you examined the label closely, you would never know (and sometimes you can't tell even with the label).

Another consequence of our highly centralized and specialized food system is that it led to distribution systems reliant on increasingly scarce and expensive liquid fuels for transportation. When oil was relatively cheap, it made more economic sense to transport food across the country. The cost of the energy and fuel to chill and ship spinach and strawberries from California to New York was low enough to be relatively inconsequential, easily absorbed into the price that consumers paid. As fuel becomes more expensive, the economic advantage of centralization and long-distance transport decreases.

According to estimates we calculated at the Kellogg Foundation in 2007, only about 2 percent of food purchased in the United States comes from local and sustainable sources. The system that brings us the other 98 percent of all our food is exactly the kind of system we would expect to evolve given the policies that have been put into place over time. Our policies—based on specialization, centralization, concentration, and globalization—encourage the production of abundant food at low cost. That's the good news. The bad news is that the system is now producing unintended consequences that most of us don't want. These consequences are all symptoms of a food system that is broken, not because the policies that created it were necessarily bad policies for the time in which they were created, but because the *context* has changed. Today we understand how careful we need to be with our finite resources of clean water and fossil fuel energy. We now see the long-term environmental cost for the broad use of chemical fertilizers and pesticides we once thought benign. Many of the consequences of our current food system we could not have seen coming when the industrial age began or when the policies were first put into place, but these unintended consequences can no longer be ignored.

Other unintended consequences of the way our current food system is organized include these, which I will explore in more depth in Chapter 2:

- Declining food quality. When fruits and vegetables are produced for long-distance transport and long-term storage, the product's hardiness—its ability to maintain shape, integrity, and appearance—becomes more important to growers than taste and nutrient concentration. Studies are starting to show that fruits and vegetables eaten many days (or sometimes weeks) after harvest have significantly lower nutrient density than those eaten within a day or two of harvest. And in terms of taste, anyone who has compared a fresh tomato from a garden or a farmers' market with those on most grocers' shelves can immediately detect the difference in quality.

- Compromised food safety. One promise of a centralized food system was that food safety protocols, such as regular inspection for disease organisms, could be standardized and implemented at a single point of packing or processing. But when a system becomes so concentrated, any glitch in safety protocol can have consequences that quickly spread far and wide, and it may take weeks (or months) to determine the source of food toxicity. Food recalls due to safety issues are becoming more common and more serious. I am writing this today on the heels of a large and deadly outbreak of Listeria in cantaloupes. In 2010, a single egg production company in Iowa (I guess we would call this a farm?) was forced to recall more than 380 million eggs produced by its hens at five plants in Iowa, due to risk of salmonella. These eggs were distributed from this one company under at least fifteen brand names across at least four states. If the same number of eggs had been produced by dozens of farmers spread out across the country, it is unlikely that the recall would have had to be so large, and a salmonella problem, if it arose, could be contained much more easily.

- Animal welfare concerns. Concentrating so many livestock in confined animal feeding operations creates living conditions that animal welfare activists find unacceptable. And when so many animals live in such close quarters, the use of antibiotics to avoid spread of disease is increased, raising concerns about the spread of antibiotic-resistant bacteria to both animals and humans.

- Soil erosion and depletion. The increasing specialization in crop production has resulted in an increasing reliance on monoculture (growing the same crop in the same field year after year). This type of farming can create many additional problems, including a greater incidence of pests and diseases. When monoculture corn is produced, for example, there is a greater risk for loss of both soil quantity and quality. Some of the practices that produce the highest corn yields in monoculture— such as moldboard plowing, turning the soil over each year, and leaving the ground bare, as opposed to using cover crops between seasons so that the ground is covered with crop residue—are also those that render the soil most susceptible to wind and water erosion.

- Water pollution. When food production is so specialized and concentrated, there is a greater need for fertilizer nutrients for crop production. One consequence of the high rates of fertilizer use is that some of the nutrients in the fertilizer (such as nitrogen and phosphorus) end up leaving the crop field and polluting either surface waters (lakes, rivers, streams) or groundwater by leaching through the soil down to the aquifers.

- Separation of crops and livestock. When crops and livestock are raised on the same farm, the waste from one part of the system (animals) becomes a valuable resource for the other (fertilizer). By disconnecting these two components of the food production system, animal manure becomes a source of pollution due to its high concentration in a small area. And synthetic fertilizers, which replace the crop nutrients formerly provided by animal manure, are applied in ways that result in additional contamination of rivers and streams with nitrogen and phosphorus.

- Loss of farmland. As our population has become more concentrated in urban areas, the threats to productive farmland have become more real and dangerous. American Farmland Trust, the premier national organization that works on this issue, estimates that we are losing prime farmland at a rate of almost 3,000 acres per day.

- Energy consumption and greenhouse gas production. According to the World Resources Institute, agricultural production accounts for just over 6 percent of total greenhouse gas emissions in the United States. Worldwide, agriculture accounts for just over 16 percent of total emissions. If we include processing, packaging, and distribution, overall the U.S. food system accounts for 15 to 20 percent of total energy use within the United States. Much of this energy comes from packaging and distribution, which are more energy-intensive as the distance that food needs to be transported from point of production to where it is eaten increases.

- Problems of food access and food security. One consequence of our highly concentrated and centralized food system is that many residents of historically excluded urban communities, and some rural communities as well, have little access to healthy, fresh food, or are food insecure, which means that all household members do not have access at all times to enough food for an active, healthy life. The USDA conducted a study to determine the number of people and families in the United States who live in what they term a "food desert." One conclusion from this study is that more than 57 percent of those living in low-income areas have limited physical access to supermarkets or grocery stores.

- Diet-related illness. Lack of access to healthy food on one hand and the abundance and relatively inexpensive cost of heavily processed and packaged food products on the other have fostered increasing rates of obesity, diabetes, and other diet-related illnesses. This is especially a problem in low-income communities but increasingly is being seen in more affluent communities as well, in the United States and around the world. It appears that one unintended consequence of a food system that focuses on abundant production of crops from which ingredients are extracted for highly processed food products is that too many of us are eating too many calories of the wrong foods and gaining weight, with all of the attendant health problems.

- Worker exploitation. Large farms and concentrated processing facilities require enormous labor forces, and many rely on migrant workers or undocumented residents for that labor. Opportunities for exploiting them abound. Most of these workers are underpaid, receive no medical benefits or disability insurance, and are offered housing that is only marginal at best. In the fields, many of these workers are exposed to toxic chemicals in the form of pesticides and insecticides.

- An aging farmer population. As farming has become more specialized and concentrated, the cost of establishing a farming operation has risen dramatically—so dramatically, in fact, that it is nearly prohibitive for young people to get into farming as a profession, unless they inherit land and equipment from a relative or are brought into the business by family at a young age. This has led to an aging of the farming population. By most estimates, the average age of U.S. farmers is close to sixty years. I am quite certain that the authors of food and agriculture policy over the past eighty years have not intentionally sought to diminish our farm population through retirement— but this unintended consequence is upon us.

As we look at all the unintended consequences of our current food system, it seems clear that we will not be able to solve these problems one by one. For starters, we can't find enough Band-Aids to fix all the broken parts of this system, and if we do try to repair the system problem by problem, we are likely to create new problems with each one we solve. Instead, we need to imagine the food system of the future, one that could serve us and the planet well for generations to come, and then think about how to embed the features of that system into both institutional practice and public policy.

Public awareness about the negative consequences of the current food system is building. Authors, journalists, chefs, and filmmakers have helped increase this awareness over the past decade. Many of us know the difference between purchasing a factory-farm-raised chicken and a free-range organic chicken and are taking steps to shift our own purchasing and eating habits. Farmers' markets are exploding in number all over the country. Organic and local foods are two of the fastest-growing segments of the grocery industry in terms of sales.

But the percentage of our food system that is local and organic is still very small. While planting a vegetable garden and supporting local farmers are great steps, they are not transformative enough on a sufficiently large scale. I am not proposing that we return to some kind of agrarian society, and I don't think that we need to abandon features of the system that are working for us now. I am a scientist and believe that many of the advances that have been made are very positive, and I am confident that future discoveries will help advance the food system in sustainable and equitable directions.

In essence, I believe that the food system has spun out of balance and out of harmony with the natural cycles on which it is based. On the continuum between specialization and diversification, we have veered too far toward the specialization side. We are similarly out of balance on the continua of centralization-decentralization, concentration-dispersion, and globalization-localization. There are policies and practices that we can collectively put into place that will help bring the system back into greater balance, but first, let's take a closer look at some of the problems caused by our current food system.

CHAPTER 2

The Problem Is . . .

I can't count the number of conversations I have had that begin with
"The *real* problem with the food system is . . . " And here we can fill
in the blank with:

- Pesticides
- Corporate agriculture
- Bad policy
- Too much sugar (or fat or salt or high fructose corn syrup) in
  our food
- Too much processed food
- All those commercials peddling bad food to kids
- Soda vending machines in schools
- Bad school lunches
- Not enough government money for school food
- Tainted food imports
- Lax food safety standards or enforcement
- Urban sprawl covering over prime farmland
- Organic food being too expensive
- Food deserts
- GMOs
- Insufficient label information
- Subsidies

- "Big Ag" lobbyists
- Overirrigation
- Overfertilization
- Migrant labor
- Soil erosion
- Unfair treatment of farmworkers
- Individuals making bad choices
- Hunger in such a wealthy nation
- Insert your answer here

At other times, I find myself in conversations with people whose view is along the lines of "I can walk into any number of super-markets in my city and buy whatever I want pretty much any time. And from spring through fall, I can go to the weekly farmers' mar-ket and purchase great local food directly from the farmer. I don't see any problem with our food system at all." To those friends, I usually say, "If you live in the right place and have enough money, it can appear that the food system is functioning just fine. Just like the health care system seems to function for those of us who have decent insurance and access to competent medical care." But if you take a closer look at our food system, the picture isn't as rosy.

The symptoms of our failing food system—whether related to the environment, diet and health, or social inequities—are real, and to fix them will take a redesign of the system, not a series of iso-lated fixes or individual measures. Scientists are generally very good at pinpointing individual symptoms, and here is what they have to tell us.

The Environment

Soil and Water

The two most precious resources for growing food are soil and water. Without them, we would all go hungry. While this may seem like an obvious statement, our food system as currently designed is not doing a particularly good job of protecting these resources for future generations. Let's first look at soil.

Soil erosion means that soil particles are dislodged from their location in a field and carried someplace else by water or wind. In most cases, the soil particles are eventually deposited as silt in rivers, streams, and lakes. In fact, this type of sediment is considered the largest contaminant of surface water when measured in both weight and volume.[1] Once these soil particles leave the field, they are lost forever as a basis for food production. Soil anchors the roots of plants so they can grow in one spot, and the soil system supplies plant roots all the nutrients (except atmospheric CO_2) and water needed for growth. As we lose soil particles in the field, we lose plant productivity. Without the addition of greater and greater amounts of chemical fertilizers, crop yields decline.

"But isn't soil a renewable resource?" you ask. Yes, soil is not like fossil fuel. Natural processes are forming it all the time. The issue is that we are losing precious topsoil at a much faster rate than it can be replaced by natural formation. It takes hundreds of years for soil to be created, while it can be lost to erosion in a single season. The average erosion rate on U.S. cropland is about four tons per acre per year, which exceeds the average rate of soil formation by ten times in the best scenario.[2]

For many decades, soil erosion has been a severe problem in many of the most productive agricultural ecosystems in the United States. Some experts tell us that half of the best topsoil in Iowa has been lost to erosion in the past 150 years of farming,[3] and due to the rolling topography of Iowa farmland and the predominance of corn and soybean production, very high rates of erosion (about twelve tons per acre per year) are still an issue there.[4] To put this in perspective, this is equivalent to losing about thirteen large wheelbarrow loads of soil on a typical quarter-acre suburban lot every year. In another highly productive area, the Palouse region in the Pacific Northwest, about 40 percent of the rich topsoil has been lost to erosion in the past one hundred years.[5]

Another issue is salinization, the process by which salt accumulates in the soil. It may occur naturally but has become a significant issue in some areas that rely heavily on irrigation for crop production. When crops are grown in areas that rely on natural rainfall, salts don't tend to concentrate in the upper soil layers. Instead, they are flushed away, so salinization is not much of an issue. With irrigation, though, as applied water evaporates, it leaves behind salts that build up in the soil and have a pronounced negative impact on crop productivity. In California's fertile San Joaquin Valley, for example, farmers have already retired more than 100,000 acres of prime cropland due to salt buildup from inadequate drainage.

The area of cropland affected by salinization is increasing, more than quadrupling from 1987 to 1997.[6] The agricultural acreage that is irrigated is also increasing, growing by 40 percent between 1969 and 2002.[7] In 2002, total irrigated cropland was estimated to be about 55 million acres, or about 12 percent of all cropland in the country.[8] Water used to irrigate crops represents the dominant use of freshwater in the United States, with 41 percent of all freshwater withdrawals in 2000 used for agriculture.[9] (A freshwater withdrawal is the amount of water diverted from surface and groundwater sources.) This amounts to approximately 159 million acre feet,[10] which is equivalent to the entire state of California being covered by a foot and a half of water.

One of the starkest examples of how our current food and agriculture system is out of balance is the drawdown of the Ogallala Aquifer in the western plains. Located deep beneath parts of eight states, from South Dakota to Texas, this sole aquifer supplies one in every five irrigated acres in the United States. Estimated to be responsible for $20 billion a year in food and fiber production,[11] it contains enough water to cover all fifty states one and a half feet deep and, if it were totally drained, would take 6,000 years to refill naturally. Of all the water pumped out of the Ogallala Aquifer, more than 90 percent is used to irrigate crops. Water is being overdrawn from the aquifer at a rate equivalent "to the annual flow of eighteen

Colorado Rivers."[12] The useful life expectancy of the aquifer, according to the experts, is between fifteen and fifty years.[13] Once this aquifer is no longer a viable source of irrigation water, we will see an entire swath of productive farmland in the middle of the country transition either to crops that require much less water (such as sorghum and sunflowers) or back into grassland (which was its native state prior to irrigation being available), or in the worst case, into desert.

The quantity of water the food system uses is one big concern. Water quality is another. Freshwater goes into the food production system at a relatively pure level, whether from rainfall or pumped from deep underground wells. Some is used directly in plant growth or to water livestock. When that water is recycled back into the environment, most often through runoff from fields, its quality is often much worse than when it entered the system.

The two most prevalent pollutants in our water that come from agriculture are herbicides (chemicals that are sprayed in most crop fields to kill weeds) and nutrients (those molecules that are essential for plant growth and crop yield, most commonly applied as synthetic fertilizer). As our food system has become more reliant on the application of these chemicals, we have seen an increase in these same chemicals in both surface water and groundwater. In *The End of Food*, Paul Roberts notes that atrazine, an herbicide commonly used in corn production, "is linked to heart and lung congestion, muscle spasms, degeneration of the retina, and cancer . . . and yet despite long efforts by federal and state regulators, it remains the second most frequently detected herbicide in drinking-water wells."[14]

Nitrogen fertilizer is another problem. It is common for a molecule of nitrogen, whether contained in synthetic fertilizer or in animal manure, to be converted to nitrate in the presence of water and oxygen. Once nitrogen is in the nitrate form, it is very soluble. Wherever water goes, it takes the nitrate along with it. A 2006 USDA report states, "As much as 15 percent of the nitrogen fertilizer applied to cropland in the Mississippi River Basin makes its way to the Gulf of Mexico."[15] When nitrogen fertilizer is applied to a corn crop, only a fraction of it is actually absorbed by the plant and incorporated into the stalk, leaf, or grain. The portion that is not absorbed by the plant can travel either downward to groundwater or laterally into surface waters. Throw in hundreds of millions of tons of nitrogen-rich manure from confined animal feeding operations, some of which leaks into surrounding water sources, and you've got hundreds of tons of nitrates finding their way into drinking water and marine environments even hundreds of miles away from the original sources.

Excess nitrogen has been linked to a number of human health concerns, including miscarriages and cancer. Public health officials in most farming areas are well aware of the issue, but the cost of abatement is staggering. For example, Des Moines, Iowa, has an elaborate mechanism for filtering out agricultural runoff, notably nitrates, from the local drinking water supply.[16] The price tag? Approximately $4 million to build and around $1.1 million per year to operate.[17]

And there's more. A national water quality assessment by the U.S. Geological Survey conducted in 2000 found "at least one of seven prevalent herbicides . . . in 37 percent of the groundwater sites examined."[18] Another U.S. Geological Survey study conducted between 1991 and 2004 found nitrate contamination in 72 percent of 2,100 private wells that were sampled.[19] This assessment also found that "nine percent of [all] domestic wells sampled . . . had nitrate concentrations exceeding EPA's drinking water standard," with agriculture identified as the major source.[20] In a 1984 report to Congress, the Environmental Protection Agency (EPA) reported that in the United States, agriculture was the most significant contributor to nonpoint-source water pollution, which means pollution that cannot be traced to a single source, such as a factory.[21] More recent evidence only supports this conclusion. A general assessment of water quality undertaken by the EPA in 2000 concluded that "agriculture is the leading source of pollution in 48 percent of river miles, 41 percent of lake acres . . . and 18 percent of estuaries found to be water-quality impaired."[22]

And then there is the "dead zone." This term refers to an area, usually an estuary along the coast, that has such low levels of oxygen in the water (a condition known as hypoxia) that virtually no life can be sustained. Dead zones occur when those areas are overloaded with nutrients, such as nitrogen, that cause algae to grow and proliferate. The Ecological Society of America, the professional society of ecological scientists, reports, "Although [hypoxia] is sometimes a natural condition, the increased area of water affected, extended length of each episode, and higher frequency in recent decades are due to human activities. . . . The effects of hypoxia include fish kills and shellfish bed losses. These losses can have significant detrimental effects on the ecological and economic health and stability of coastal regions."[23]

In the United States alone, there are now estimated to be 150 dead zones in coastal waters.[24] The largest of these is in the northern Gulf of Mexico near where the Mississippi River empties into it, and is linked to nitrogen loading into the Mississippi River. A 1999 report to the White House Office of Science and Technology Policy found that agricultural nitrogen fertilizers and animal manure contribute about 65 percent of the nitrogen entering the Gulf of Mexico from the Mississippi.[25] This dead zone varies in size each year, but in 2008 it was the second-largest ever recorded, larger than the land area of Massachusetts (almost 8,000 square miles).[26]

The dead zone is perhaps the most obvious and glaring environmental symptom of a food system in which farmers spend $28 billion on agricultural chemicals and apply them to more than 225 million acres of land.[27]

Land Use

One characteristic of a healthy system is that it self-adjusts for changing conditions. A system so critical to the survival of our species, guided by some of the most intelligent and science-savvy leaders we can find, surely must be adjusting now for future scenarios that we know are coming. While a few scientists (a dwindling number) are still arguing about climate change and the true causes of global warming, nobody denies the exponential increase in the human population worldwide, which means we will need to feed an additional three billion people, at a minimum. It would make sense to protect our most productive farmland for future generations, right?

The statistics tell a different story. According to American Farmland Trust, America's agricultural land is at risk.[28] Each year more than one million acres are taken out of current or potential production. The reasons are many, but not one of them can trump the need for future generations to feed themselves. As the average age of American farmers increases and farmers find it more difficult to make a living on their farms, some see selling their land to developers as the only way to raise sufficient funds for retirement or other needs.

The geographic pattern of farmland loss is even more troubling. Farms closest to our urban centers are both those most likely to be used for development and those that produce much of our fresh food, including 63 percent of dairy products and 86 percent of fruits and vegetables. Because local food production is becoming more desirable—in part to reduce the economic and environmental costs of long-distance food transport—protection of farmland in areas surrounding our cities is even more critical. The issue is not only the loss of farmland; it is the loss of our most productive land. The rate of conversion of what's known as "prime" farmland—the best, according to the USDA—is 30 percent faster than the rate for nonprime rural land. This can result in more marginal land being used for growing crops, and making more marginal land productive usually requires using larger amounts of resources such as water and fertilizer.[29]

Climate Change

The food system contributes to the production of greenhouse gases. It also holds the potential for removing greenhouse gases from the atmosphere by sequestering carbon dioxide in soil organic matter. Organic matter is that part of the soil composed of high carbon-containing compounds and is formed through the activity of soil organisms. As organic matter increases as a percentage of total soil volume, atmospheric carbon dioxide can be transformed into organic matter, thus taking it out of the air and "sequestering" it in the soil.

The primary greenhouse gases emitted by agricultural activities are methane and nitrous oxide. Much of the methane is a result of livestock digestion and anaerobic decomposition of manure (when manure breaks down in an oxygen-starved environment, such as a manure pit or lagoon, one of the resulting gaseous compounds emitted is methane), while nitrogen fertilizer production and use is the greatest contributor of nitrous oxide.[30] Both methane and nitrous oxide are considered to contribute to climate change to a much greater extent than carbon dioxide on a ton-per-ton basis. And agriculture accounts for 67 percent of all nitrous oxide emissions in the United States.[31] While agriculture per se is not a huge direct contributor to carbon dioxide emission, every mile we transport food adds to the carbon footprint of the food system overall.

Diet and Health

Perhaps the starkest symptoms of a food system that is broken are hunger, malnutrition, and starvation. Each year, 3.5 million adults and children die of malnutrition.[32] Hunger is rampant not only in developing nations but in the United States as well. And by many measures, things are getting worse: according to the Food and Agriculture Organization of the United Nations, the number of undernourished people worldwide has increased from just under 842 million in the early '90s to an estimated 1.02 billion in 2009.[33] While the vast majority of chronically undernourished people live in the developing world, as recently as 2010, close to forty-nine million individuals in the United States lived in "food insecure" households.

Food insecurity occurs whenever the availability of nutritionally adequate and safe food—or the ability to acquire these foods without relying on food pantries or soup kitchens—is limited or uncertain. While food security is as dependent on affordability as access, most communities in which the prevalence of food insecurity is high are also communities in which food access is limited. According to the USDA Economic Research Service, in 2010, 17 percent of all urban U.S. households experienced food insecurity. When rural households are also included in the calculation, the numbers drop to 14.5 percent of households.[34]

Healthy Food Access

Almost everyone intuitively understands that in order for people to have healthier diets, they need access to healthy foods. Admittedly, even those with access may need to learn more about how to prepare fresh fruits and vegetables and how to cook with whole grains; working and/or single parents may have an especially hard time carving the hours out of their day to prepare more nutritious meals for their families. But without *access* to foods that are healthier and affordable, there's no chance that people can enjoy better diets and lead healthier lives.

It doesn't take much to find the evidence of poor access to healthy, fresh food—just drive down most low-income urban streets or walk into the convenience and liquor stores that are prevalent in these communities. Yet only recently has this issue become the focus of published research by both independent researchers and the USDA. Mari Gallagher, one of the leading researchers in this area, defines "food deserts" as "areas with no or distant grocery stores and limited access to nutritious food options." The term "food desert" is typically used to describe geographical areas of food imbalance, defined as a place in which the average distance to a full-service grocery store or supermarket is greater (sometimes by as much as a factor of three) than the average distance to a "fringe" location, such as a gas station, liquor store, pharmacy, convenience store, or fast food restaurant.[35] Even after controlling for income, education, and race, Gallagher concludes that "diet-related health outcomes . . . are worse in areas of food imbalance." In Detroit, she found more than 500,000 residents living in areas that are so out of balance in terms of healthy food options that "they are statistically more likely to suffer or die prematurely from diet-related disease."[36] In Chicago's particularly out-of-balance communities, she found a diabetes death rate greater than twice that of more in-balance communities. On average, rates of obesity were 24 percent higher, and rates of hypertension 27 percent higher in out-of-balance communities.[37]

I am not particularly enamored of the term "food desert," and I use it with caution due to the way it is usually defined. Because many researchers focus on the lack of full-service grocery stores as a "problem," it naturally follows that the solution is to attract new grocery stores or expand those already present. Of course, I am not against more full-service grocery stores in low-income neighborhoods. But if we put all of our efforts into attracting grocery stores and forget that there are many other ways to create greater access to healthy, fresh, and sustainably grown food, we will not have "solved" the problem of a broken system. We merely will have created more opportunities for residents to purchase (usually at higher prices than in the suburbs) primarily highly processed foods in a way that also very rapidly siphons money away from their community.

The lack of access to healthy, fresh foods has also gotten the attention of the federal government. The Food, Conservation, and Energy Act of 2008—the new nomenclature for what many still call the Farm Bill—called for a USDA-led study on the incidence of food deserts, defining a desert as "an area in the United States with limited access to affordable and nutritious food, particularly such an area composed of predominantly lower-income neighborhoods and communities."[38] The USDA study was also intended to identify strategies to reduce the incidence of these food deserts, such as community and economic development initiatives; incentives for retail food market development, including supermarkets, small grocery stores, and farmers' markets; and improvements to federal food assistance and nutrition education programs.

This study, released in June 2009, indicates that while a mere 5.7 percent of overall households in the country face food access limitations, the situation appears much worse when we look specifically at low-income communities (places where more than 40 percent of households have an income at or below 200 percent of the federal poverty level threshold, which was $22,350 in 2011). In these areas, nearly 22 percent of all households are located more than one-half mile from a grocery store and do not have access to a vehicle. In urban low-income areas, more than 57 percent of inhabitants have limited physical access to supermarkets or grocery stores.

The industry-standard definition of supermarket or grocery store, which was used in the USDA food desert study, is a retailer with "all the major food departments found in a traditional supermarket, including fresh meat and poultry, produce, dairy, dry and packaged foods, and frozen foods." Yet, according to the USDA study, of the 166,000 outlets that are authorized to accept SNAP (Supplemental Nutrition Assistance Program; also known as food stamps) benefits, only a paltry 34,000 would be considered supermarkets.[39] So where else can people get their groceries? Primarily at the aforementioned corner stores, convenience stores, drugstores, and liquor stores, where fresh fruits and vegetables are in short supply at best, and where junk food is offered in abundance. Food stamp dollars are spent on soda, candy, and potato chips—not a prescription for a healthy diet or a healthy life.

This same study tells us that the majority of the research examining the relationship between store access and dietary intake found that better access to a supermarket or grocery store means healthier food intake.[40] Other studies have corroborated this finding. For example, researchers looking at more than 10,000 adults in urban, suburban, and rural communities found that African Americans who live in a census tract where there is a supermarket are more likely to meet dietary guidelines for fruits and vegetables, and for every additional supermarket present, produce consumption increases by 32 percent. Among whites, each additional supermarket leads to an 11 percent increase in produce consumption.[41] It's also interesting to note that while better access to a supermarket is associated with a reduced risk of obesity, better access to convenience stores is associated with an increased risk of obesity.[42]

Diet-Related Illness

Obesity has become a serious health concern for both children and adults, and is directly related to the types and quantity of food available and eaten. The fewer fruits and vegetables one consumes, the more likely that obesity and diet-related illness become problems. From 1980 to 2006 the prevalence of obesity increased for all children and teens, and 32 percent of all children in the United States are now categorized as overweight or obese.[43] Among adolescents, the greatest rise in numbers, for both boys and girls, has been among non-Hispanic blacks and Mexican Americans.[44] A 2008 Centers for Disease Control and Prevention (CDC) study found that more than one-third (34 percent) of U.S. adults age twenty and older are obese.[45]

The other serious health concern is diabetes, a disease associated with high levels of blood glucose and closely associated with obesity. Since 1990, the prevalence of diabetes in adults has risen more than 5 percent each year, likely tied to the growing rates of obesity.[46] Although type 2 diabetes historically was thought of as "adult onset" diabetes, it is being diagnosed more frequently in children and adolescents, especially in conjunction with the increasing rates of overweight and obesity. Diabetes is now one of the most common chronic diseases among U.S. children. We see racial disparities with incidence of diabetes very similar to the disparities seen in weight. Type 2 diabetes incidence is highest among American Indians, followed by African Americans, Asian/Pacific Islanders, and Hispanics. It is considered to be at low incidence for non-Hispanic whites.

While common sense tells us that both obesity and diabetes are strongly connected to poor diet and often with the inability to access or afford a healthy diet, CDC research has confirmed that nutritional intake for children who have type 2 diabetes is poor.[47]

Diabetes is not the only disease that has been associated with poor diet; certain types of cancers, hypertension, and heart disease also place a huge burden on our health care system. Imagine the cost savings to individuals and the government if we could decrease the incidence of these diseases by redesigning the food system so that more people—especially those currently most prone to these diet-related diseases—enjoyed a diet that promoted greater health. Individuals need to make different choices, but first they need to have the option to make those choices. Our food system needs to be redesigned to offer greater access to and increased affordability of healthy foods.

Food Safety

In the United States, there are approximately seventy-six million cases of food-borne illness each year, resulting in 5,000 deaths and costing up to $6 billion annually.[48] Each time we hear about a major food scare or recall—whether it's *E. coli* 0157:H7 in spinach, salmonella sickening 1.4 million U.S. consumers annually,[49] melamine in imported pet food, five hundred million eggs potentially tainted with salmonella, or pesticide residue on produce—we also hear calls to strengthen our food inspection and regulatory mechanisms. In a sense, each food safety issue is seen as one more problem to be solved rather than yet another symptom of a broken system.

Many of these food safety issues are actually the result of how or where we raise the livestock or produce the crop. For example, because growers in the Salinas Valley in California are under so much pressure to increase produce production at the same time that they are being pressured to turn the land over to developers, they have expanded their fields to include the foothills surrounding the valley. These areas, unlike the valley floor, had been occupied by both cattle and dairy operations and contain the habitat for wilder animals, such as feral pigs. Regarding the 2007 *E. coli* spinach scare in Salinas, author Paul Roberts concluded, "It's probably not a coincidence that the spinach field identified as the source of the *E. coli* 0157:H7 strain found in bags of Dole spinach was not only next to a Salinas Valley cattle ranch but was itself a cattle pasture only a few years earlier."[50]

Others attribute the problem to the sheer size of many of our food processing operations. Jeff Benedict, an investigative reporter who has been working on a book about the largest *E. coli* outbreak in U.S. history—the Jack in the Box restaurant tragedy of 1993, in which four children died and hundreds were seriously sickened—concludes, "Any time you have such grand scale mass production as we currently see with beef, pork, chicken, and eggs and so many other products, there are going to be problems. . . . We have gotten so far away from consuming locally grown fruits and vegetables and locally raised meat and poultry. The food system has gotten so big and so complicated that most people have no idea where their food comes from, who produced it, or how it got from farm to fork. In fact, a lot of food today doesn't come from farms. It comes from what I'll call factories. The risks go down when you know who, when, where and how your food was produced."[51]

Perhaps one reason why food safety seems like such an intractable problem is that it is unclear who is responsible for and/or has authority over the producers. As mentioned, at the federal level, it is the job of the Food Safety and Inspection Service, the public health agency in the USDA, to ensure that the nation's commercial supply of meat, poultry, and egg products is safe, wholesome, and correctly labeled and packaged. The Food and Drug Administration (FDA) is charged with protecting consumers against impure, unsafe, and fraudulently labeled products. The FDA, through its Center for Food Safety and Applied Nutrition, regulates foods other than the meat, poultry, and egg products regulated by the FSIS. Meanwhile, the CDC leads federal efforts to gather data on food-borne illnesses and monitor the effectiveness of prevention and control efforts to reduce them. In addition to all the federal agencies, state and local governments also have authority over food safety at the local level.

Antibiotic Resistance

The Union of Concerned Scientists considers antibiotic resistance in humans to be a "growing crisis." The organization estimates that 70 percent of all antibiotics used in this country are employed in livestock production, primarily in confined animal feeding operations, where they are mixed with animal feed and water to accelerate growth and prevent diseases that can spread rapidly in the very crowded conditions under which these animals are raised.[52] While other estimates are lower (the Animal Health Institute's figure is around 30 percent),[53] there is not much dispute about the increasing incidence of antibiotic-resistant strains of bacteria that are affecting humans. In fact, the Infectious Disease Society of America has declared that we are experiencing an epidemic of antibiotic-resistant infections.[54] Close to two million patients in U.S. hospitals contract bacterial infections annually and 90,000 of those patients later die from those infections. In approximately 70 percent of such cases, the bacterial strains responsible for the infection are resistant to at least one first-line antibiotic treatment. Increasingly, bacterial strains are resistant to multiple treatments.[55] The specific reasons why feeding antibiotics to livestock increases their growth rate is not fully understood, but over the past fifty years this has become the common practice of many livestock producers and is starting to be used in aquaculture and some plant agriculture as well.

Congress is now paying attention. The Preservation of Antibiotics for Medical Treatment Act, an active bill, would require the FDA to review all previous approvals of antibiotics for animal feed. Any practices that are deemed unsafe will have their approvals rescinded. Needless to say, there are many alternative ways to produce meat that do not require the use of antibiotics. (In later chapters you will meet some livestock producers who are successfully implementing these other approaches.) The bill has not passed yet, but the issue has come under increasing scrutiny and the bill was reintroduced in the 2011 Congress.[56]

Social Inequality

Without the largely invisible workforce of people who labor to produce, process, and serve our food, most of us would go hungry, yet these individuals are treated as if they are expendable—one more symptom of our broken food system.

On the Farm

One of the reasons why the agricultural labor force is relatively invisible is that far fewer people actually work on farms today than in the past. According to the U.S. Census Bureau, in 1950, 12.5 percent of the labor force was employed in the agriculture sector. By 2006, that figure had dwindled to less than 1.5 percent. Of those who work to grow our food, about two-thirds are self-employed farmers and their unpaid family members, and one-third are hired farmworkers. The USDA considers the hired farmworker labor force unique because "it includes a relatively disadvantaged and sometimes mobile workforce, a large proportion of whom lack authorization to work in the United States."[57] Some of the reasons why hired farmworkers are disadvantaged are that they are younger, less educated, and less likely to speak English compared to the overall workforce of salaried employees. Largely due to seasonality of work, unemployment rates for farmworkers are double those of all wage and salary workers. In 2008, the median weekly earnings for full-time hired farmworkers were $400, and farmworkers were twice as likely to work more than fifty hours per week compared to non-farm workers. Only 2 percent of hired farmworkers have union membership,[58] compared to more than 12 percent for all wage and salary workers.[59]

Because they cannot afford to pay for more expensive temporary housing, many farmworkers rely on housing provided by their employers, which is often substandard and crowded, with deficient sanitation. In addition, because more than 25 percent of these buildings are in direct proximity to fields where pesticides have been applied, there is an additional risk of chemical exposure for the tenants.[60]

Other health risks for farmworkers include dehydration and heat stroke from lack of access to drinking water and health risks due to unsanitary conditions resulting from lack of access to washing water. Meanwhile, few farmworkers carry any health insurance for non-work-related injuries or illnesses. On the other hand, almost 75 percent of farmworkers do have some type of health insurance that covers injuries, and about half of them receive some compensation from their employers if an injury prevents them from working.[61]

In the Processing Plant

It is not only workers on the farm who face such challenges: those in food processing plants are also treated poorly. Though this sector is experiencing employment growth (there was a 150 percent increase in employment in the poultry processing industry alone between 1972 and 2001), real wages (wages paid adjusted for inflation) have remained unchanged. What used to be an urban-based, unionized, skilled workforce in supermarkets, butcher shops, and production plants has become, since the 1950s, a rural-based, non-unionized, low-skilled workforce mostly in large processing plants.[62] And the living and working conditions of meat-processing workers are often similar to those of farmworkers.

In the Restaurant

Data on the working conditions of those who prepare our food, bus our tables, and clean our dishes in restaurants are scant. We hear

much more about celebrity chefs and high-profile restaurant owners. For most of us, our contact during our dining experiences is
with hosts or hostesses and servers, not with those who toil in the
"back of the house." The little information we do have paints a
dreary picture. The Restaurant Opportunities Center (ROC), an organization dedicated to improving working conditions for restaurant workers, has published the results of a survey of restaurant
workers in New York City showing that in 2000, average annual
earnings were slightly less than $20,000, which is less than half of
the average earnings in the private sector. In addition to being paid
low wages (only 20 percent of those surveyed reported being paid a
livable wage—above $13.47 per hour) and working long hours,
many of the respondents also reported having no workplace benefits, such as health insurance, paid vacation or sick days, or even
legally required overtime pay. A full 90 percent of the workers had
no health insurance through their employer, and nearly three-quar-
ters had no health coverage whatsoever. This survey paints a vivid
and disturbing picture of an industry with disproportionately large
numbers of Asian and Hispanic workers, two-thirds of whom were
born outside the United States. On-the-job injuries are common (46
percent of workers report work-related cuts and 38 percent report
being burned on the job), as are labor-law violations.[63]

　　More recently, ROC United, the national organization created
from the New York group, asked five hundred restaurant workers in
New York, New Orleans, Chicago, and Detroit about their work
experiences. While there are a few "good" restaurant jobs in the industry (meaning good wages and working conditions), most jobs
are characterized by very low wages, few benefits, and limited opportunities for upward mobility or increased income. The national
median hourly wage for food preparation and service workers is
only $8.59, including tips, which means that half of all restaurant
workers nationwide actually earn less.[64] More than 90 percent of
restaurant workers surveyed reported that they do not have health
insurance through their employers, 78 percent do not have paid

vacation days, and 90 percent do not have paid sick days. In 2008, their average income was only $12,868, compared to $45,371 for the total private sector. Workers also reported discriminatory hiring, promotion, and disciplinary practices, and a wage differential of $3 per hour between white workers (where the median was $14.70) and workers of color (only $11.50). Now that close to one-half of all our food purchases are occurring in restaurants and other food service venues outside the home,[65] the way in which our food workers are being treated is not only unconscionable, it's also unsustainable in the long term. It is hard for me to imagine a healthy food system that does not include safe working conditions and adequate pay for the army of people who actually handle our food, whether in the field, the processing plant, or at a restaurant.

By now, I hope it is as obvious to you as it is to me that we need to change our food system. The symptoms of its profound dysfunction cannot be tolerated if we want abundant, healthy food for future generations—and the soil and water necessary to produce it.

What exactly should our redesigned food system look like? For starters, it should provide healthy, nutritious, and safe food for everyone, grown in a manner that stewards the natural environment. Based on a more equitable distribution of resources, it should respect the wisdom of natural systems and produce a variety of crops and livestock, all grown in a manner that recycles the waste from one part of the system for use in another. This food system would actually reduce the production of greenhouse gases that threaten untenable warming of our planet. At the same time, it would buffer us against the effects of climate changes that we know are coming. And, perhaps most important, this food system should recognize the strength of ethnic, racial, and cultural diversity and challenge the structural racism and classism that for so long have determined who has access to healthy food.

Though there have been experiments in designing a centralized food system, most of them—such as the state-run collective farms in the former Soviet Union—have failed. You can't expect design engineers to create the "ideal" system, as there are too many variables, such as climate, soil, topography, and cultural preferences. A better approach is to think about what design "principles" are essential to include in a redesigned food system, search out examples of where these principles are already being effectively put into practice, and then replicate those examples. A fair food system needs to retain certain positive features of our current system, such as efficiency, high crop yields, and convenience, and balance them with some new principles. The four principles I think most crucial to a functional, sustainable, redesigned food system are equity, diversity, ecological integrity, and economic viability for all participants in the food supply chain.

You might wonder whether these are the "right" principles. Are there others that are better or more important? Possibly, but these four principles are necessary if we're going to bring the system back into balance and rein in features such as centralization, concentration, specialization, and globalization that have pushed the system too far in one direction. While we could spend lots of time thinking through what additional principles to consider, if we work toward including equity, diversity, ecological integrity, and economic viability in the system, we will start to create the balance we need.

In the four chapters that follow, I will introduce you to people and projects that exemplify what our food system could look like in the future. Not every illustration has every principle embedded within it, but if we want to rebalance and redesign the food system, we need to shine a spotlight on those models that are making such features as equity and diversity come alive. You will meet leaders who are designing and implementing new kinds of farms, food businesses, and modes of distribution based on the features we need in a fair food system—and they are making these models work in their communities.

For example, I will introduce you to George Shetler, who almost two decades ago put his dairy cows back on pasture and then started direct marketing some of his dairy products. The Shetler dairy is now making a good living for three families on smaller acreage and with fewer cows than most experts would say is possible. Of course, I don't think that in the future every dairy should look like the Shetler farm; that's not my point, but many more livestock operations can take the lead from George's example and create farm systems that are more environmentally friendly and community oriented—and can make a good living doing it. And many more consumers in other cities, towns, and rural areas can support this kind of system by purchasing their food closer to home. A future fair food system is not one that is based on a specific formula or recipe. It is a system that evolves from the creativity and innovation that I know is in this sector, by enterprising people who are committed to creating a more positive future.

How do we get from small, independent models to something that resembles a "systems change"? There are two ways to describe my theory of change. One is more metaphorical and the other is based in systems theory.

In 1988, it would have been nearly impossible to find a political analyst predicting the fall of the Berlin Wall. Yet, one year later, that is exactly what occurred. It surprised everyone. So how did this happen? I think of all the political activists in East Germany who spent years working to erode an ineffective political system. In metaphorical terms, they each had a small chisel and hammer and were chipping away at the wall day by day, each in their own way, often disconnected from each other. And then these same folks used actual hammers and chisels to start banging against the stones. A point occurred in 1989 when enough activists had been at work with their tools that the political infrastructure and the foundation of the wall were sufficiently weakened, and the wall came tumbling down.

In the same way, we have had food systems activists chipping away at the current broken food system for many years. Countless farmers, gardeners, leaders, students, teachers, writers, politicians, businesspeople, academics, and moms and dads, with the equiva-

lent of chisels and hammers in their hands, have been challenging
the current food system brick by brick. Every time someone decides
to get their food at a farmers' market, establishes a small-scale organic farm, or develops a new sustainable supply chain for their
company, they are attempting to change the current system, one step
at a time. Just as we will never know who removed the actual brick
that caused the Berlin Wall to collapse, we don't know which specific innovation will serve as the tipping point for change in the food
system, but it will happen, sooner or later. My fear is that we don't
have enough time to wait. Can we let another generation or two go
by before we have sufficiently redesigned the food system to ensure
a sustainable future for our progeny? I think we need to act more directly and forcefully now.

Buckminster Fuller, the late scientist and engineer, said, "You
never change things by fighting the existing reality. To change things,
build a new model that makes the existing model obsolete." The
new models are in place, as the following chapters make clear. How
do we move from isolated models to systems change? Through reforming policy. We need to recognize and reinforce the interaction
between market forces and public policy if the small models of
change are going to expand into something that resembles a redesign or a shift in the system. This happens in part by encouraging
demand in the market for food being produced in a manner that in-
corporates our four principles. And this means not just individuals
and families, but institutions, too. That increased demand sends a
signal to farmers, processors, distributors, wholesalers, and retailers
that will lead to more people taking the risk either to start farming
to produce the kinds of goods desired, or to expand their current
operations. As the supply continues to increase, we will see the quality of locally and regionally produced foods improve and the prices
go down, which will further increase demand. Systems theory tells
us that a positive reinforcement loop will emerge, where demand
and supply are feeding each other for this new system, and all of
these models start to expand.

However, there is one blind spot in this theory of change that must be acknowledged. By way of example, let's look at what has happened with organic farming. Back in the late '60s and early '70s, when interest in this method was just starting to build, organic farmers were almost exclusively small farmers who were also incorporating many of the desired food systems' principles. Organic farming was part of an entire food system that included small consumer-owned co-ops, locally owned natural food stores, and independently owned restaurants. As the market for organic food started growing, larger farms, distribution companies, and grocery stores took notice and started incorporating methods of organic production. Some of the smaller organic farmers got bigger, and some farmers who already farmed on large acreages started converting some of those acres to organic. Today we have an organic industry that does not look at all like it did back in the '70s. There are still small and midsize organic farmers producing for local markets, but it's also now big business, with large acreages of monoculture crops, producing organic food for global processing and distribution. Many of the best-recognized organic brands are now divisions of the largest multinational food companies. The organic food system may still have embedded within it such principles as ecology and diversity, but some of the organic farming world has lost touch with the principles of equity and economic viability (described in Chapter 6). With some exceptions, food and farmworkers in large-scale organic businesses are treated similarly to workers in other large-scale food operations, and disparities in access to healthy, fresh food are magnified when we consider the cost premium of organic food to consumers.

As organic food companies became successful businesses, many of them were purchased by larger corporations, providing very healthy returns to the individuals who started the companies. There is nothing wrong with individual entrepreneurs making money by selling their businesses to multinational corporations; this is often the business model sought after by many entrepreneurs. If we are not careful, though, this is what will happen with every single successful innovation in the food system. We need to make sure that the ownership structures in our food system are such that as these new businesses thrive, their economic successes will benefit the local communities as well as individual entrepreneurs.

The best way I know to make this theory come alive is to share with you some actual examples. Let's begin by taking a closer look at each of the key principles of a redesigned food system and some of the food system "modelers" who are paving the way, hammers and chisels in hand.

PART II

Principles of a Fair Food System

CHAPTER 3

A Fair Food System

Let me start by returning to a point I made earlier: when any of our systems are broken, the pain is usually felt first—and worst—in those communities that historically have been excluded from opportunity and access. In the United States, this usually means inner-city, low-income communities, which are often communities of color. For example, of all the people receiving federal food assistance in 2007, most—close to 80 percent—were families living in inner-city communities.[1] Yet if you are well-off enough to live in a community with full-service grocery stores, farmers' markets, CSAs (community-supported agriculture), or restaurants that feature locally grown and organic ingredients, you might even wonder whether the system is really broken.

Equity is an important principle for a successful food system; everyone must have equal access to healthy, safe, and fresh food. Our choices about food should not depend on where we happen to live. If we believe that everyone should have the same opportunity for a good education and access to quality health care, then it's only reasonable to agree that everyone should also have a right to good food. In truth, equal access to healthy food will do more to level the playing field than anything we might change in our health care system. And equity has to be built in from the start: we have to make sure that those in historically excluded communities gain local control of their food sources; that these residents have access to the same kind of foods as their suburban neighbors; and that public health isn't being compromised because of inadequate choice, access, or affordability.

We've seen that the "trickle-down" theory of economics is a misnomer. Just because a few of our wealthiest citizens are making more money doesn't necessarily mean that those at the bottom receive more. Similarly, just because more wealthy neighborhoods have greater access to an abundance of healthy food options doesn't mean that good food somehow "trickles in" to inner-city neighborhoods. It is time to try a "trickle-out" approach: if we ensure that those on the bottom rungs of the economic ladder have access to good food, perhaps we will have a better chance of creating a healthy system for everyone.

Equity in the food system means more than access to healthy food. It also means more equitable access to healthy jobs so that those people working in the system can support their families, and it means more equitable access to land and water, the essential resources needed for farmers to make a living and for more local and regional food systems to thrive. In the following pages, we'll explore what equity in the food system looks like from these different perspectives.

Equal Access to Healthy Food

Farmers' markets and buying clubs are great alternatives for those of us who are reinventing our own personal food system. At the same time, it's important to note that most people get their groceries from retail grocery stores or supermarkets. And in historically underserved communities, food retail often means a liquor or convenience store. Efforts are under way to encourage these storeowners to carry a greater array of fresh foods, especially fruits and vegetables. The Food Trust in Philadelphia is a leader in this effort.

Since the early 1990s, The Food Trust has been working to improve the health of children and adults, promote good nutrition, increase access to nutritious foods, and advocate for better public policy. It is not unusual for the children in North Philadelphia—most of whom are being supported by food stamps—to eat Cap'n Crunch sandwiches on white bread as an afternoon snack and to view obesity and diabetes as the norm. Nutrition awareness has been stifled by limited financial means and few healthy food choices. However, once these children are exposed to the programs of The Food Trust, they begin to see food options through an entirely different lens. For more than 50,000 children, ages five to nineteen, food choices are changing dramatically, based on access to produce that is brought in fresh from the farm.

What began as farmers' markets in low-income areas evolved into school-based nutrition programs. A recent evaluation of the trust's community-based nutrition and food systems programs concluded that the number of kids becoming overweight was cut in half, an unparalleled accomplishment. But we all know that food access efforts need to go beyond farmers' markets in recreation centers. The organization's current focus is on the Healthy Corner Store Initiative, encompassing an initial network of forty stores in North Philadelphia. The Food Trust developed this program to increase residents' access to healthy food and to educate young people about healthy snacking.

The Food Trust's research shows that in the neighborhoods they serve, much of the caloric intake of fourth through sixth graders—roughly six hundred calories a day—comes from corner-store purchases. Averaging twice a day at $2 per visit, these numbers represent a shocking $16 million a year in revenue for local storeowners.

In response to these findings, a survey was conducted to explore what the youth might eat that was different from standard corner-store fare, and how much they would be willing to pay for it. As a result, fresh fruit salads and bottled water are now being sold for $1 each from refrigerated barrels. The storeowner profits 40 cents to the dollar, and one of the owners has profited even more by acting as the supplier, cutting up and packaging the fruit himself. This initiative led to the formation of the Philadelphia Healthy Corner Store network, which links corner-store owners, community organizations, and local farmers to create and sustain healthy corner stores. It doesn't cost the store owner anything to join, and as members, the owners can receive small refrigeration units to stock fresh fruit salads, assistance to make changes to their store layout to increase shelf space for healthy foods, marketing materials to promote sales of these foods, and consulting services and training to improve business practices.

This idea is catching on in many places beyond Philadelphia. For example, a group of students at the University of Michigan started a project in Detroit called Fresh Corner Café, in which they deliver fresh and healthy grab-and-go meals through corner stores in underserved areas of Detroit. Initially branded as "Get Fresh Detroit," the project started with the team packaging and delivering mixed vegetable packs, but they found that customers' negative perceptions of corner stores would not allow them to develop the demand necessary to sustain a business model. After taking a step back and conducting close to five hundred surveys and interviews, they found that corner store shoppers did in fact value fresh and healthy food, but that they valued convenience even more. The team now has a product line of fresh salads, wraps, and soups stocked inside countertop coolers that they provide for each corner store. As their capacity grows, they plan to incorporate a wide variety of locally produced fruit cups, yogurt parfaits, grain salads, healthy dessert alternatives, and even mixed vegetable packs into what they dream of as the "true café experience in corner stores across the city." By the end of 2012, Fresh Corner Café plans to sell 15,000 healthy meals per month through a network of one hundred corner stores in Detroit.

The Food Trust was also a major force in creating the Fresh Food Financing Initiative in Pennsylvania, the first state policy that provides grants and loans to help develop and expand healthy food choices in grocery stores in underserved neighborhoods, such as those in North Philadelphia. In 2004, as this initiative got under way, the Pennsylvania state government invested $30 million in the program. This leveraged an additional $90 million in economic development and private funding. In just over six years, the initiative helped finance the development of eighty-five new retail outlets, each of which offers healthier food choices, one of the requirements for receiving financing. Estimates of the number of jobs either created or preserved due to this initiative stand at 5,000, most of them being filled by neighborhood residents. In Philadelphia alone, 400,000 residents now have improved access to healthy foods in retail grocery outlets.[2] The Fresh Food Financing Initiative has been so successful in bringing retail grocery stores with healthy food options back to "food desert" neighborhoods in Philadelphia that it is being used as a model for a national Healthy Food Financing Initiative, which is currently being funded by the federal government.

While the number of stores and jobs created is impressive, what is even more striking is how some of these stores are becoming new anchors of economic and social revitalization in their communities. I drove through Philadelphia recently to witness the results of the Fresh Food Financing Initiative. In addition to new grocery stores, there are vibrant retail establishments of all kinds clustered around the stores. And these are not the run-down, paint-peeling façades of many of the stores I have seen in Detroit or West Oakland, but clean, well-lit, fully stocked grocery stores that are some of the highest revenue-generating stores in the area. Jeff Brown, a third-generation grocery retailer in Philadelphia, was responsible for helping to institute the Fresh Food Financing Initiative policy in Pennsylvania, and he took advantage of the financing available to build or expand several new ShopRite stores in inner-city Philly.

But the innovation that really caught notice was how Brown connects these new stores to youth entrepreneurship opportunities in the neighborhood. He calls it "ultra local." Within three blocks of each store, he has identified a group of youth and a vacant lot. In addition to testing the soil and working with nonprofit organizations to organize these "microfarms," Brown has guaranteed that he will purchase and sell in his store every vegetable that the young farmers can grow. And he works with them to make sure they are growing the organic vegetables that will be in greatest demand in his stores. So far, the farmers are not making a huge profit on their production, but they are earning some cash and paving the way for future expansion.

This is the kind of innovation that will lead to a redesign of our food system. It takes us beyond our own kitchen and local farmers' markets, out of the elite boutique grocery stores and high-end restaurants, and smack-dab into the middle of this country's food deserts. Jeff Brown is now on a mission to use this model elsewhere in Philly and in other cities, including Detroit.

Though I am often asked, "Why did the grocery stores and super-markets leave the inner cities?" I really do not have a good response. Assumptions abound—and frequently the person asking the question already has an answer—usually having to do with higher crime rates, lower population density, decreased spending power, or lack of a well-trained and dependable workforce. One expert in the field approached the issue from a different perspective, theorizing that retail grocery stores find it less desirable to locate in inner-city neighborhoods because of the difficulty of assembling enough land for a large store, higher perceived expenses for public safety, and higher costs, especially in the first year, to develop the workforce compared to suburban stores.[3] One of my assumptions is that it simply has been more profitable for the large grocery retailers (most of them regional or national chains) to follow the model of the big-box store— a large suburban footprint with lots of parking. This is a model that works better in the suburbs than in the inner city, where land tends to be in smaller parcels, and where many people rely on public transportation. Whatever the reasons, I am convinced that we need to re-populate our inner cities with vibrant grocery stores. Some of them may be locally owned and independent and some of them might be cooperatively owned by community members and/or employees. And some of them will be regional and national chains.

Take Detroit. Over the past year, I have had a chance to meet with grocers who are considering reentering this market. The most intriguing of all is Whole Foods Market. The store is known among some of my friends as the high-priced alternative, and it is odd to think about Whole Foods being the first national grocer in over a decade to build a new store in Detroit—but that is exactly what is about to happen. The desire of Whole Foods leadership is not just to open a new grocery store, but also to become part of a broad-based community effort that builds a healthy food ecosystem in one of the starkest food deserts in the country.[4] The intention is not only to become a prominent retail outlet for healthy food, but also to house a small processing kitchen and classroom that can be used by individuals and organizations in the community, and to help generate income for the suppliers of locally grown and processed products to be carried in the other five Whole Foods Markets in southeast Michigan as well as the one in Midtown Detroit. There is a recognition by Whole Foods leadership that for their project to be successful, the food system infrastructure also has to shift. In Detroit, this means connecting with community-based organizations such as Eastern Market, a regional food hub, so that there are more seamless connections between local producers and processers and larger-scale retailers.

If three years ago someone had told me that the first major national chain grocer to come back into Detroit would be Whole Foods, I would have asked them what they had been smoking! A company known for providing high-quality merchandise, natural and organic products, and healthy prices to go along with its healthy food does not seem at first blush the ideal candidate to set up shop in an inner city. But Jeff Brown's recent success in Philadelphia—as well as that of New Seasons Market in Portland, Oregon, which I'll talk about in more detail later—should have us all thinking about new ways to reinvent the food system.

In my recent conversations with Whole Foods executives, it is clear that they are rethinking the conventional model of their store for the context of inner-city Detroit—everything from the store's footprint to its product mix to the locally grown and value-added products (such as Avalon baked goods, McClure's pickles, and Garden Fresh salsa and chips) they will carry. It may not look like the Whole Foods Market I am used to in Ann Arbor—nor should it. Detroit is a different place with different needs. But these are exactly the kind of outside-the-box thinking and actions it will take to redesign the food system so that it is sustainable in the long term and offers everyone access to healthy and fresh food. And now Whole Foods is not the only chain grocer developing new stores in Detroit. Meijer, a regional chain based in Michigan, is considering building two new grocery stores in the city.

How will these new food retail stores and food processing companies find the local produce to fill their needs? Similar to the approach Brown has taken in Philadelphia, John Hantz, an entrepreneur and Detroit native, is taking a hard look at an abundant local resource. Hantz was startled to hear that more than 5,000 acres of public land lie vacant within Detroit's city limits. With the help of Michigan State University scientists, Hantz Farms is now on a mission to turn some of this vacant land into the country's largest urban farm. "Hantz Farms will transform this area into a viable, beautiful and sustainable area that will serve the community, increase the tax base, create jobs and greatly improve the quality of life in an area that has experienced a severe decline in population," he said in a press release. While not everyone is thrilled that a wealthy businessman is planning to create the largest urban farm in the past one hundred years in the middle of their city, it points to the scale of solution that is starting to be considered.

Whole Foods and Hantz Farms are just two aspects of a shift that is occurring with the food system in Detroit. Later in this book I discuss in more detail exciting community-based projects (such as the Detroit Food Policy Council and Greening of Detroit's community gardens) that are also transforming the landscape there.

Food Assistance and Local Farmers

Farmers' markets are another way to provide residents of under-served communities with healthy, fresh food, but it's not always easy to make this connection, in part because in many cases, the markets have served primarily (or exclusively) relatively well-to-do families in upscale city or suburban neighborhoods. They have been slow to serve lower-income families and communities. One of the people connecting the dots is August "Gus" Schumacher, the former director of the Massachusetts Department of Agriculture and Environment, World Bank executive, and undersecretary of agriculture at the USDA during the Clinton administration.

Schumacher comes from a farming family. His father first farmed in New York City. When land became too expensive there, he moved to what is now suburban Boston to continue growing healthy food for city residents. One Saturday in 1980, Gus helped his brother deliver and sell pears at a farmers' market in downtown Boston. That particular morning, he accidentally dropped a crate of pears and some of them fell in the gutter and were damaged. As he continued hauling the rest of the boxes to the market stand, he noticed a woman down on her knees collecting the damaged fruit and putting it in her bag. Shocked, Gus handed her some unblemished pears to take home.

This encounter stayed with him, as did its implicit lesson that seniors with limited incomes could not afford to purchase the healthy, fresh food they need for an adequate diet. In 1988, as Massachusetts commissioner of food and agriculture, he created the Senior Farmers' Market Nutrition Program. It started small, but thanks to Schumacher's focus and considerable powers of persuasion, we now have a federal program with mandatory funding of $20 million per year. Though federally funded, this program is administered through each state, generally through the same administrative unit that handles SNAP. Low-income seniors are sent coupons worth $28 to $50 per person that can be redeemed for locally grown fruits and vegetables at farmers' markets or farm stands. This took care of one specific population of low-income residents, but Schumacher did not stop there.

During my tenure as a program director at the Kellogg Foundation, with Schumacher as a key consultant, we supported early efforts to provide incentives at farmers' markets to encourage low-income families to spend their food assistance dollars on healthy, fresh, and locally and sustainably grown food. This became more challenging when the food stamp program switched from paper coupons, which farmers could accept and redeem at any market, to what is called EBT (electronic benefit transfer). For the past decade or more, those who are eligible for federal food assistance have relied on what is essentially a food debit card. Each month the amount to which they are entitled is loaded into their account. They access these funds by using their EBT card to purchase food, just as they would with a debit card. Stores need to meet certain requirements established by the state SNAP agency in order to accept EBT cards.

Now farmers' markets are becoming certified to accept EBT too. In most cases, rather than each individual farmer receiving certification, which would mean that each farmer would also need a special machine to swipe the EBT card, the organization that manages the farmers' market becomes certified to conduct EBT transactions. When SNAP customers want to spend their food assistance funds there, they go to a central location where there is an EBT machine, swipe their card, and let the farmers' market manager know how much they want to spend that day. The manager then gives that shopper tokens or coupons that can be used to purchase any eligible food items at the market. At the close of business, the farmers turn in their tokens or coupons to the market manager in exchange for cash.

Some farmers' markets are establishing the capacity to accept EBT with the support of USDA funding or through state governments. With almost 350 farmers' markets and one of the greatest percentages of farmers' markets that accept EBT (close to 24 percent), Michigan is leading the way. Additionally, the state has seen a large increase year-to-year in the amount of SNAP sales at farmers' markets. Even so, the amount of food sold to low-income shoppers at farmers' markets is a very small percentage of the total purchasing power of this population.

In Detroit alone, residents received $481 million in SNAP benefits in 2010. About 75 percent of these benefits are redeemed within the city. The other 25 percent is spent outside of the city proper, mostly at the full-service grocery stores in the Detroit suburbs.[5] Of the roughly $361 million of SNAP benefits spent within the city in 2010, farmers' markets accounted for less than $200,000, which is equivalent to 0.06 percent of the total. One way to create a healthier food environment for Detroit residents while also benefitting local farmers is to increase the amount of SNAP dollars being spent at farmers' markets. So the nonprofit organization I founded, Fair Food Network (FFN), decided to try a grand experiment: provide monetary incentives to Detroit SNAP clients to encourage them to spend their food assistance dollars at farmers' markets. Schumacher and I first saw this idea put into practice when the Kellogg Foundation gave a small grant to a farmers' market in Takoma Park, Maryland, and the incentive seemed to draw more low-income shoppers into the market. This experiment, started in 2007, led to several others in New York, Boston, Holyoke, and San Diego, supported by a nonprofit organization known as Wholesome Wave, founded by Michel Nischan, a well-known chef and food systems activist. Because the healthy food access issue is so acute in Detroit and because it is also the home of Eastern Market, a large and thriving farmers' market, it seemed like a natural place to try an incentive program on a larger scale.

Here is how it works in our program: when customers use their SNAP benefits at a participating farmers' market, they receive an equal amount of tokens that can be used at the market to purchase any *Michigan-grown* fruit or vegetable. We decided to offer a benefit of "double your money" up to $20 per market day. By spending $20 of SNAP benefits at the farmers' market, the shopper comes home with $40 worth of healthy, fresh, regionally grown produce. Two local foundations in southeast Michigan, in addition to Wholesome Wave, agreed to fund the program, and in fall 2009 we established a small pilot project. We began "Double Up Food Bucks" at Detroit's Eastern Market and four other farmers' markets in the city, including one mobile market (a delivery truck retrofitted to deliver fruits and vegetables door to door throughout Detroit's neighborhoods). All the markets (and the truck) were outfitted with EBT machines, so SNAP customers could easily use their EBT cards for purchases.

As the pilot program was proceeding in Detroit, I was invited to represent FFN at a meeting in Lansing with staff from several foundations and directors of several state departments. The purpose was to share ideas with representatives of the Special Fund for Poverty Alleviation from George Soros's Open Society Foundations in New York. One of our generation's greatest philanthropists, Soros had decided that he wanted to use some of his foundation's resources to help our state, which has been hit particularly hard by the recent recession. Fair Food Network's Double Up Food Bucks was chosen as one of the three projects to fund, with two provisions: that we take the program statewide over the next three years, and that we match dollar for dollar the funds we receive from his foundation. Fair Food Network has obtained commitments for matching funds and now has a $6 million project in Michigan to double the value of SNAP purchases at farmers' markets throughout the state. Our early results indicate that we are on course to triple the funds low-income customers spend at participating farmers' markets, which will benefit consumers and their families as well as the farmers who sell their produce at the markets.

During the 2011 farmers' market season, Double Up Food Bucks were offered in fifty-four farmers' markets in Michigan and resulted in more than $1.3 million in revenue to local farmers. More than 40,000 people received the Double Up Food Bucks tokens, and more than one-fourth of them were first-time shoppers at the farmers' market.

Two encounters in the early days of the project told me we were on to something that could improve the lives of many people. One day, a farmer who has been bringing fruit and berries to Eastern Market for years made the effort to find me. When he did, he reached into both pockets of his jeans and pulled out handfuls of Double Up Food Bucks tokens. He told me that he had sold out of everything he had brought to the market that day—the first time that had ever happened—and he credited the huge sales to our project. Later that same afternoon, as I wandered around the market, I noticed a young man I had seen earlier at the Welcome Center with his toddler. He recognized me as one of the project leaders who had described the program to those waiting in line. When he saw me, he put down his bags, which were overflowing with fresh vegetables, took my hand, and thanked me for giving him the opportunity to bring home so much fresh and healthy food for his family. And he told me that for the very first time, he was thinking about where his food came from and who was growing it. Remember, in order to use the Double Up Food Bucks tokens, he had to determine which farmers were selling products grown in Michigan. The signage was evident, but it was the first time he had paid attention to it. Clearly, this program is making a difference!

 www.doubleupfoodbucks.org

Fair Access to Good Jobs and Healthy Working Conditions

Most of us know a bit about the plight of farm- and food workers in the United States—the low wages and lack of access to health care and education for their children. In part this is due to the work of Cesar Chavez, who organized farmworkers a generation ago and led successful consumer boycotts to ensure these workers had the right to unionize. But such efforts continue today and are still necessary. Only a small percentage of farm- and food workers are represented by a union or have collective bargaining rights.

In the Field

Even in situations where collective bargaining rights may never exist, some courageous farmworkers are teaming up with students and others to build more equity into the system, one penny at a time. They have banded together to create the Campaign for Fair Food, which since 2001 has been working on behalf of the two million to three million migrant field workers in the United States, starting with the tomato workers in Florida. Their approach is different than the one taken by traditional union organizers. Rather than struggling to achieve agreements with growers—which one activist characterized as "fighting for the scraps," since the growers are also being squeezed by their buyers to sell at low prices—the Campaign for Fair Food is working to get concessions from the part of the system that actually has some flexibility: the retail sector. By working with top executives at some of the companies that purchase tomatoes from the Florida growers, historic agreements are being reached.

The Alliance for Fair Food, which is running the campaign, now has more than 190 organizational endorsements.[6] Much of the campaign's success stems from the Coalition of Immokalee Workers (CIW) and their leader, Lucas Benitez, who came from Mexico to the United States as a teenager to work the fields with his family. He has seen firsthand how workers who do not speak English are treated: hard labor and nearly unlivable conditions in run-down trailers the farm owners rent at exorbitant prices. Some workers are treated more like slaves than employees. By the time Benitez was in his early twenties, he realized that his life's work would be in service not to the fields, but to the farmworkers.

Immokalee is a small town surrounded by tomato fields in central Florida. In 2005 I drove from the lushly landscaped enclaves of the Miami area through the swamplands of the Everglades to the flat, hot tomato fields of Immokalee to meet Benitez. Signs in Spanish lined the dusty road to the run-down town center. Old mobile homes were scattered haphazardly along the road. At the time Benitez was about thirty years old, the elder statesman in the community center/office/grocery store where we met. With very few words, he took me on a walking tour of the town, giving me a visceral sense of what it is like to live in these conditions. With pride he showed me the almost bare cinderblock interior of a new radio station where he broadcasts news and information to workers. In the small store, he explained the economics of purchasing large quantities of staple foods that he then subdivides into smaller packages to be sold at the lowest possible prices to the workers and those few families who accompany them north.

He strategically ended our tour in the dusty parking lot and pointed to one of the rusted singlewide trailers, asking me to consider the number of shoes out front. I counted fourteen pairs. More than a dozen men lived in that trailer, with a single hot plate, one small bathroom, and fourteen mattresses lining the floor. For this, they each paid $100 per month, meaning that the monthly rent for the trailer came to $1,400. My daughter was then attending NYU in Manhattan, one of the highest rent districts in the world, and she pays $200 less per month for about the same amount of space. By the time I was in my car heading north, I had some sense of the patience and power of Lucas Benitez, a man who knows he must take one courageous step at a time, even in the most desperate of situations.

When he could not get the farm owners to budge on fair-pay issues or working and living conditions, he decided to follow the trail of the tomatoes once they left the field. He went to the packinghouses, to the distribution networks, and ultimately to the end users—restaurants and food service. It took him four years, but he was able to negotiate an agreement with Taco Bell in 2005 and two years later with McDonald's, both companies agreeing to pay a penny more per pound for the tomatoes coming from Florida to ensure that the workers receive fairer wages, their working and living conditions improve to a standard agreed upon by the workers and the growers, and the coalition has access to the growers' records.

More recently Bon Appétit, a food service company with four hundred institutional outlets in thirty-one states and serving 120 million meals each year, most including fresh tomatoes, also penned an agreement with CIW and the growers whose tomatoes they pick. After Bon Appétit, other food service companies, such as Compass, Aramark, and Sodexo, followed suit. In total, nine national companies (including Whole Foods Market) now have signed on to Benitez's penny-more-per-pound initiative.

Why did the companies agree to these concessions? CIW banded together with student activist groups on college campuses across the country and threatened boycotts of food outlets that did not negotiate with CIW for fairer wages and conditions; these students were able to help bring about change. Within the past year, some of the tomato growers have voluntarily started to participate by increasing the payment to the workers by a penny a pound. And in October 2010, Pacific Tomato Growers pledged to improve its working conditions and pay harvesters a penny more per pound, which could raise annual wages from about $10,000 to as much as $17,000.[7] The total number of workers covered by these agreements is estimated to be about 5,000. There are at least 30,000 migrant farmworkers in Florida's $400 million tomato industry, from which 95 percent of the nation's tomatoes come between October and June. It may be small at the moment, but the model being created with tomato growers and workers could be replicated with other crops and by other organizations. "The Campaign for Fair Food could become the blueprint for farmworker justice in the 21st Century," commented one of the organizers.[8] If a small group of young farmworkers and college students can create a more equitable food system for the Immokalee workers, imagine what can happen as the movement grows, as other low-wage workers join in, and as these workers start to organize across sectors, from field to processing plant to food service.

In the Restaurant

In the kitchens of many restaurants, the food preparation workers and dishwashers are treated almost as poorly as the farmworkers who plant and harvest the food that comes in the back door. Yet this is big business: the restaurant and food service industry includes approximately thirteen million workers in the United States. In 2007, the restaurant industry contributed more than $515 billion in revenue to the nation's gross domestic product through employment and sales at more than 550,000 establishments. Despite the recent economic recession and slow recovery, the restaurant industry continues to grow, with employment growth outpacing that of the overall economy. Since formal credentials are not a requirement for the majority of restaurant jobs, the industry provides employment opportunities for new immigrants, whose skills and prior experience outside the United States may not be recognized by domestic employers, for other unskilled workers, and for young people just starting out in the workforce.[9] Unfortunately, the wages received by many of these workers are far below average.

One great irony in the food system is that these workers, who toil to make good food available to others, often don't have access to healthy food for their own families due to the financial constraints of low-wage jobs. But just as with the farmworkers, strong individuals and organizations are stepping forward to change this, including Saru Jayaraman, a passionate young lawyer from Brooklyn. When I met her, she was teaching at Brooklyn College Law School while organizing workers through the Restaurant Opportunities Center (ROC). She now lives in the San Francisco Bay Area but is still active in helping to organize local affiliates of ROC in Detroit, Chicago, New Orleans, and Maine.[10]

Jayaraman's passion is demonstrating on the front lines. A petite and fiery woman with long, wavy, dark hair, she is uncompromising in her belief that fair wages and healthy working conditions are an absolute right for all workers in the food system, and that these are achievable goals. She also believes it's her job to show naysayers the error of their ways so that they join her in the battle. She created the nonprofit ROC to train restaurant workers, currently toiling for poverty wages and no tips, to move into "front of the house" jobs that will enable them to earn a decent living. At the same time, the center challenges restaurants to take the high road— that is, to pay livable wages and create fair working conditions for all their employees.

When the Windows on the World restaurant in the World Trade Center was destroyed on September 11, 2001, those restaurant workers who did not lose their lives lost their jobs. This intrepid young woman helped them regain a foothold in the food world— not by helping them find other low-paying jobs but by helping them create their own worker-owned restaurant, COLORS, in Manhattan's trendy NoHo neighborhood. In this comfortably appointed, sophisticated establishment, the dedicated staff prepares and serves meals in the evening. But during the day the restaurant is a training center where restaurant workers learn skills such as waiting tables, bartending, and hosting, so they can move into higher-paying jobs in the industry. On the heels of its initial success, COLORS is expanding to a location in Harlem, and in fall 2011, a new COLORS restaurant opened in Detroit, complete with a training center similar to the facility in New York.

I got my first glimpse of Jayaraman's commitment and energy at a meeting we both attended in 2008. We'd been invited to a mountaintop retreat in Vermont to discuss food justice issues. The retreat was structured with time for meditation each morning, followed by one-on-one conversation. While some of us children of the '60s found this approach comfortable, she was visibly agitated every time we took to our mats for contemplation. "How can we sit in quiet when there is so much work to be done?" she lamented. For those of us who equated food justice with food access or farmworkers' rights, Jayaraman taught us the importance of including the plight of food workers in the discussion.

Less than one month later, I was moderating a panel at the national Slow Food Nation conference on food justice and creating a fair food system. The young Brooklyn lawyer had had such a strong impact on my thinking that I asked her to come. She brought a dose of reality to an event that attracted thousands of people to the beautiful San Francisco Bay area. While upper-middle-class folks were learning how they could access the finest artisan foods and exquisite wines, she brought a more sobering message that sensitized some of these slow-food aficionados to the inequities of our system. Since that meeting, San Francisco has become the first major municipality in the country to have the mayor issue an executive order stipulating the need for food procurement from local and sustainable sources and including health and welfare protections for food systems workers.

Slow Food USA, the organization that sponsored the San Francisco conference, is now also on a path to incorporate food justice and social justice for food workers into its efforts, encouraging local chapters to advocate for fair food provisions in local and national policy.

Equitable Access to Water and Land

For families living in urban food deserts, access to healthy food is their main concern; for workers in the food system, it's equitable access to decent-paying jobs. But for those families living in more rural areas of the country, those who are struggling to maintain small-scale farming as a way of life, the issue is fair access to productive land and water. As the population of the western United

States has grown, federal projects to dam, store, and distribute water were able to keep up with the growth for a period of time. More recently, tapping underground water supplies has given us the additional water needed for the increasing urban population and irrigated agriculture. But with inadequate rainfall and a larger population, this entire region is facing the reality of a limited and finite water supply. If water is needed for urban or suburban development, it will have to come from sources traditionally used for agriculture. In most cases, these water rights need to be transferred from their owner to a new user. In general, this transaction is controlled by a government agency, and many of the decision-makers argue that water should be allocated to those businesses or institutions that generate the most money. This means that the needs of small farms, and the families who own them, are often ignored.

As a society, we need to decide whether we will treat water as an economic commodity, sold to the highest bidder, or as a basic right. Will we respect traditional uses of water to support small-scale agriculture or will we allow small farms to die off as they lose access to one of their essential resources?

A key organization working to protect the traditional water rights of small-scale farmers is the New Mexico Acequia Association, led by Paula Garcia. She was born in Mora, New Mexico, where she still lives with her husband and young son. When I visited her in this northern corner of the state, she and Antonio Medina, her mentor, told me about the struggle of small-scale farmers to make a living here. Developers and city planners in Albuquerque are thirsty for new sources of water as development spreads. The farmers have to divide their time between growing crops and raising livestock the environment can support and doing the political work necessary to ensure that their traditional water rights are not taken away by the New Mexico state legislature. So far, their campaign is succeeding with the help of Kellogg and other foundations.

The acequias are an age-old system of water rights and community governance that originated in a Muslim area of northern Africa and traveled through Spain to Mexico and then to New Mexico. This system allocates very precious water in the high desert areas to individual farmers based on the amount of water running from the snow melts each season, the amount of land each individual farmer owns, and the amount of water they need and when they need it. It is a way for a community of farmers to work together to get what they need while stewarding its most important resources. Nonetheless, the New Mexico state constitution legally guaranteed water rights to its citizens, treating these rights as private property, rather than being connected to the land itself. It wasn't until the 1980s and 1990s that the lack of water in New Mexico led to land developers attempting to buy water rights and transfer them from rural and farming communities, creating an openly adversarial situation.

Slowly the acequias began protesting this encroachment on their essential rights and eventually took legal action in a test case that sought to put the community in charge of the water rights, allowing those rights to be transferred only through acequias with full regulatory authority rather than by individual landowners.

In the fall of 2008, the state Supreme Court ruled that the New Mexico Acequia Association has self-determination in water decisions and a voice in deciding the future of its communities. The court upheld the right of the acequias to deny transfer of water to an applicant/developer. Water rights would be treated as a communal resource and not bought and sold on the free market, establishing a legal precedent for a core cultural value of the acequias. The case upheld the constitutionality of a 2003 law passed by the New Mexico legislature, the culmination of a ten-year battle to recognize the exclusive rights of the acequias to determine who had the rights to the water being used by small farmers. All decisions concerning the allocation of water must now be made by the local acequia. No one may sever the connection between agricultural land and its water without the support of the acequia in that specific locale.

The court victory galvanized the Acequia Association under the capable leadership of Paula Garcia and is helping her build a stronger organizational base in local governance to enable each of the eight hundred acequias to incorporate this new authority into their rules of operation. She is now working with the local acequias (each one supporting the water rights of up to one hundred families) to update their governing rules to enact this new power, and to prepare for any legal challenges that might come.

Though soft-spoken, Garcia has the toughness and determination to make a good community organizer in the midst of a traditionally male farm organization—and to gain their trust and respect. She knows that it is not by laws alone that the future will be ensured for her community and is cultivating the next generation to embody the values she holds dear, including community self-determination, love of people and place, and reverence for water. They are becoming "guardians of the water." She comments, "Our young people are proud to have a cultural identity they can feel good about—to be connected to land and place and water. They were brought up to think they should leave the village and get educated, but now they have a different perspective."[11]

The type of communal control over water use exemplified in northern New Mexico is also seen throughout the state, as well as in parts of Colorado and on Indian reservations. While the acequias' approach is not widespread, it is an example of how it can be done, and Garcia is now in demand as a speaker and teacher as others attempt to learn from her success.

While small landowners in the Southwest are concerned about access to water, many African American farmers in the South are focused on maintaining access to and ownership of farmland. There has been a devastatingly sharp decline in black-owned farmland and farm operations in the southern United States. In 1920, 926,000 farms (14 percent of all farms nationwide) were operated by black farmers on 16 million acres of land. Today only 29,690 farms in the U.S. on 7 million acres of land are owned by black families. This is a 97 percent decline in the number of black-owned farms, a situation that affects nearly every black man, woman, and child in the rural "black belt."[12]

Many of those directly affected, and those who have supported them over the years (including the Kellogg Foundation), agree that structural racism both in community attitudes and on the part of government services underlies the basic inequity in access to land and clearly explains the significant loss of land among black farmers. From the time immediately after the Civil War, black farmers were systematically denied access to fertile land due to patently discriminatory practices by the federal government and refusal of white landowners to sell land to blacks or suffer violence at the hands of their community for doing so. This resulted in black farmers staking their claims on the least desirable land, far from critical resources such as water and railways.

Rural poverty also seriously affects African American communities and leads to a host of other challenges, such as inadequate health care, nutrition, and housing. In 2000, 88 percent of the Mississippi Delta counties had a per capita income below the national average of $23,044.[13] Hand in hand with this grinding poverty comes lack of access to quality education, which often has prevented rural black children from gaining even basic literacy skills. Farmers with less than adequate literacy rates and few or no computer skills face significant obstacles in accessing government assistance programs that require computerized applications and higher-level skills, effectively eliminating the candidates who most need help.

All of these factors lead to discrimination in the provision of government assistance, such as credit, subsidies, conservation, and other farm programs. Rather than leveling the playing field, inequitable practices in applying USDA policies have placed black farmers at a disadvantage and prevented them from retaining the land that was the source of their families' sustenance.

In 1981, groundbreaking research on heir property in the rural South found that land owned by black families was more vulnerable to land grabs by developers and the government.[14] The federal government has admitted that it has been primarily responsible for the decline in both black farmers and black-owned land in America.[15]

Even though the Farmers Home Administration, which Congress created in 1946, was mandated to be "the lending institution of last resort" for all farmers, it failed to live up to this responsibility for many black farmers.

If equity is indeed a crucial principle of a redesigned food system, then how do we overcome the structural racism that has led to this situation? Committed and thoughtful activists have been tackling this question, including some who have been working at the Federation of Southern Cooperatives/Land Assistance Fund (the Federation) and the Land Loss Prevention Project (LLPP), which was formed by the North Carolina Association of Black Lawyers in 1982.

To ensure that historically excluded communities and farmers have access to land so they can maintain their farming operations, they must be able to draw on the same resources that are available to everyone else. Key among them is the kind of operational capital and credit through the USDA that has been readily available to other farmers. Another is equitable access to quality education, which teaches farmers in rural black communities the skills needed to apply and advocate for credit, subsidies, and other government programs.

The Federation, founded in 1967, was created to help farmers acquire these important skills and resources. When it merged with the Emergency Land Fund in 1985, it was better able to address the challenges of saving land resources and assisting farmers through the formation of rural cooperatives that provided a wide range of critical services such as credit unions, business training, housing assistance, technical assistance with farm management, and debt restructuring.

Savi Horne, LLPP executive director, says that advocacy from her organization and the Federation has shown clear results.[16] For example, in 1990 they successfully advocated for new legislation passed by Congress, the Minority Farmers Rights Bill (section 2501), which provides technical assistance to black farmers. A "Caravan to Washington" of black farmers in 1992 continued to bring this issue to the attention of the public, the USDA, and Congress.[17] Since 2004, LLPP's Fair Lending and Home Defense Project has helped farmers and their families restructure debt so they can maintain their farm operations.[18]

Along with the Federation, the lawyers in the LLPP are the key group that has tackled the actual litigation required to gain compensation for past inequitable treatment by the USDA. In 1990 the first lawsuit against the federal government was filed on behalf of all black farmers. It was the second lawsuit, *Pigford v. Glickman*, where black farmers finally were designated as a "class" in the legal sense, when attorneys from both sides agreed to a settlement that gave many black farmers the compensation they had been denied. Horne and Shirley Sherrod, her colleague at the Federation, are working to make sure that as these farmers regain control of their land, and that they have the support systems required to ensure their economic success and future sustainability—everything from advisers in forestland management and assistance in sustainable fertilization practices and crop rotation to financial and estate planning and access to cooperative marketing structures that can support the collective marketing of farm products.

It's one thing to be denied access to the land, water, credit, and capital needed to make a living as a farmer, but there is an entire people, Native Americans, who historically have been denied access to their food culture and traditions along with many of these physical resources. As a result, their communities have rates of diet-related illness, such as diabetes, that are astronomically high. One of these communities, or tribes, the Tohono O'odham in southern Arizona, has a documented diabetes rate of more than 50 percent of the total population, the highest rate in the world. More than 76 percent of sixth to eighth graders in the community are obese or overweight. It is only in the past sixty years—with the introduction of processed foods—that the loss of the traditional food system has had such a devastating effect on the people, particularly on the children.[19]

Driving down the almost empty highway from Tucson to the Tohono O'odham reservation in southern Arizona through mile after
mile of arid desert, I finally reached one of the only stores that serves
the food needs of the tribal community. A few nearly dead tomatoes and moldy onions compose the "produce" section of this gas
station/food store that is full of potato chips, white bread, and other
processed foods. It is here that I met the two codirectors of TOCA
(Tohono O'odham Community Action), Tristan Reader and Terrol
Dew Johnson, who later treated me to a dinner of traditional native foods back in their small office.

These leaders of the only nonprofit organization on the reservation realized that in order to improve the physical, emotional,
and spiritual health of their community's residents, they needed to
redesign their food system. Their goal is to create "a healthy, sustainable and culturally vital community on the Tohono O'odham
Nation."[20] In essence, they are looking forward by looking back-
ward to food traditions that may have been lost to the land, but
not to their memory. According to Reader, "Over the past two
decades, several scientific studies have confirmed what the Elders
had known: traditional Tohono O'odham foods—such as tepary
beans, mesquite beans, acorns and cholla (cactus) buds—help reg-
ulate blood sugar and significantly reduce both the incidence and
effects of diabetes."[21]

In 1930 the tribe was cultivating 20,000 acres of land using traditional farming methods, which took advantage of the natural
flooding of the land for irrigation. In 1936 they harvested 1.6 million pounds of tepary beans. By 2000 they harvested less than one
hundred pounds of beans—and this was after Reader and Johnson
started their small one-quarter-acre community garden of tepary
beans, corn, squash, and carrots.[22]

Starting in 2003, TOCA initiated a small community garden and
in 2007 established the Food System and Wellness program to help
support physical, economic, and cultural health in the community
through reintegration of traditional foods. A grant from the Kellogg

Foundation allowed the community to scale up production and purchase basic machinery and tools for the return to the cultivation of
traditional foods. Currently they lease 130 acres and produce half a
million pounds of traditional crops on their two farms, which provide most of what the tribe serves and sells at two establishments,
the Desert Rain Cafe and the Desert Rain Gallery, under the label of
the Tohono O'odham Trading Company.[23]

In the past three years, TOCA has focused on education. They
have developed a curriculum to introduce culturally appropriate
foods back into the community through the school system. In 2009,
they created a pilot project where these foods were offered as part of
the school lunch program. In 2010, they provided a total of 40,000
meals for children from Head Start (early childhood) through high
school. These foods are starting to have a positive impact on the
community, both through the physical effort it takes to grow them
in the harsh Sonoran Desert and the favorable effects they have on
the metabolism of members of this community.

Their food systems program is both reintroducing the young people of the community to the foods that kept their ancestors healthy
and becoming a source of revenue as they produce and sell their traditional crops to schools, hospitals, and lunch programs for the eld-
erly. All of this economic activity provides much-needed jobs and
increases the self-sufficiency of the community—providing an excellent model that can be replicated elsewhere. And the program has
done this by tapping into the tribe's collective memory to create a
solution that is culturally appropriate for them.

What's happening in the Tohono O'odham community is not
an isolated case. Working with Mike Roberts at the First Nations
Development Institute, I have become aware of dozens of projects
in Indian communities that focus on reintroducing their native
foods.

As you can see, there are many models of food systems change that
we can adopt, from focusing on equitable access to healthy food,

good jobs, healthy working conditions, land, and water to reinstating a fading food culture. As more food systems leaders start to understand that "food justice" means equity on all these levels, we have the opportunity for more people and organizations to support one another's work and build a stronger movement. Many of these same leaders understand the need for every part of the food system to embrace the principle of diversity, which is the topic of the next chapter.

CHAPTER 4

Strength Through Diversity

One principle of nature is that a more diverse system is more resilient, better able to withstand disruption, and more sustainable long term. This should also be a principle of a redesigned food system. We need more diversity in what we grow and how we grow it—on individual farms and across farm enterprises. But we can't stop there. We also need diverse economic and ownership structures, and we need to incorporate much more social diversity—multiculturalism—not only because it is the right thing to do, but also because it will make our system stronger and more resilient.

Conservation biologists warn us about the disappearance of species in rain forests and other ecosystems because as these species are wiped out, our planetary ecosystem becomes more fragile. As our food system has evolved over the past few generations, we have come to rely on a very few plants and animals to provide most of the food we eat. In 2003, the Food and Agriculture Organization of the United Nations reported that more than 40 percent of the food calories consumed worldwide came from just three crops—wheat, corn, and rice. In the United States in 2008, more than 50 percent of all harvested cropland grew only two crops, corn and soybeans. And nearly 100 percent of those corn and soybeans are produced in vast monocultures. Even though most farmers know the advantage of robust crop rotation, in which the same field produces the same crop only once every three to five years, our current economic incentive system, driven largely by public policy, steers them toward monoculture production. The entire agricultural industry has also geared itself largely to monoculture production, with the array of large-scale machinery and agrichemicals ill suited for anything but vast fields of a single crop.

With the drive toward more and more acres of fewer and fewer crops (mostly grown with synthetic fertilizers and pesticides), we are also reducing a form of diversity that is perhaps even more important—the array of microorganisms in the soil, which has an effect on soil quality. As we continue to support a food and agriculture system that limits crop diversity aboveground, we are also limiting soil diversity, which in the long run may produce even more dire consequences. While I would not advocate for a food system in which every field had a great diversity of crops in it every year, we do need to move toward a balance of greater agronomic diversity in the system.

In all my years of working with and around farmers, I have come to know them as some of the most independent and innovative entrepreneurs around. With small but significant shifts in public policy to create incentives for more diversity in production and greater biodiversity in the soil, I believe we would see an explosion of creativity and diversity on our farms. At the same time, there are some pioneering farmers who are not waiting for public policy to change. By embracing diversity, these farming heroes are demonstrating what is possible with ingenuity and hard work.

Integrating Crops and Livestock in Diverse Systems

Early in my career as an agronomist focused on sustainable farming systems, I had the opportunity to travel to different parts of the country to visit farms that were managed by innovative farmers, including Dick and Sharon Thompson. The Thompsons had already initiated a collaboration with the Rodale Institute, one of the first sustainable and organic research centers in the United States, to conduct on-farm research that demonstrated more sustainable approaches to corn and soybean production and integrating crop production with cattle and hogs. When I drove from Des Moines to Boone, Iowa, in midsummer, all I saw stretching out for miles and miles were corn and soybean fields. But as soon as I parked in the Thompsons' driveway and looked around, I noticed the colorful array of crops interwoven in neat checkerboards, along with the welcoming smiles of Dick and Sharon. Wearing his usual work overalls, Dick had the weathered face and raspy voice that indicated a man unafraid of hard work in the elements. As Sharon showed me the multitude of posters in the barn chronicling their farming experiments, it was clear that she was equally enthusiastic about their pioneering work in crop rotation and integrating animals into the productive work of the farm.

While most Iowa corn and soybean farmers plowed each field each year, planting row after row of corn or alternating between corn and soybeans, the Thompsons were successfully experimenting with a system known as ridge-till. Rather than plowing the entire flat field before seeding the crop, which turns the soil over and exposes new weed seeds that germinate and create a need for control measures, they had developed specialized equipment that cultivates only a very narrow band of soil at the top of small ridges that run the length of the field. These cultivated strips on the ridges are just wide enough to plant the small seeds. The rest of the field that is not on the ridges is left alone, so that the soil organisms can thrive without their environment being disturbed, and new weed seeds are not exposed to germinate and create a need for weed-control measures. The Thompsons have also developed ways to diversify beyond the limited crop rotation now typical on most Iowa farms to include small grains, such as oats and barley, into their system.

I recall Dick telling me, "When I plant the small grain in a field that formerly grew corn, I have a chance to control the weeds without using herbicides." This is because the small grain crop outcompetes weeds trying to grow in the early spring, and the weed plants never get a chance to mature. He continued, "And the different crops pull different nutrients out of the soil, so the crops' fertilizer needs are taken care of more naturally." He maintains his soil fertility levels by planting legume cover crops. A cover crop is one that gets planted between seasons, solely for building soil quality and improving the soil nutrient content for the following crop. Legumes are a group of plants particularly well suited for use as cover crops because they have the ability to take nitrogen gas from the atmosphere (which contains more than 70 percent nitrogen) and "fix" it into a form that can be used to provide the plant with this essential nutrient for growth and maturity. Once these legume cover crops are turned back into the soil, they can provide the nitrogen to the following crop in a form that is more stable in the soil (which means much less potential for nitrate contamination in the ground or surface waters). So instead of farming with a system that leaks nitrates into groundwater or into the river system, the Thompsons created a system that both saves money and protects the environment. They were successfully experimenting with redesigning one of the most predominant cropping systems in the Midwest long before many of us even realized the necessity.

And in terms of diversity, the Thompsons didn't stop with their crops. In an area and era in which most crop farms had already specialized to the point that there were no animals in sight, they decided to reintegrate cattle and hogs back onto their farm. I also recall Dick telling me, "I can make more money on my corn, soybeans, and grain if I feed them through my livestock and then sell the meat. And the manure from the livestock gives me rich organic fertilizer for my crops—and I don't need to buy it from a fertilizer supplier. It's a win-win."

There are certainly reasons why many farmers specialize in specific crops and why livestock have disappeared from many farms, only to be raised in confined animal feeding operations. Economies of scale, discussed in Chapter 1, is one of these reasons, and lack of information from our land-grant universities and extension services on how to manage diverse farming operations is another. But the predominant reason we see so little diversity on farms these days is that farmers know there is a higher risk involved in farming without the safety net of government programs, which are provided to farmers who maintain their monoculture systems. Public policy has driven the system in this direction, as well as toward the concentration of larger farms and fewer farmers. But working together, we can change this.

Diversifying Crops and Customers

Another farmer, who cultivates many fewer acres than the Thompsons and grows an array of crops to sell directly to his customers is Ari Kurtz, who happens to be my brother-in-law as well as the force behind Lindentree Farm in Lincoln, Massachusetts. Ari, his wife, and their son, farm twelve acres nestled in an inviting, peaceful spot within walking distance of Walden Pond. While they own the house and the two-hundred-year-old traditional New England barn, renovated mostly thanks to Ari's own skillful carpentry, the town of Lincoln owns the bulk of the land they farm. Many years ago the township leaders, seeing the intense pressure for development in a location so close to Boston and Cambridge, decided to purchase some tracts of land and set them aside in perpetuity as "conservation land." This land can never be sold for development. Some Lincoln conservation land is used for public trails and mountain bike paths and some, like the land Ari leases, is used for agriculture.

When I first met Ari more than twenty years ago, he was just finishing rebuilding the barn, from stone foundation all the way to the rafters, and carefully attaching a used greenhouse to its outer wall, taking advantage of the sun in the early spring to start his seedlings. The field next to his house and barn had been leased to a local farmer who had grown sweet corn on the land year after year.

The system that farmer used was simple: spread chemical fertilizer and herbicide before the corn is planted, use insecticide if insects attack the corn, hope you get sufficient rain to make the crop, and sell the sweet corn at a roadside stand or to local grocery stores when the crop ripens in late summer. Though this system made a profit for the farmer in most years, it was also wearing out the soil.

Ari had a small garden plot next to the house and had spent time working on some of the other small farms in the area. He grew up in Pittsburgh, miles from any sign of a farm, hating vegetables, since his only knowledge of them was from a can, yet somehow found himself strongly drawn to spending his days outdoors learning how to grow vegetables in his own garden. He also had an eye on the field next door. So when the sweet-corn farmer had an accident and could no longer farm, Ari made his case to the Lincoln Conservation Commission, and the land was his to lease.

On any Tuesday or Thursday afternoon, the cars start arriving. Sometimes the drivers have on business suits sans ties, on their way home from work in Boston. Other drivers are smiling young moms with babies or toddlers in tow waiting to pull their first flowers from the multicolored raised flowerbeds full of sweet blossoms that Ari's wife tends along with her herb garden. They all gravitate to the basement of the barn, where the day's harvest awaits them.

You may be wondering what they're doing there. Lindentree Farm operates as a CSA (community-supported agriculture) enterprise, one of many in the country. According to the U.S. Department of Agriculture, in 2007 more than 12,000 farms in the United States reported marketing products through a CSA arrangement. It is called community-supported agriculture because the only way it works is if a large enough community provides financial and physical support to the farm. Each winter, CSA members buy shares in the coming year's harvest for a set amount (in the case of Lindentree Farm, $650–$800). For this up-front fee (which becomes the de facto operating capital for the farm), each family shares in the weekly harvest. In addition to paying the fee, in many CSAs, each member also commits to spending several hours during the growing season providing labor on the farm—planting, weeding, and harvesting. As the harvest starts in the spring, each "share," which is what a member is entitled to that week, is distributed. The CSA farmer is responsible for splitting each week's harvest into equal shares to distribute to the members.

In a bountiful week or season, members get lots of great veggies. If a week's harvest is short due to cold weather, wet fields, late planting, or plant disease (as with the 2009 tomato blight), then the shares that week are uniformly smaller. The members share the bounty and share the risk as well as the satisfaction gained from reconnecting to the land and participating directly in food production. On this hot August day, each family takes home peppers (three varieties), eggplant (Italian and Japanese), okra, four kinds of greens, green beans, several kinds of squash, cucumbers, the year's first pick of sweet corn, melons, raspberries, and the prize of the CSA—heirloom tomatoes! The diversity of food that each member brings home mirrors the diversity in the fields.

Ari carefully plans his crop rotation, making sure that no crop grows in the same place more than once in three or four years. He takes advantage of all that the Thompsons have learned about weed control and soil fertility. For the extra fertility that Ari needs to keep his crops healthy, he uses legume cover crops and composted animal manure that he hauls from nearby horse farms. Over time, he has converted his farm fields to "organic," which means they are now certified by the USDA as having been untreated with synthetic chemicals for at least three years. This provides him a premium for the produce his customers buy, and also lets him sell his overflow as organic produce at the local farmers' market each Saturday.

Ari is certainly a local hero to the many families who eat his healthy vegetables and learn about how food is grown by spending time on his farm. They also chuckle while reading his weekly newsletter, *The Real Dirt*, which chronicles the various challenges of climate, weather, and critters he tackles and presents recipes for tasty use of the produce, thus bringing his community more fully into the process of growing the food they eat. He is also a hero to the local food bank. He sets aside one field each season as his "field of greens." When it is time, volunteers from the food bank and his own CSA members harvest nearly 8,000 pounds of food for distribution through the food bank and soup kitchens in the Boston area, creating a modern-day version of sharing the food we glean, as described in the Old Testament.

While many of the largest corn and soybean farmers in the United States receive thousands (at times, hundreds of thousands) of dollars in taxpayer subsidies, known as commodity payments, CSA farmers like Ari Kurtz receive none. They are acting as stewards of our diverse natural resource base and are helping a generation of children learn about where their food really comes from. Imagine how many more smaller-scale farmers we would see producing the diversity of food we need and protecting the diversity in the soil if they also received help from our government policy makers.

Redesigning the food system from an agronomic perspective means adopting different approaches in different places. In Iowa it might mean introducing two or three new crops to the rotation and integrating animals. In a rapidly urbanizing environment like Lincoln, Massachusetts, it can mean growing fifty different crops in a field that for many years grew only one—and by doing so, building a community with the farm at its center. In the case of Lindentree Farm, it also means diversifying the system both agronomically and financially. Without the customer base to work with, it would be nearly impossible for Ari to make a living growing such small quantities of so many different vegetables. The diversity of customers and the diversity of crops all contribute to healthier soil and food and a healthy lifestyle for the farmer.

Diverse Business Structures

The importance of diversity in the food system does not end with production. Just as we know how important (and possible) diversity is in the natural world, it is equally important in terms of economic structure—both how firms are organized as well as their size.

In the natural world we need a variety of species coexisting side by side, while in the economic world we need a balance of small and large firms, global corporations and local businesses, publicly held companies, and small LLCs or sole proprietorships. I often hear people say that big companies are bad and that "small is beautiful." But some of the largest food companies in the world are working to make changes that, given their scale, will have enormous impact, even if the change itself is small. On the other hand, Michael Shuman, author of *The Small-Mart Revolution*, argues that small companies are actually out-competing large ones in many sectors.[1] His most recent research points to the many reasons why local and small businesses are competitive and succeeding locally.[2] They include:

- Quicker innovation
- Direct delivery and local distribution
- Owner loyalty
- Better taste and fresher products
- Better labor practices
- Better service
- Giving customers a sense of community

Nowadays we can travel to almost any size town or city and find thriving local food businesses—from Zingerman's Community of Businesses in Ann Arbor to Flour Garden Bakery in Nevada City, California, to Small Potatoes Urban Delivery in Vancouver, British Columbia, to the Ashland Food Co-op in Oregon, to Seven Stars Yogurt in the Philadelphia area, and The Farmers Diner in Vermont. The Business Alliance for Local Living Economies (BALLE) claims a network of more than 22,000 locally owned businesses in thirty states, with 20 percent of them doing business in the food system, diversifying our food economy in creative and exciting ways.[3] These are not the businesses advertised on television or the ones with fancy billboards featuring Hollywood stars or sports figures peddling their products. They are run by families and entrepreneurs who have a commitment beyond all else to keep their businesses rooted in the local community. Most of the jobs in these companies are held by local folks, and the money that customers spend circulates in the local economy to a much greater extent than food dollars spent in regional or national chain grocery stores or restaurants. According to BALLE, when dollars are spent with large corporations they almost immediately leave the community, while dollars used to purchase local food products circulate within the community, dramatically improving the value of what is bought.[4] According to Shuman, "A growing body of evidence suggests that locally owned businesses generate two to four times the economic benefits—income, wealth, jobs, taxes, and charitable contributions—that non-local businesses do."[5] If you have an interest in reading more in-depth case studies of locally owned "community food enterprises," an excellent report was recently produced by the Wallace Center at Winrock International in collaboration with BALLE.[6]

Two of my favorite heroes of the movement to create a fair food system in Detroit are Jackie Victor and Ann Perrault, founders and owners of Avalon International Breads. Known by customers and locals simply as Avalon Bakery, the establishment's start and success were as unlikely as the Detroit Lions winning the Super Bowl. Jackie and Ann both grew up in the Detroit suburbs and traveled very different paths to the city. Ann followed a childhood dream to live in the city after delivering the *Detroit News* in her Grosse Isle neighborhood; Jackie was a politically active student at the University of Michigan in the 1980s. In her typical spontaneous and outgoing manner, Jackie relishes telling her story. "When I needed a break from protesting and social activism," she says, "I would stop by the Wildflour Bakery in downtown Ann Arbor and help slice bread." Wildflour, which has since closed, was a venture connected to the local food co-op.

Jackie and Ann met in Detroit in the early '90s, when both were involved in community-building activities with legendary activists

James and Grace Boggs. Neither had any experience in business or in commercial baking but both kept thinking about how they could contribute to reviving this city that had fallen on such hard times. Inspired by the Boggses, who encouraged people to open businesses where they could "bake their own bread, fix their own shoes, sell their own food," the partners drew upon Victor's brief experience at Wildflour and decided to open a bakery, a literal "hearth" in a city that could feel pretty cold at the time.

An acquaintance who has experimented with many types of business once told me, "Every business needs three elements: discipline, patience, and courage." I don't have much experience with Jackie's discipline. And she never impressed me as a particularly patient person. But her courage makes up for whatever she lacks in the other departments.

As she tells it, "One day, after buying less-than-fresh bread at the Cass Corridor Food Co-op in Detroit, I started thinking about a bakery in Detroit that would nourish body and soul, like the one I had worked at in Ann Arbor. I was thinking what a bakery like this would be called—an oasis in the middle of Detroit—and the word 'Avalon' came clearly into my mind." She figured that the one tangible skill she had learned in college was baking—and she had kept the recipes from the now-closed Wildflour Bakery.

From the start, the partners' vision was to have a socially conscious, environmentally responsible business in a neighborhood that would help revitalize the city. They found a space in the area known as the "Cass Corridor," one of the toughest neighborhoods in Detroit, where abandoned buildings with broken windows lined the street.

Their original plan was to bake bread in the neighborhood, hire local residents as the business grew, and sell wholesale primarily to restaurants and upscale groceries in the wealthier suburbs that ring Detroit. As Jackie and Ann started bringing in ovens and renovating the space for the bakery, many curious residents came by and peeked in, wanting to know what was going on. In fact, so many curious visitors stopped by during their build-out phase that when they finally opened, more than 750 people showed up at the grand opening to try the breads and pastries, made with 100 percent organic flour. The word quickly spread, and the retail bakery took off from day one in the most unlikely of neighborhoods. Today, five hundred to a thousand customers a day come through the front door on Cass and Willis.

Now, if any astute business student (or experienced business investor) were tasked with putting together a business plan for a new organic bakery with retail space for neighbors to buy goodies and enjoy a cup of good coffee as well as purchase bread to take home, he or she would look for a location with the demographics of a Whole Foods or Trader Joe's, or at least a Starbucks. He or she certainly would not pick a former speakeasy in the Cass Corridor in Detroit. Yet Avalon International Breads is one of the real local food success stories in the city.

The business now employs forty-five workers (full-timers receive a living wage with health benefits), thirty of whom live in Detroit. Sales in 2009 topped $2 million, and the store is expanding to a space three times its current size due to increasing demand both for the wholesale baked goods (which the store still ships daily in three trucks) and the retail store.[7]

Although the story of Avalon Bakery's success makes for good reading, it is literally only one of thousands of examples from across the country of local food entrepreneurs creating economic opportunity while also bringing good food to neighborhoods and families that have limited access to healthy, fresh, and sustainably produced food.

The Role of Multiculturalism

As we consider redesigning the food system to incorporate more biological, agronomic, and economic diversity, we need to consider the social perspective as well. Like that of many progressive movements, the leadership of this fair food movement was for many years primarily white and middle class. At the same time, those who are being most negatively affected are on the lower rungs of the economic ladder and often live in communities of color. If we are to succeed in redesigning the food system to provide healthy food for all, we need to take very seriously the challenge of including the voices of people who have historically been excluded from the conversation. While we do have a lot of work to do, the good news is that there are people in the movement who have taken on issues of structural racism and are looking to multiculturalism as part of the solution.

The Food Project is one model of an organization that is forging connections among young people of diverse race, ethnicity, and class while focusing on food systems development in their community. It was started twenty years ago by a farmer named Ward Cheney, who brought together teenagers from Boston and the surrounding suburbs to grow organic food for their families and other residents of their communities. In their first year of operation, they produced 20,000 pounds of vegetables on a two-acre plot owned by the Massachusetts Audubon Society.

Because this was the first project of its kind combining youth development and sustainable food systems, they had to figure out how to get teenagers to eat the vegetables they grew and how to provide a safe and secure environment with youth from very different backgrounds and neighborhoods. According to a retrospective evaluation published by The Food Project seventeen years after its start, "In the early years we worked hard to develop our model[;] we also struggled to convince funders, the media, educators, and the community that what we were doing, using sustainable agriculture to grow youth and food, made good sense. Times were different then; organic was still associated with granola, convenience and low cost trumped taste and quality in food purchasing, few people thought about where their food came from, and the idea that teens could be (food) producers instead of just consumers was novel." From the outset, I could see the intrinsic appeal of young people helping to build healthier communities by growing good food for people of all economic levels in urban, suburban, and rural areas—and understood that it was an opportunity to marry social diversity and sustainable food systems efforts with a focus on youth. But many folks wondered whether the idea of diverse young people changing the food system would work.[8]

Fast-forward to my first visit to The Food Project four years after its start. A fundamental challenge of most youth-focused food programs is that they operate from a perspective of "hunger and nutrition." Are the kids getting something to eat for breakfast, lunch, and dinner? There is an understanding that most of these youngsters (as well as many in the communities that these programs serve) are not eating a diet with enough fresh fruits and vegetables to give them a healthy start in life. And most of the programs that have the ability to do something about nutrition find that they are up against huge barriers: budgets too lean to provide fresh food; lack of time to prepare food from scratch; no facilities for food preparation; difficulty in accessing the kinds of foods that would provide healthier choices for the youth; and lack of staff knowledge about what to do with fresh, whole foods even if all the other barriers did not exist.

Approaching this situation as a single problem to be solved does not move us forward. What makes more sense is to see this situation as one more manifestation of our broken food system. Young people grasp the inequities of unsustainable food systems, which are apparent in their own neighborhoods. The youth living in these food deserts are affected by increasing rates of childhood obesity and diet-related illnesses, such as diabetes and hypertension. The broken system affects the products on the grocery store shelves, which in turn threaten the health and well-being of our youth.

Programs such as The Food Project, which is finding success with altering young people's diets while providing structured physical activity and positive youth development opportunities, approach the issue from a food systems perspective rather than from a hunger/nutrition perspective. These organizations realize that connecting young people to the soil and the source of healthy food, helping them experience the food system from seed to plate, makes all the difference. Youth attain invaluable life skills that increase their chances for success and, in some cases, survival. In addition, these organizations are creating the next generation of food systems activists, especially in historically underserved urban communities.

An overwhelming percentage of youth food systems organizations are engaged in urban gardening, most in urban areas with a population of 11,000 or more and 40 percent in our major metropolitan areas.[9] For many of these garden projects, sustainable food is the focus but youth enrichment is the core priority, so they evolve into community development programs that incorporate youth enrichment and food systems as strategies to build community. A fundamental principle of community organizing is that change must come from the community itself, so this approach empowers not only the youth but also the whole community to develop an awareness of the importance of consuming healthy food and maintaining a healthy lifestyle, and provides the tools to create changes within the family and community.

Because most of these programs emerged from a desire to address community food insecurity and/or the lack of opportunities for at-risk youth in the community, most programs are highly structured and promote self-discipline. As a result, the participants develop a positive group identity and many move into leadership roles from within. These young people are like the gardens they tend, growing into a productive life.

The Food Project, located in both the upscale suburb of Lincoln, Massachusetts, and the inner-city community of Roxbury, is a stunning example of a national model that has continued to engage youth in personal and social change through sustainable agriculture by remaining true to its mission: "to grow a thoughtful and productive community of youth and adults from diverse backgrounds who work together to build a sustainable food system."

Currently five farms provide meaningful work to teens and volunteers. Each season, they grow nearly a quarter-million pounds of chemical-pesticide-free produce, which is donated to local shelters and sold to community-supported agriculture crop shares and farmers' markets. They also produce and market their own products, such as Farm-Fresh Salsa.

But these are not just gardens. These youth are part of a social movement. Youth of every generation have found the cause that imprints on their psyche and that spurs them to action. Generations past have flown the flags of civil rights, women's rights, environmentalism, and war protests. I am sensing that some youth of the current generation are finding "food justice" to be the cause they are willing to invest in and work for.

Twenty years ago Ward Cheney had a hard time finding even one program trying to achieve his dual goals of multiculturalism and sustainable food systems with youth. Today there are dozens of organizations with similar enough approaches that they are starting to share resources and provide guidance for one another. There are also now regular opportunities for staff and youth to network with their counterparts in other communities. Young people are providing millions of meals for farmers' market customers, members of community-supported agriculture programs, clients at shelters and soup kitchens, and their own families. These young people are educating one another about healthy eating and exploring what food justice means in the context of their communities. I can think of no better way to shift the food system in the long term than to engage youth so that, as they mature, creating a fair food system is in their blood.

Diversity is one of the key principles of our redesigned food system because without it we weaken the system biologically and economically. And because creating a healthier system also means including the voices of those who have historically been excluded, social, racial, and ethnic diversity is also critically important. As we craft more diverse food systems, though, we also need to be sure that those systems remain environmentally sound, which is the topic of the next chapter.

CHAPTER 5

Nurturing the
Land That Feeds Us

Can we produce enough food for the expanding global population without sacrificing the natural resource base on which our food system depends? Is it possible to create an environmentally sustainable agriculture and food system? Some experts claim that the only way we can answer in the affirmative is by "feeding the world through pesticides and plastics."[1] Or that only through intensive agriculture, nurtured by high levels of synthetic fertilizers and pesticides and fueled by huge amounts of fossil fuel energy (for everything from powering tractors and irrigation pumps to manufacturing nitrogen fertilizers) can we avoid a future of mass starvation. Others are convinced that in time most of the remaining rain forests will need to be cleared for food production.

I refuse to believe that with a growing population and limited land, our only recourse is to sacrifice our natural resource base now, making it even more difficult (or impossible) for future generations to feed themselves. There are individuals who have already implemented innovations that point to a different future, one in which agriculture is practiced in concert with nature, more closely mimics natural systems, and reduces or eliminates the potential for pollution and environmental degradation. These farmers, researchers, and educators are establishing production and distribution systems that rely much less, if at all, on chemical inputs; they are practicing production methods, such as the Thompsons' cover cropping in Iowa, that save our precious soil and protect it from eroding into rivers and streams; and they are showing us how to raise healthier meat on pastures rather than in confined animal feeding operations. We are also starting to see some of the largest agribusinesses in the world take these issues seriously and develop food supply chain protocols that ensure more ecologically sound production, processing, packaging, and distribution. In each of these arenas—from research to farm production to distribution and sales—there are leaders showing us the way.

Reducing the Chemical Load

As detailed in Chapter 2, the environmental consequences of a food and agriculture system so dependent on agrichemicals are severe, particularly because of the nutrient and pesticide loads ending up in our water. Debates continue among scientists and advocates about whether large-scale organic farming can produce sufficient yields to support our food needs. Research indicates similar yield potential exists for organic and nonorganic systems, depending on the specific soil, weather, and crop rotation.[2] In addition, although not defined as "organic," there are many successful systems that use judicious amounts of specific fertilizer or pest control chemicals, but much less than the norm.

Of all the farmers I have met who have experimented with farming without chemicals, none is more articulate than Fred Kirschenmann. A longtime advocate and practitioner of farming with the protection of nature in mind, Fred is tall and broad shouldered, from sturdy German farming stock, and looks like the kind of guy who can throw a calf over his shoulder and haul him to the next pasture. He grew up in south-central North Dakota on a grain and livestock farm that his parents started farming in 1930, in the middle of the Dust Bowl years. His father understood that these dust storms were not just about drought and wind, but were also due to the way the farmers were treating their soil.

From the time Fred was a boy, his father instilled in him an ethic of soil conservation. Like many young farm-raised boys, when Fred had the chance he left the farm for an education and a more genteel career. After studying divinity and philosophy and receiving a PhD from the University of Chicago, he became a teacher. A student of his who was a farm kid from Nebraska started telling him about how organic farming systems could create superior soil, and Fred started sharing this information with his father. In 1976, when the older farmer had a heart attack and needed to find someone else to manage the 3,100-acre farm, his son decided to move back to take over the operation. But he did it on the condition that he could use organic methods, which meant growing the crops and raising the livestock with no synthetic chemicals.

Many home gardeners proudly harvest organic vegetables for their own meals, and increasingly small- and large-scale organic vegetable and fruit production is meeting the growing organic market segment. But the challenge of converting an enormous grain farm to organic was a huge undertaking, especially since no other farmer in that area had any interest or expertise. During Fred's first year back on the farm, his organic fields yielded more than the nonorganic fields of his neighbors. What he hadn't realized was how ideal the weather conditions had been for an organic system. It became clear the next year, when his fields underperformed due to a cool spring, and the weeds, without herbicides, outcompeted the crop seedlings.

When Fred became the first organic farmer in the area, most of his neighbors thought he had left a piece of his mind in Chicago. They were concerned about the farm that the senior Kirschenmann had worked his whole life to build and how his son was going to ruin it. But Fred understood the importance of protecting the soil and the danger of our overwhelming dependence on chemicals and

fossil fuels. It took him eight years to fully convert the Kirschenmann Family Farm to organic status. The most important practice
that he instituted, in contrast to his neighbors, was a complex crop
rotation scheme. No field has the same crop growing on it for more
than one year out of several. He rotates cool- and warm-season
crops (buckwheat or sunflowers following wheat), grasses and
broadleaves (rye and alfalfa or clover), and deep-rooted and shallow-
rooted plants. This type of crop rotation controls weeds, insect pests,
and plant diseases and taps different soil layers in different years for
the necessary plant nutrients. He also maintains natural habitat on
the farm (for example, hedgerows separating fields) to encourage
natural insect predators. He uses legumes in the crop rotation often
enough to maintain soil nitrogen levels sufficient for good yields of
his grain crops without adding any synthetic fertilizer. In 1982, he
learned how to make compost by connecting with farmers in other
areas who were starting that practice; since then, regular additions
of composted manure from the farm's cattle are part of what makes
the system work. Today, the Kirschenmann Farm is viewed as one of
the most environmentally and economically sustainable large-scale
certified organic grain farms in the United States.

His crop rotation is not only good for the soil—it is also good for
the bottom line. As Fred tells it, when he first started farming organically, he "didn't even know that there was a market for organic
grain. A grain trader called me one day looking for high-protein organic wheat." As he learned more about what the organic grain
market wanted, he was able to develop his crop rotation to meet
the demand. For example, he started raising buckwheat (a warm-
season, broadleaf, shallow-rooted plant) because of the demand for
organic buckwheat flour.

The challenges of large-scale organic farming are not to be un-
derestimated. And they come from all sides, including natural pests
and government policy. One of the rotation crops that fits well in
the system on the Kirschenmann Farm is sunflowers (a warm-season,
broadleaf, deep-rooted plant), and it doesn't hurt that there's a good

market for organic sunflower seeds. Unfortunately, they are also beloved by blackbirds, which are abundant in North Dakota and need a high-energy food to fuel their migration south every fall. Sunflower seeds fit the bill. By the early 1990s, some of Fred's neighbors had caught on to his crop rotation ideas and several farmers in the area were also growing sunflowers. Even though the birds attacked, as long as there were many sunflower fields across the area, each farmer lost only 5 to 8 percent of his yield, which could be tolerated economically. Then came the Farm Bills of the 1990s, which prevented farmers from collecting their government payments on land that did not stay in corn or another "program" crop. Fred's neighbors could no longer afford to devote fields to sunflowers. Fred, who had never been part of these government programs in the first place, continued to include sunflowers in the rotation. As the only source of sunflowers in the neighborhood, he lost 60 percent of his crop to the blackbirds, and he lost sunflowers as a rotation crop.

Another challenge came with the advent of genetically engineered Roundup-ready canola. Canola is a cool-season, broadleaf crop that fits well into the crop rotation and has a good market (organic canola oil). But because canola is an insect-pollinated crop and no genetically modified organisms (GMOs) can be used in organic farming, organic canola farmers need to maintain a two-mile buffer between their canola field and any that are planted with GMO canola (this assumes that the insect pollinators will stay within a two-mile radius). When many farmers in the area started planting GMO canola recently, the Kirschenmann Farm lost canola as a rotation crop. It troubles me that these critical rotation crops are being forced out. We need to do everything possible with market forces and government policies to encourage more, not less, of these kinds of practices. They are what will sustain us into the future.

Being a teacher as well as a farmer, in the mid-'80s Fred began to speak out about his experiences and the need to alter government policy so that more farmers had the economic freedom to create more sustainable practices on their farms. His first public speech was at a Senate hearing in Washington, D.C., as the 1985 Farm Bill was being considered and the very first sustainable agriculture research program (LISA—Low Input Sustainable Agriculture) was created at the USDA. Now, as then, Fred speaks with the voice of a farmer who is deeply connected to the land and crops, but there is a twinge of an evangelist preacher and scientist mixed in. For example, he'll relate a story about a Japanese farmer who, rather than using herbicides to control weeds in his rice fields, began raising a particular breed of ducks in the rice paddies. These ducks don't have much of a taste for rice seedlings, but they relish the weeds that grow alongside them. But there are additional benefits: the ducks also provide an important source of fertilizer, and this farmer now has a second product to sell—duck meat! Kirschenmann uses such anecdotes to point out that solutions are available if we think more holistically and look at our farms as ecological systems rather than as machines meant to produce a single crop.

Putting Cows Back on Grass

George Shetler, a dairy farmer in northern Michigan, is an unassuming man who would rather talk about the weather or his family than lofty subjects like food systems and sustainability. But he does love to talk about his dairy cows. When I first met him, he had signed up to participate in the sustainable agriculture leadership group that eventually formed the Michigan Agricultural Stewardship Association. He was looking for answers to a dilemma that was about to tear him away from the land and the cows he loves so much.

Like most small-scale dairy farmers in the Midwest, Shetler had precisely followed agriculture extension recommendations. He owned about forty milk cows and used his acreage to grow some of their feed.[3] What he could not produce (such as corn grain and soybean meal, grown farther south), he purchased. The cost of feed was a significant part of his expenses each month. He also owned lots of farm equipment to plant the crops, till the soil, fertilize, and spray for pests (with the additional cost of fertilizer and pesticides), harvest the feed he did grow, cut and bale the hay, and haul it to his cows in the barn. This system also required lots of storage space for animal feed. He kept his cows confined, mostly to a barn or small outside paddock, fed them daily, milked them twice a day, 365 days a year, and with additional equipment, fuel, and labor, hauled the manure and bedding from the barn back out to the fields to spread it on his cropland. His system was so labor intensive that he needed help (if he could find it) and had to pay for it.

Soon after I met him in 1990, I learned that he was on the verge of losing the farm. The price he received for his milk from the milk co-op, which blended his cows' milk with milk from farms all over the county, was not covering his expenses. He would soon be out of business; he'd have to move his family off the farm and start looking for another job. It was a sad situation, and I could read the grief on his face.

Then Shetler started learning about a different way to manage a dairy operation, one that had been used successfully in New Zealand for many years. At that time the island nation was responsible for less than 2 percent of the milk produced worldwide, yet it accounted for almost 25 percent of dairy products traded around the globe. How could this be? Apparently dairy farmers in New Zealand had adopted a new mind-set and implemented new technologies that enabled them to become the lowest-cost milk producers anywhere. The technology was simple: high-tensile electric fencing that can be easily moved by one person. The mind-set change was revolutionary: they shifted their focus from the cows to the land and began seeing themselves as grassland farmers, not dairy farmers.

I watched Shetler make the same shift in northern Michigan, striking out on a new path despite a lifetime of a more traditional approach to dairy farming. Instead of buying his feed from hundreds of miles away, hauling and storing it (along with the hay he grew on his own land), and then hauling and spreading the manure back on the fields, he started focusing on managing the feed in the

field—in other words, letting his cows eat the grass in the pasture.
He divided his fields into discrete paddocks of no more than a couple of acres each, used New Zealand–style fencing to separate the
paddocks, and moved his cows instead of moving the feed and manure. Each day he shifted his herd to a new paddock that had grass
at the proper growth stage for maximum nutrition. The cows ate
the tender, nutrient-rich grass in the field, and exercised their legs
twice a day walking to the barn for milking. Each small paddock is
allowed to "rest" for about thirty days after it has been grazed so
the grass plants can recover and be ready with a new round of feed
for the herd.

Here are the ways that Shetler's new system is more ecologically
balanced:

- No more large-scale equipment for crop production (in fact,
  he sold it all and made some money).
- Less fuel used, significantly lowering his fuel bills.
- No more money, fuel, or labor spent on spreading manure. The
  cows spread their own manure as they graze; as their sharp
  hooves walk across the fields, they work it into the soil.
- A diverse mixture of grasses and legumes grown in the pastures—
  no more monoculture. Between the legumes "fixing" the nitrogen and the nutrients deposited along with the manure, there is
  no need for synthetic fertilizers. In most of Shetler's fields, he
  does not even need to seed the grass and legume plants. Simply
  by letting the cows keep the forage at the right stage of development and by resting each paddock sufficiently, the grasses
  and legumes needed for the system started to populate the pastures on their own.
- No pesticides or herbicides required; the natural mixture of
  plants and the fact that they are grazed so often have eliminated the need for chemical pest control. What used to be considered weeds in the corn and alfalfa fields are now part of his
  cows' nutritious breakfast!

- Using fields for perennial pasture rather than annual crop production creates a "sink" for CO_2, one of the greenhouse gases
  causing global climate change; the roots of the pasture plants
  sequester carbon underground and turn it into organic matter.
  Shetler's new system actually contributes to reducing global
  warming.

Within a couple of years, Shetler had turned his financial situation around and was solidly in the black, but the story gets even
better. He instituted what is known as "seasonal dairying," which
means that he times the births of the calves each year (by artificially
inseminating his cows on a specific schedule) so he can "dry" his
cows for a few months in the winter before they give birth, thus rewarding himself with an annual vacation. For all the years Shetler
milked every day, he could never go away. Now he has given himself
and his wife the gift of their own renewal each year, which is just as
important as giving the grassland a break between grazings.

And it gets better still. Shetler realized that the milk he was producing on this grassland was of a different quality—much tastier!—
than the milk he used to produce with cows that consumed grain and
soybean meal. He saw the glimmer of demand for locally produced
food before most of us realized it. In 1998, he started bottling his own
milk and selling it directly to local stores, rather than mixing it with
milk from the surrounding area and selling it through the milk co-
op. Today you can find glass bottles (returnable with a deposit) of
Shetler's Dairy milk and cream in most stores in the Traverse City
area. And if you go to his family's on-farm store, you can buy rich
and thick Shetler Dairy ice cream. George is a great example of how
ecological integrity and economic viability can work together.

Happily, Shetler is not the only dairy farmer to make the transition
back to pasture-raised cows and local creameries. From the Strauss
Family Creamery in Northern California to Francis Thicke's dairy in
Fairfield, Iowa, to Seven Stars Farm in Chester County, Pennsylvania, dairy farmers in every part of the country are demonstrating that

this kind of agriculture can work for the environment and for the farm families that are stewarding it.

Alternatives to CAFOs

In order for more farmers to transition to systems like Kirschenmann's and Shetler's, we need an ongoing stream of research from our land-grant university scientists. I am encouraged that some of these scientists (admittedly in the minority) are challenging conventional thinking and voicing bold new ideas about how our food production systems need to change. They are not content to bury their heads in biochemistry or genetics labs or economics charts. They understand that the mission of the land-grant university system is to engage with the communities they serve to find real-life solutions to the issues their constituents face. One such scientist is North Carolina State University's Dr. Nancy Creamer, whom I first met when she led a team of researchers and farmers applying for a grant from the Kellogg Foundation in a program we called University/Community Partnerships. She was working with this group to explore alternatives to confined animal feeding operations (CAFOs) as a way to profitably raise hogs in North Carolina.

A Californian by birth, Creamer went to Ohio State University for her education in horticulture and was on the agriculture faculty at North Carolina State. There she wanted to start a new institute (the Center for Environmental Farming Systems, CEFS) that would focus on researching more environmentally sound production systems for the major crops and livestock operations in the state. It was clear when I met this tall, tanned, and lean woman that she spent more time in the fields than behind a desk. What fascinated me was that this young Jewish horticulturalist from Southern California was leading a team of researchers and farmers from the Deep South in an attempt to create a more ecological and humane way to raise pigs.

In this country, most pigs (or hogs, as they are called by most pig farmers) are born in small cages to a mother who has no room to move other than to eat and nurse her young. Endless rows of these cages are lined up in buildings known as confined animal feeding operations. As described by Jeff Tietz, "Pigs live by the hundreds or thousands in warehouse-like barns, in rows of wall-to-wall pens. There is no sunlight, straw, fresh air, or earth. Sows are artificially inseminated and fed and delivered of their piglets in cages too small to turn around in. Forty fully-grown 250-pound male hogs often occupy a pen the size of a tiny apartment."[4] Once they are weaned, these hogs are fed for maximum weight gain per day, along with receiving growth hormones and antibiotics to speed up their development and prevent the kinds of diseases that tend to spread when so many animals live in such close quarters.

Although more than 90 percent of all pork produced in the United States comes from hogs raised in CAFOs, there is a growing demand for pork from hogs raised with access to fresh air and pasture and without hormones or antibiotics. For example, there has been a recent resurgence of Berkshires. Known for its excellent quality and tenderness, the Berkshire breed increased fourfold in registrations and litters in the ten-year period from 1994 to 2004.[5]

Consumers who prefer pasture-raised or organically produced pork are primarily interested in the health or quality aspects of the meat, but there are significant ecological benefits as well; the kinds of benefits found in George Shetler's pasture dairy system are also found when hogs are raised on pasture. North Carolina produces more hogs than any other state. When Creamer worked with the administration at North Carolina State University (as well as North Carolina Agricultural and Technical University and the North Carolina State Department of Agriculture) to help secure funding for CEFS, she also wanted to research an alternative to CAFOs for hog farmers in North Carolina who wanted to raise their livestock with ecology and animal welfare in mind.

Since Creamer and her group obtained the Kellogg grant and established the CEFS in 1994, thirty-five faculty members representing twelve departments at the two universities have directed research programs, twenty-nine graduate students have conducted their thesis research there, and the center has trained almost one hundred interns and apprentices. Notable projects include alternative swine housing, and connecting hog producers who are using more environmentally sustainable production methods with consumers in North Carolina who want to purchase pork raised in more environmentally and humane ways—the first "pork CSA" in the country.

Sustainability Is for the Big Guys, Too

Some leaders of the fair food revolution are focused on smaller-scale farming systems, but others are setting their sights on the bigger players. The Sustainable Food Laboratory (SFL) project brings together leaders in the nonprofit, for-profit, and government sectors from North and South America and Europe to learn about each other's perspectives, build relationships, and accelerate the shift of sustainable food from niche to mainstream. From the start, this project has been led by Hal Hamilton, who began his career as a dairy farmer in Kentucky after graduating from Stanford University in the early 1970s. After his direct experience with the farm crisis of the 1980s, he reluctantly gave up on farming as a way to make his own living, but he did not give up on family farming as a way of life. Many farmers have found inspiration in his work and support.

In 2003, Hamilton asked me if I would consider authorizing a grant from the Kellogg Foundation for a project that would become the SFL. I knew if I could get the foundation to fund this project, I wanted to be a participant. We often funded projects that stayed in existence only for the life of a grant. This one had the potential to create far-reaching change that would endure long after the foundation funding had run out.

In June 2004, I attended the first Sustainable Food Lab meeting in Bergen, Netherlands. By the end of the first chaotic day I wondered whether this vision I had bought into was a pipe dream. When

I wasn't listening to the nonprofit leaders berate the big food and agriculture corporations for befouling the environment and exploiting their workers, I was hearing corporate leaders disdainfully accuse nonprofits of fixating on elite organics while people all over the world were starving to death. As one of the participants, an executive of one of the largest meat companies in Brazil, put it, "Our first job is to keep people from dying of hunger. And anyone who doesn't focus on that one job simply doesn't understand the real meaning of sustainability. Forget about organics. We need more food to feed people."

Not everyone at the first meeting of the Sustainable Food Lab made it to the second meeting, and some of the leaders on both sides dropped out. But enough stayed engaged, the process of trust-building kept improving, and a few key people joined, so some very significant gains were made at these first meetings. The Sustainable Food Lab continues and is the only significant venue to bring together representatives of some of the largest agrifood companies in the world (including Costco, General Mills, Unilever, Nestlé, Starbucks, M&M Mars, and Sysco) and nonprofit leaders involved in issues related to the environment, sustainable agriculture, and farm workers' rights. Together they develop standards and practices to create environmentally friendly and socially responsible supply chains for their products.

I have observed Hamilton taking plenty of heat from his friends in the nongovernmental organization (NGO) world for getting too chummy with the "corporate enemy" and from corporate leaders for acquiescing too much to the idealistic concerns of NGO partners. But the SFL is working because he is able to help mediate the competing interests and keep everyone's focus on a larger goal. We can point to significant successes that demonstrate the power of bringing these diverse leaders to the table, all of whom are focused on how we embed new principles, such as ecological integrity, in the current food system. Sysco's work to bring integrated pest management to hundreds of thousands of acres is one such success.

Sysco has a $39 billion annual revenue stream. It is the largest food distributor in the United States and is responsible for much of the food and supplies delivered to restaurants, cafeterias, and food service establishments. For ten years, Rick Schnieders was its CEO. Soon after he took the reins in 2000, he started talking with his colleagues about the negative impacts of the food system on the environment and the large carbon footprint of their own company. He asked them to imagine the positive impact Sysco could have if they took a leadership position in changing agricultural practices among their suppliers.

When some of the younger leaders at the company heard about Schnieders's commitment and concerns, they started taking action. Shane Sampels, a quality assurance manager who had been working at Sysco with his boss, Craig Watson, on procuring asparagus, saw an opportunity; they created a project within the company that is reaping huge environmental rewards. In the late 1990s, Sysco found it necessary to source asparagus from South America because the company's needs had outgrown the volume available in Michigan and the Pacific Northwest. They found what they needed in Peru, but they also found, according to Watson, "huge abuses of land and way too much pesticide use, primarily due to a lack of knowledge." Sysco decided to work with the growers on better nutrient management, water conservation, and more prudent use of pesticides.

They turned to Cornell University, an institution known for integrated pest management (IPM) research, for assistance. IPM is a way to use synthetic pesticides only as a last resort when growing a crop, and even then, application is carefully timed to the pest's life cycle so the smallest effective amount possible is used. This is contrary to more conventional approaches, which use pesticides as a preventative measure or on a calendar schedule. IPM relies on knowledgeable "pest scouts" to monitor the fields for early signs of pest outbreaks. Control measures are recommended only when the pest population reaches a threshold that would cause economic damage to that crop. If that threshold is approached, the scout can recommend a range of control measures, including traps that release pheromones (insect sex hormones) to attract insects, releasing beneficial insects that naturally control pests, and using pesticide application as a last resort. The Peruvian growers began using IPM and were able to alter the production process of their asparagus significantly, to the benefit of the growers and Sysco's customers.

Schnieders soon asked Watson to take on the role of vice president of quality assurance and sustainable agriculture. In that role, he would bring the system they had developed in Peru to the production of all fruits and vegetables that Sysco sources domestically. They both knew they would need help from outside the company to implement this very innovative project, and they turned to colleagues in the nonprofit world they had met at the Sustainable Food Lab. They asked Tom Green, president of the IPM Institute in Wisconsin, to help develop standards for all the company's growers and suppliers. Green's organization independently audits growers and suppliers each year to ensure that the IPM practices are being followed and reported accurately. The Sysco program, now managed by the IPM Institute, includes three levels of performance evaluation: (1) Suppliers to Sysco draft and submit a written program for review and scoring. The program must detail how they will address pesticide and fertilizer use, water and energy conservation, and waste recycling. The IPM Institute grades the program; suppliers must resubmit until they earn a passing score. (2) Suppliers undergo an annual third-party audit using standards related to everything from water quality, pesticide application, and waste management to energy use and worker safety. Suppliers must get information from their growers about their performance in all of these categories. The auditor typically spends a day and a half with each supplier and visits one or two growers in addition to the processing plant. (3) Suppliers submit an annual self-report assessing their performance according to indicators and standards.[6]

Most of Sysco's auditing and reporting refers to the "amounts of pesticides or fertilizers avoided" due to shifts in practices on the farm and in the processing plant. They also report on tons of waste materials recycled and energy savings.

What have the results been so far?

- More than 900,000 acres of land are under IPM management, or about 6.5 percent of all "specialty crop" acres in the United States,[7] representing more than 4,900 growers, 160 processing plants, and 59 suppliers of fruits and vegetables to Sysco.[8]
- More than 2 million pounds of pesticide applications have been avoided in the five years of the program.
- In 2009, 3 million pounds of synthetic fertilizer applications were avoided, 227 million tons of organic material was recycled in the field as compost rather than disposed of as waste, and 290 million pounds of materials were recycled rather than being sent to landfills.

Most land-grant universities have IPM recommendations for specific crops in their state or region, but a national standard that could be applied to many different crops did not exist before Sysco developed this program. Green describes the initiative as "the largest effort ever undertaken by a North American food distributor to improve sustainable agriculture and IPM practices for the food products it distributes." Sysco has offered to share the details of the program with other food companies, including its competitors. "We offered to allow others to use the program specs but no one has joined us," Watson recently told me.[9]

Why did Schnieders take the company in this direction so quickly and on such a large scale, with little apparent immediate economic benefit? "It's about the long-term sustainability of this company," he told me. "There will be a point in time when farmers who are treating the soil well and suppliers who are treating the environment well will prosper, and those who are not will fail." But rather than beating their chest publicly about their accomplishment, they keep it quiet because they believe it's just a start. I heard some frustration from Watson, who told me, "We don't yet have an industry-driven program. Without strong partnerships among companies in the industry, we won't make the kind of difference we need to make. We need a call to action industry-wide."

Even so, Sysco is not sitting still in its march toward food system sustainability. Its next big innovation will focus on more local procurement—locally grown fruit and vegetables delivered on Sysco trucks to local restaurants and cafeterias. The company believes that there is potential for at least 7.5 percent of its produce nationwide to come from local sources. Given Sysco's size, this will mean a new market of more than $500 million for local farmers. It is also moving into the arena of sustainable seafood, working with another nonprofit, World Wildlife Fund, to assess how to create reasonable goals and standards to ensure that its procurement will help steward the marine environment for future generations.

There are also huge opportunities for Sysco to play a role in distributing locally and regionally produced food. After all, Sysco is really a distribution company; that is where its expertise lies. And this is one bottleneck identified by many in the local/regional food systems world. The company is currently experimenting with hybrid truck engines and looking at much more energy efficient new technology for truck refrigeration than what is currently in use.

The achievements with the Sustainable Food Lab and at Sysco show what can happen when leaders from the corporate and nonprofit sectors get together and take some risks to build a system with ecological integrity. Creating these kinds of partnerships is also a good way to make sure that these innovations are not only ecologically sound but also economically viable. Without that feature, these models will be short lived.

CHAPTER 6

Feeding the Green Economy

While equity, diversity, and ecological integrity are critical features of a redesigned food system, the success of any system redesign depends on its economic viability. Every link in the chain that brings food from production to processing to distribution to point of purchase needs to have economic viability as part of its DNA. We can learn a lot from studying a variety of food systems businesses—both those that succeed and those that fail. We can also learn by doing. My own experience with creating an economically viable food enterprise happened when I was young and possessed virtually no business training. I'm including my story here to underscore the point that an important route to economic viability in the food system is innovation.

As a twenty-two-year-old, I was an idealistic organic farmer living in Santa Cruz, California, which was becoming a center of organic and natural food in the country. Each day, along with the other young members of the University of California–Santa Cruz Farm, I tended the vegetable beds on a hilltop overlooking the ever-changing Pacific Ocean. As our group continued to produce a bountiful array of organic vegetables, we found we were producing way more than we could eat. And there were some foods we needed (such as grains, dairy products, fruits, nuts, and seeds) that we were not yet producing. So we started bartering with the health food stores in Santa Cruz, offering organic lettuce, carrots, squash, and tomatoes for them to sell to their customers for an equivalent value of grains, nuts, and cheese.

Early one morning the produce manager from the Integral Yoga Institute food store (one of the natural food stores in Santa Cruz in those pre–Whole Foods days) came to the farm to help us gather that day's harvest. As he prepared to haul back his share to the store, he asked a simple question that sent my life in an unexpected and highly rewarding direction. Several of his customers had been asking for alfalfa sprouts. In those days, some of the most health-conscious folks were growing sprouts in Mason jars on their kitchen counters, but virtually no sprouts were commercially available anywhere in the country. Did we have any interest in growing sprouts so he could sell them along with our vegetables? The farmers discussed this, and two of us started growing sprouts in big plastic tubs, bartering them along with our produce. We didn't know much about sprouts, but some of us had grown small jars of them and thought we could just use bigger jars to grow more sprouts, which we did.

A few months later, one of the young earth mothers on the farm was planning to give birth in a tepee in the middle of our fields. When the chancellor of the university caught wind of this upcoming blessed event, a rule was instituted that disallowed any overnight stays in the tepees. Clearly we needed to find somewhere else to live. After securing a far less joyous communal housing situation in town, most of the farmers decided to head off to Arkansas, where they hoped to buy a farm together.

I was not ready to leave California, and I was especially not ready to head off to the Ozarks. So when the rest of the group loaded up the trucks and moved, I inherited the fledgling sprout business. This meant scraping together $75 to purchase a bag of alfalfa seeds and sprouting them myself in the big mayonnaise buckets. Three times a week I delivered the sprouts on my bicycle to the three health food stores that had started purchasing them.

Little by little the business grew as demand for this new product was building. Soon I was delivering sprouts in my 1953 GMC pickup truck (which I still own) to many of the sandwich shops and delicatessens in the Santa Cruz area. As sales increased, I started hiring some local folks to help me with the growing and delivering and started thinking about how I could produce a sufficient quantity of sprouts to fill the rapidly expanding market. I soon developed a new method using an automatic watering system in a temperature-controlled room so I did not need to babysit my sprouts and water them every three to four hours, something I had done for two years. As a result of this new growing system, the sprouts had three to four times the shelf life compared to the product I harvested from the mayonnaise buckets.

As the company expanded, I wore many hats. I was the production manager, the sales staff, the accounts receivable department, and the research and development leader all wrapped into one. By the time we employed five or six staff, I was selling sprouts as fast as I could grow them. I had started with a small "retail" route, delivering the sprouts to the end users, both small grocers and sandwich shops. As I built the capacity to grow a greater volume, I started looking at higher-volume buyers. This led me to the wholesale produce terminals in San Francisco and Oakland and to the chain store warehouses.

Within a few years 'Ome Grown Sprouts and Living Fresh Foods, the two companies I started, employed more than twenty people, produced more than nine tons of sprouts a month, and sold them from Los Angeles to Sacramento. Our alfalfa sprouts were the first ever sold in Safeway stores, and for several years the only sprouts sold in the San Francisco Produce Terminal. We shipped our product to the Los Angeles wholesale produce market and even had some customers request air shipments to Chicago (which I thought was ridiculous because they were paying to ship a product that was 90 percent water).

In hindsight, I could have spent more years developing specialty food products and likely could have made a very good living doing so. But I had other fish (and eggplant) to fry, so I re-enrolled in college, now with a focus on plant science and agronomy, and started my journey toward a PhD. I sold my business to a local entrepreneur about the time I started graduate school, and made enough money to buy a house and pay for my education.

As my story illustrates, we don't need to leave the innovation to large companies with big research and development departments. In every community there are examples of individuals who have developed viable businesses in sustainable food-related enterprises— from small-scale growers like Ari Kurtz and his CSA to bakers like Jackie Victor and Ann Perrault at Avalon Bakery in Detroit to local food system entrepreneurs like Paul Saginaw and Ari Weinzweig at Zingerman's Delicatessen in Ann Arbor to George Shetler and his delicious milk. What these people have in common is the ability to see new economic opportunity where others don't.

Of course, innovation in the food business is not new. We could just as easily think about creating a novel enterprise that supports our broken food system as one that embodies a redesign. What makes a business part of the redesigned system rather than one that simply supports the status quo? In addition to incorporating the other essential principles—equity, diversity, and ecological integrity— I believe that there are at least two distinguishing factors to consider: the extent to which the business is enmeshed in the local economy, and whether the supply chain for that business is helping to create economic viability for all of those engaged in bringing the product to the end user.

What does it mean for a business to embed itself in the local economy and community? It does not mean that the business solely sources or sells locally but that, as the business grows, some of its value accrues to the community that has supported it over time. In the real world, it is much easier to find organic or natural foods businesses that, as they have become successful, have been acquired by large multinational food companies, such as Cascadian Farms, which was acquired by General Mills, Stonyfield Yogurt, now partially owned by the France-based Groupe Danone, or Ben & Jerry's, which was sold to Unilever. I don't have a problem with these few entrepreneurs making a lot of money through their own hard work. However, going forward, we need to find ways for successful companies to return value to the communities that helped them grow, rather than essentially becoming the research and development arms of giant multinational food companies.

Managing Around the Blind Spot

One way of creating a business to ensure that its increased value accrues to the community over the long run is to vest part or all of the ownership in a community-based nonprofit organization. As long as the focus of the revenue-generating business is consistent with the charitable mission of the nonprofit organization, this is a great way for that nonprofit to fund its mission while at the same time creating an ownership structure that benefits the community. By law, the assets of a nonprofit organization cannot be transferred to an individual—they must stay with the organization. And if that organization folds, the assets must be transferred to another community-based nonprofit.

In many places in the United States, there are now nonprofit organizations focused on food systems change. One example is Appalachian Harvest, which is one of two revenue-generating businesses wholly owned by Appalachian Sustainable Development (ASD), a fourteen-year-old nonprofit organization headquartered in Abingdon, Virginia, and founded by another hero of the fair food movement, Anthony Flaccavento. A rugged and slightly stocky man, he walks with determination, is quick to smile, and has a passion and commitment to sustainable development in this economically depressed section of Appalachia. When he finished college, Flaccavento was intent on using his knowledge and energy to help others become more economically self-sufficient. At first he thought he might work in international development, but instead took a job with the social justice program of the Catholic Diocese in the hills of eastern Kentucky. After learning about the community and its needs, he decided it was time to focus on his real passion, sustainable development. In 1995, he founded ASD with a mission to revive the region's economy and protect the environment. Flaccavento explains, "What we've been trying to do is to redefine what a healthy economy is and what economic development is."

Along with his ASD colleagues, he recognized the plight of local tobacco farmers as tobacco subsidies disappeared and the ability to make a profit dwindled along with the emergence of markets for organic produce and free-range eggs. Here was an opportunity to put ASD's mission into practice—not by telling others what they should do, but by doing it themselves. They helped a group of Virginia tobacco farmers completely switch their production to eggs and vegetables. In order for farmers to make such a change, they need to learn a whole new way of farming, including seed selection, when and how to plant different varieties of vegetables and their irrigation needs, methods of crop rotation, and composting to build soil quality and resist pests. ASD also offers technical support and training so each farmer can become certified for organic production by the USDA and helps them fulfill buyers' qualifications for high-quality produce.

Flaccavento found that a significant part of the work of his non-profit organization focused on training farmers on how to make this switch. This was particularly challenging because most of the farmers do not work full time on their fields and hold other jobs elsewhere. He says, "Convincing farmers to join was a challenge, particularly at the outset, although it continues to be to this day, even though we have very large, relatively well-paying markets virtually guaranteed, everything in place to take care of grading, packing, and shipping, and a very strong education and technical assistance program in place. I think that the farmers in our area may be especially risk averse, having heard promises about alternatives to tobacco farming for over 20 years."[1]

At the same time ASD was working with the farmers, they also set up a weekly market where the farmers could sell their produce. As sales started to grow, they sought out new markets for these high-quality food products in some of the smaller grocery stores and chains in the area. When it became clear that what was missing in the chain of production between the farm and the store was a facility to wash, grade, pack, and cool the vegetables and eggs, ASD built it. Flaccavento realized that it was important to have some measure of control over the process all the way from the field to the consumer. As a nonprofit organization, ASD was able to fund the building through grants and donations. They are now making money as a local food business and generating revenue to help the nonprofit organization continue its educational mission of local sustainable development.

Looking at Flaccavento today in his jeans and work boots, you would think that he might be the son of an immigrant farmer carrying on his family's legacy. But it didn't take me long to learn that he is from a very well-connected family in New York, where he grew up. Perhaps part of his success is due to his ability to operate in different milieus, gaining the trust of a traditional community of small farmers in Virginia while obtaining the absolute best price for his tomatoes from a supermarket chain. There are now more than sixty-five farmers in ASD's network, most of them former tobacco farmers raising organic produce and free-range eggs. They grow more than thirty different vegetables, everything from green beans, broccoli, and cabbage to peppers, squash, and tomatoes. They get their produce and eggs graded and packed in a new 15,000-square-foot facility owned and operated by Appalachian Harvest, the brand used for the products these farmers grow. Three refrigerated delivery trucks haul their bounty to several major supermarket chains both locally and regionally, including Ingles, Whole Foods, Ukrop's, Earth Fare, and Food City, to name just a few.

"We've gone from mom-and-pop chains, and now we have seven supermarket chains while we're in season. That adds up to about six hundred individual stores," notes Flaccavento. "When we explored the purely local markets, what we determined was if we were purists about it and only sold in a hundred-mile radius, there is no way we could generate enough market to create the incentives for these tobacco farmers to transition," he adds. "They didn't want to grow a few rows of arugula. They wanted to put out a couple acres of bell peppers. That's the way they're used to."

Farmers can join with any size plot of land; the smallest field is only a quarter of an acre. More typically, acreage dedicated to the project ranges from one to ten acres, with the largest producer cultivating around sixteen acres. On the retail level, ASD has helped the Abingdon Farmers' Market grow from seven or eight vendors to arguably the finest in the region. According to Flaccavento, "It's an amazing market. It has about thirty-four or thirty-five vendors and 1,600 shoppers on a Saturday morning, and for a town of 8,000 that's great."

The enterprises owned by ASD are generating well over $1 million per year in the marketplace. It's not huge—but it's a start. And the good news is that as these businesses become even more profitable, the economic benefit will remain in this Appalachian community forever.[2]

Locally Owned Retail

Another example of a local food enterprise that continues to focus on supporting the community that sustains it can be found in retail grocery. In an era in which the three largest companies sell 42 percent of all retail groceries, there is a niche for the smaller-scale, locally owned grocer. Sometimes these smaller players can offer benefits to the community that the big guys can't (or won't). One example is New Seasons Market in Portland, Oregon. Founded by three families in 2000, New Seasons Market started with a single store and, eleven years and nine stores later, continues to be locally owned and operated. Its mission has always been to offer the service and atmosphere of an old-fashioned neighborhood market along with a selection of foods and other products for today's lifestyle (including local, sustainable, and organic foods).

"Being locally owned and operated means playing an active role in the community," says Brian Rohter, president of the operation.

"New Seasons is committed to supporting those organizations that make our neighborhoods a better place to live for all of us."

The company donates 10 percent of after-tax profits to nonprofit organizations in the Portland area, especially those dedicated to feeding the hungry, educating youth, and improving the environment. In 2007, this translated into $400,000 donated to more than five hundred community organizations. They also give first preference when purchasing products to local farmers, ranchers, and fishermen. With more than 1,750 employees (who get paid a living wage with health benefits), New Seasons Market is one of the largest employers in Portland and a dedicated partner to many community organizations working to keep the region a great place to live, work, and play.

So far, this story could be about almost any company. In my own community of Ann Arbor, for example, the Whole Foods stores, while not locally owned and without a stated mission to give a percentage of profits back to the community, are in fact very community-minded and support many good causes, including Fair Food Network's Double Up Food Bucks project. But New Seasons Market's strong dedication to the Portland community really became evident five years ago when the company decided to open a natural foods grocery in one of the lowest-income neighborhoods in the city. The biggest stumbling block was finding financing. Over the years, New Seasons had been financed by the original capital of the families who started the business as well as traditional bank financing. Though New Seasons had paid back every loan in full and on time, these sources refused to finance the new store in this primarily African American and Latino neighborhood. The conventional wisdom was that it was too risky and that the demographic could not support this type of grocery. Rohter and his colleagues were persistent and eventually found a nonconventional financial institution to fund the development of the new store—ShoreBank Enterprise, one of the first banks focused on supporting businesses that have a commitment to conservation and to the community.[3]

The result? In its first year of operation, this store became the highest grossing establishment in the chain, and now many banks are vying for its business. New Seasons is a great example of a locally owned food business embedding within it the principles of a redesigned food system (providing accessible and affordable food in underserved communities, supporting local/regional and sustainable farmers, diversifying ownership among community-based employees, giving back to the community) and succeeding because of it.[4] As this story makes clear, locally owned businesses will at times take calculated risks in alignment with their mission in a way that a national or multinational firm may be reluctant to do.

The Power of a Local Food Economy

If more people were using their food-buying power to purchase food that is locally grown, processed, and prepared, and more local food companies were returning value to their communities, what might a local economy look like? In 2006, Fair Food Foundation commissioned a study to find out. The result: if shoppers within the city of Detroit shifted 20 percent of food spending to food that is grown, processed, and distributed by locally owned companies, the estimated annual impact on the economy would be a boost of nearly half a billion dollars. More than 4,700 jobs would be created, and the city would receive nearly $20 million more in business taxes each year. Were this spending shift to occur in the five counties surrounding Detroit, the increase in the regional economy would be roughly $3.5 billion, nearly 36,000 jobs would be created, and government entities in the region would receive $155 million more in business taxes.[5]

In this study, we modeled an increase of 20 percent in such areas as:

- More local production of dry goods, dairy, processed fruits and vegetables, and all kinds of beverages

- More local processing of beef, pork, chicken, and fish
- More local production of eggs
- More local growing of fruits and vegetables
- More local restaurant spending

In each case, "local" means the activity is being conducted by firms that are locally owned. For example, with restaurant spending, it means that an additional 20 percent of all food purchases in area restaurants is spent in establishments that are owned by residents of the community (not by companies outside the local area or national franchises). While this kind of economic modeling is an imperfect science (and results can vary depending on the assumptions used), it points to a huge missed opportunity for many communities that are looking for ways to ease the economic pressure of job losses, factory closings, and reduced tax revenue. Rather than focusing solely on attracting or retaining jobs with large national or multinational companies, communities could bolster their economic futures by focusing on what I call the "first economy," the food economy. The big question is whether we use this primary generator of funds to help create jobs and revenue for local residents or whether most of those food expenditures turn into profits for large food companies located outside the community.

With more people spending more of their food dollars on locally grown and processed food purchased in locally owned stores and restaurants, the food system could be viewed as a driver of economic development in every community. In fact, a number of studies have shown that a dollar spent at a locally owned business within a region can generate two or more times the multiplier benefit of an entity that is not locally owned. Some of the reasons for this increased multiplier are that local owners tend to spend more on local employees, who in turn spend their money in the locality; these owners tend to spend their profits in the local economy rather than distributing them to shareholders far and wide; and area merchants tend to provide greater support for local organizations and activities.[6]

As we consider how to shift our entire economy to include more green jobs and businesses, let's not forget that we can also benefit our local communities by feeding the green economy with a local food system.

Reimagining and Remodeling Food Supply Chains

I don't want you to think that the only route to economic viability in this new fair food system is through small, locally owned businesses. In Chapter 4, I emphasized the need for economic as well as biological diversity. That means the presence of large companies, such as Sysco, as well as small and medium-sized ones. In any size company, redesigning systems is not easy. It takes people who can understand the tangled web of interrelated parts and players and who have the passion and commitment to work through the knots that such a complex system can create. Of the many examples of large food companies starting to redesign their systems based on some of the principles discussed in this book, Costco stands out. Because of its size, one small change in the company's practices can have a profound ripple effect, so I am deeply impressed by the commitment and passion of one of Costco's employees, Sheri Flies, a hidden hero of our fair food future.

For many years, Flies was corporate legal counsel to the CEO of Costco. I don't know many folks in this kind of high-powered role within a $70 billion company who would say to their boss, "Let me work in the warehouse for a year to learn how our business really functions, because I want to move out of the legal department and help create a more sustainable food chain for all of our products." But that's the indomitable Sheri Flies.

Now the general merchandise manager for two divisions in Costco's corporate food procurement section, she is responsible for more than $4 billion in sales per year. The reason Flies made this move is that she is committed to sustainability in the food supply chain and believes that Costco has an important role to play. When

I asked her what it was like to move from a focus on legalese and words to a focus on products and numbers, she said, "Until you're in it, you don't know how hard it is. It takes tremendous passion and commitment to push this string uphill."

I first met Flies at a Sustainable Food Lab meeting in 2006. She was clearly out of her element when talking about food and farming issues. She really didn't even understand the business of food retail. What she had, though, was an unrelenting commitment to use her position to make a difference. While Costco is focused on creating product supply chains that result in greater environmental sustainability and economic vitality for all those involved, it is something the company doesn't talk about much in public because it believes that sustainability should be a part of how it does business and not a marketing tool. You may find this hard to believe, as it stands in sharp contrast to Wal-Mart and its Sam's Club chain (Costco's major competitor), which has undertaken a highly publicized sustainability campaign. But it is true.

One of the first endeavors Flies initiated was the procurement of high-quality French green beans using a supply chain that ensured good prices to the farmers producing the vegetable. This project became possible because it was an effort of the Sustainable Food Lab, enabling Flies to access its members' expertise in redesigning the supply chain and take advantage of SFL's relationship with a nonprofit like Oxfam, which was trusted by those in Guatemala who were producing and aggregating the beans for wholesale.

For years, Costco, like any major retailer that needed to import produce to meet the volume its customers expected year round, would identify a distributor in a South or Central American country to provide a "turnkey" operation. Costco would place the order at an agreed-upon price and expect that the right amount of the right quality product would arrive at its U.S. distribution centers. As long as the beans arrived at the warehouse in good shape and at the right price, Costco could remain unconcerned about the economic conditions of anyone involved in getting those beans there. Even if the hundreds of farmers producing the beans were living in abject poverty, Costco could claim ignorance.

One consequence of this approach was that some of these farmers would eventually decide to leave their communities for a better life elsewhere (either in an urban area in their country or in the United States). This would threaten the supply chain on which Costco relied. As Flies thought about how to create a more sustainable and equitable supply chain, one that would provide fair economic rewards for all, that would not rely on exploitative conditions, and that would keep the farmers with their families and in their communities, she thought about these French green beans.

Flies is a very persuasive person. She convinced executives at Costco to let her try to build a model for green bean procurement that would exemplify a sustainable and equitable supply chain— and that could ultimately be emulated with other products. For this project, an equitable and sustainable supply chain means that it "must provide a decent return to participating actors, especially small farmers, their families and their organizations in rural Guatemala without undermining the resource base."[7]

What resistance she encountered from her colleagues was softened by her participation in the Sustainable Food Lab. Her superiors had given their permission for Flies to become involved in this "community of practice," and they had heard stories of how other large food companies (such as Sysco) had made positive changes. But things were much more complicated than Flies and her colleagues had imagined. Initially, Costco bought green beans from a Guatemalan grower cooperative thought to consist of three hundred individual farmers (about whom Costco knew very little). But when the Costco team looked more closely, it discovered that this cooperative was actually getting beans from more than 5,000 Mayan farmers in the deep mountain pockets of Guatemala. The team soon realized that to do this project well, it needed to undertake a value chain analysis, which looks at the role of all players in the supply chain and how they are compensated. It requires a tremendous de-

gree of transparency, a willingness of all the parties involved to open
their books, expose their revenue and cost structures, and justify
their share of the profits. The analysis looked at the flow of goods
and money between Costco, the wholesaler, the cooperative, and
the farmers. Each of the supply chain stakeholders was involved in
the decision-making and the analysis, each company was able to review the report on its own data before sharing it with the rest of the
supply chain, and no information was shared publicly without the
company's approval. Some of the questions they were trying to answer in this analysis were:

- Are indigenous farmers getting a fair price for their product,
  one that fosters a sustainable improvement in their lives?
- Would Costco use the information about the value chain to
  squeeze out the "middle man," in this case a key distributor in
  the United States, and perhaps even the cooperative?
- Would these companies be able to conduct an honest, objective assessment of the social, economic, and environmental impacts of French green bean farming?
- Would information about the businesses leak to competitors in
  the French green bean business in Guatemala, Mexico, and the
  United States?

In the process of conducting the analysis, the Costco team spent a
lot of time and effort building trusting relationships among all the
supply chain members. In Costco's typical role as a buyer, building
trust is not always high on the agenda. Instead, the company tended
to ensure quality while looking for cost reductions wherever possible. In a typical supply chain relationship, the wholesaler (the party
selling to Costco) would not want to encourage a direct relationship between Costco and the cooperative out of fear that the large
company would cut out the middle man to save money. On the
other hand, the cooperative would hesitate to share information

about its costs and the prices paid its farmers for fear of encouraging buyers to push for cost reductions.

Flies believes that the trust she and her team established enabled the value chain analysis to be completed. The report on the analysis included a review of the overall functioning of the French green bean supply chain from farmers' fields in Guatemala to retail outlets in the United States. It included a schematic representation of the supply chain showing the value that each actor receives from the chain and an assessment of its overall efficiency; an analysis of the effects of French green beans on the economic sustainability of the cooperative and its ability to function as both a viable business and a catalyst of social change and development; and an analysis of the impact of the supply chain on the farms and families. The value chain analysis also assessed how profits from French green beans contributed to the broader processes of social development, including such issues as access to education and health care.

Flies says, "If we focus on the people, what each person has to contribute and what each person needs as compensation for that contribution, it all works out. Focus on the people first; the money part of it works itself out." Flies and her colleagues believe that this project has been a success, which they define as "economic profitability, good land husbandry and social investment including access to education and health care." They can now document that the farmers receive a substantially higher income from green bean production than they would have received for growing other crops. Sufficient value is being created in the supply chain, and social services that were not previously available are being provided to the farming community.

Even though Costco is clearly not a locally owned business, it is doing a pretty good job of upholding the principles of a redesigned food system, with equity (access to fair income and healthy working conditions), diversity (both in terms of crops—bringing more beans into an area that has primarily grown maize—and supporting an ethnically diverse population), ecological integrity (ensuring that the natural resource base for production is being protected), and economic viability (for everyone in the supply chain).

What does it mean in practice to put a values-based supply chain into operation? According to Don Seville, a leader in the Sustainable Food Lab who helped put this one together for Costco, "The heart of a values-based supply chain is that there is some coordination that goes beyond simple price and quantity transaction. The 'values' at the center may differ—quality, fair labor, organic/sustainable, new product innovation—but the coordination and commitment to collective problem solving is key. For example, instead of buyers simply switching who supplies them, a commitment is created to proactively work towards multiple goals and solving problems and not simply giving up and moving on at the first cheaper sourcing alternative."

According to Flies, putting this value chain into practice means that now, in every Costco store, all of the French green beans that are sold come to the customer through a supply chain that distributes the profits so that farmers receive a final benefit of approximately 28 cents per two-pound bag. These profits are as much as four times the money per acre that they get from maize production, which is their traditional crop.

One additional benefit to the community of this new supply chain approach is the creation of a community foundation in the Guatemalan mountains, an area of intense poverty where the green bean farmers live. The foundation was created to support health care access and educational scholarships for workers' families. Specific projects under way include community computer labs, a low-cost ophthalmology clinic, and the revitalization of children's playgrounds.

Dale Hollingsworth, a Costco buyer who works with Flies, says, "This commitment we have is different than any other way that we do business." With Costco's other suppliers, the company would not spend the time to understand the details of the supply chain and have extensive discussions beyond aspects of product quality and quantity. Normally it would set up a competitive supplier (which in this case would have undermined the ability of the cooperative to

invest so much in its farmers and its communities). Hollingsworth
continues, "We have to step back and look at the whole situation
from a different perspective. For example, sometimes we have to
look at additional reasons behind why they may need a price increase on their end. It's very unique, and very different. . . . What
makes it unique? The people. This is all about the people. I know
why we are buying this product. We are buying it so that people
in . . . Guatemala, are improving their lives, . . . they are getting resources, they are being educated. . . . This is more than just business, this is about livelihood. We must look at it that way."[8]

While the French green bean example may be unique, Flies tells
me that Costco is starting to delve into this kind of sustainable supply chain effort with many more products, including organic and
cage-free eggs. She says, "Just like with the green beans, at first it
looks like a simple prospect—but to find organic egg producers with
sufficient volume and consistent quality is no easy chore. Add to
that our animal welfare standards, which are some of the most stringent in the industry, our concern about food safety, packaging made
from recycled plastic, our concern about how the manure is managed, and making sure that trucks don't drive back from deliveries
empty, so we can reduce our carbon footprint—means that we have
a pretty complicated system to deal with." Now Costco is able to
bring its customers hundreds of thousands of organic eggs that Flies
knows are being supplied in a way that provides great economic
benefit all along the supply chain.

With the principle of economic viability solidly entrenched in our
food system, we can look forward to a time when everyone from
farmers to retailers (and everyone in between) receives fair compensation for the contributions they make. And as our economy
"greens" with renewable energy and sustainable building materials,
all the ingredients are in place to feed this green economy with a redesigned fair food system.

PART III

From Conscious Consumer
to Engaged Citizen

CHAPTER 7

Becoming a Fair Food Activist

On one of the last episodes of *Bill Moyers' Journal*, the journalist was interviewing Michael Pollan about the food system and what needs to change.[1] Toward the end of the conversation Moyers asked, "What can people do, ordinary people, who are not farmers?"

I thought to myself, "Here is a chance that this movement does not get very often—a prominent, nationally known television journalist asking a best-selling author what millions of people should do, many of whom have probably never thought about being involved with fixing the food system. Our time is coming."

Without missing a beat, Pollan responded, "You can vote with your fork. . . . You have to shop strategically and be prepared to cook." Unsatisfied that he had the whole answer yet, Moyers pushed Pollan. "What else? Give me a list, quickly, of what we can do to make a difference in this reforming the food system." Pollan's response: "Well, plant a garden." And I thought, "What a missed opportunity!"

Now, don't get me wrong. I have immense respect for Pollan's work and think that he has been a remarkably good publicist of the symptoms of our broken food system. And he made sure to connect "voting with your fork" with supporting a more local food economy. And I also agree that growing a garden is great. In fact, I have a vibrant vegetable garden right outside my kitchen door. The more people gardening, the better! But if we think that this is the most we can do to repair our broken food system, we are selling ourselves short. And if all we do is grow more gardens, I am afraid our system will never change. We are at a stage in this movement where we can focus on more impactful, and more collective, action.

If Bill Moyers had asked *me* that question, I would have responded, "We need to shift from conscious consumers to engaged citizens." If you are convinced, as I am, that our food system needs a major overhaul for the healthy future of our children and grandchildren, then we need to not only eat local or plant gardens but start engaging as fair food citizens to alter the larger policies and institutional practices that are driving the system in its current direction.

Now that I have introduced you to the key principles of a revamped food system and some of the fair food heroes who are implementing these changes, it's time to get personal. In this part of the book I'll show how each of you can become a hero of the Fair Food Revolution. Here you will find a variety of actions you can take, from altering your food-buying and eating habits at home to leading change in your community to encouraging your government representatives to revise public policy. Some of the suggestions will be illustrated with examples of people making the changes that lead to improved personal and planetary health. Others will point you to people, organizations, and websites that will put you on the path of empowerment and change. The final chapter offers an extensive list of resources, including those organizations mentioned throughout the book. I am convinced that, armed with these myriad suggestions, you can use your creativity and passion to have a positive impact on this issue that is so critical to our future.

In Your Kitchen and Community

If you have come this far in *Fair Food* or are enough of a food activist to turn to this section of the book, you are probably doing (or thinking of doing) at least some of what you are about to read in this chapter. While "voting with your fork" or "changing the system with your food dollar" will not, in my opinion, ever be enough to bring about a redesign of the food system, it is an important start. Every time one of us chooses to spend our food dollars at a farmers' market or CSA rather than a conventional grocery store, we are sending a message. And as more of us do the same, that message will be heard by farmers who grow our food, and by food processors, distributors, and retailers. So let's keep sending these messages and eating great meals while we are at it.

Eat Seasonally, Shop Locally

In almost every area of every state, you can find information on the Internet or in local newspapers about farmers who are selling their products directly to consumers without a middleman (also known as direct marketing). In most cases, this contributes to a more local or regional system, cutting down on the number of miles the food travels to get to your plate—which means that the food is much fresher and often much tastier since it does not need to travel for days to get to you. And because the farmer doesn't need to be concerned with his or her products maintaining quality during long-distance transport, he or she can harvest at a riper stage of development. For many fruits and vegetables, this means their freshness and taste are unparalleled. There are many ways that farmers are direct marketing these days; you can find them and their products at local farmers' markets and at farm stands.

A note of caution: I have learned when shopping at farmers' markets that I cannot be assured that the farmers are selling only what they have grown. Some markets require "producer only" status for vendors, which means that merchants are required to sell only what they have grown on their farms. Other farmers' markets allow vendors to sell both what they grow and/or what they can broker that has been grown by others. In some cases, such as at Eastern Market in Detroit, some farmers sell exclusively what they grow; others offer a mixture; and still others only resell what they buy from a produce broker.

How do you know if the vendor actually grew what he is selling? You can ask, although you may not always get a straight answer. It helps if you are aware of the seasonality of fruit and vegetable production in your area. For example, when I find a vendor at a farmers' market in Michigan selling pineapples and bananas, I know he didn't grow these products, because there are absolutely no tropical fruits grown anywhere near the state. It gets a little trickier when there are strawberries in the market in August. Yes, Michigan grows great strawberries, but the season generally starts and ends in June. The weather here is too hot in late summer for the delicate fruit, so they are probably being shipped in from somewhere else, and the vendor is functioning as a middleman.

One good resource for information on the seasonality of produce in your area is the manager of the market where you shop. In my experience, the managers know their vendors well and can steer you in the right direction if you are interested in purchasing from the folks who actually grow the produce. Another way to learn more about what is in season is by contacting the local cooperative extension office; you can find them in the phone book or online. Usually housed in county government offices, they will likely have a point person you can talk to or a resource guide. You can also look at the websites listed in Chapter 10 under "Resources for Conscious Consumers" to find guides to seasonality of produce for different regions of the United States.

Eating seasonally is one way to play a role in decreasing the number of miles that food is transported to get to your plate. Many grocery stores now feature local and seasonal produce, too. And for those who want and can afford the convenience of home delivery, businesses such as Fresh Picks in Chicago and Basis in New York deliver local, seasonal produce right to your door.

I have often heard the idea of eating local criticized because in northern climates the growing season is so short. It is true that in these areas, tomatoes and peaches picked at their peak will be available for only two or three months of the year, depending on where you live. But two simple technologies are helping many people extend the season for eating local. One is the freezer: you can freeze locally grown fruits and vegetables when they are at their best and then eat them out of the freezer during the rest of the year. A few years ago, one enterprising woman started a business called Locavorious in our area. She purchases choice fruits and vegetables from local farmers, washes and freezes them, and distributes them to customers throughout the year. Locavorious operates like a CSA in that the customers get a share of the "harvest" each week during the winter and early spring for a preset amount of money that they paid the previous summer.

The second simple technology that has been developed to extend the growing season for local foods, especially vegetables, is the hoop house (or high tunnel, as some call it), which is simply a frame made of plastic or metal, covered by greenhouse-grade polyethylene plastic. It is high enough for a person to walk into (and literally looks like a high plastic tunnel) and is covered at both ends so it is fully enclosed. One of the first farmers in the northern United States to successfully experiment with "four-season farming" is Eliot Coleman in Maine. He has been perfecting techniques of winter production in hoop houses for many years, and sells vegetables grown on his farm year round. He has also written several books on the subject.[2] Now there are programs that train farmers in cold climates to grow vegetables in hoop houses to extend the production and marketing season. One of the very best of these programs is at the Michigan State University Student Organic Farm. An eight-month training program runs each year from March through November, teaching farmers and aspiring farmers how to grow and market organic vegetables and fruit using this season extension technology. In addition, the USDA offers funding (through the Natural Resource Conservation Service) for farmers to build hoop houses on their land.

Many families are joining CSAs like Lindentree Farm, bringing the freshest, healthiest food into their kitchens while helping families make a decent living on small acreages, often near urban or suburban centers. The CSA approach has become so popular that in many places, CSA farms are at their capacity and prospective customers are being put on waiting lists. Most CSA farmers use organic methods and are careful stewards of our natural resources. There are several good resource lists that can help you find a CSA near you.[3]

If you are ready to make the small effort to purchase some of your groceries locally, the infrastructure is developing to help you. It is not yet perfect and can be clumsy at times, but by joining these efforts now, you will help them emerge into the mainstream. You can find farmers who work in your area and sell directly to customers on a number of website directories listed in Chapter 10.

The advantages of purchasing food directly from farmers and through locally owned businesses go beyond freshness, taste, and good nutrition. Buying local means supporting the local economy as well, which means creating jobs and a stronger tax base for local government and services. Supporting the local food economy will keep farmers on the land and preserve farmland and open space for the future. For anyone interested in learning more about local economies and their positive impact, read Michael Shuman's wonderful books, *Going Local* and *The Small-Mart Revolution*. The organization I mentioned in Chapter 4, BALLE (Business Alliance for Local Living Economies), can help guide you in exploring this aspect of redesigning the food system.

Earlier I described the changes made by George Shetler on his dairy farm. By shifting the milk production to a grass-based system and bottling the milk on his own farm, he has taken steps to protect the land and water in his area while creating an economically viable business. This works only if the rest of us do our part—by buying Shetler's milk and ice cream at local stores. Whenever I go to the Traverse City area and need milk, I always buy these dairy products as a way of supporting the kind of food system I want to see in all our communities. You can do the same. It may take a bit more effort, but by asking questions about local dairies in your area (see the list in Chapter 10), you can play your part in ensuring a fair food future.

Is Organic the Answer?

It is not unusual for me to be asked this question. The short answer is "partly." Most of us who were farming organically back in the 1960s and '70s or who were involved in the organic food movement in one way or another were conscious of the principles I am suggesting for a redesigned food system. Many present-day organic farmers are also working hard to continue to incorporate the principles of ecology and diversity into their systems. Along the way, organic food has also become a growing market niche, providing a price premium for those farmers who carry the USDA organic certification and big business for food processors, distributors, and retailers.

In order for a product to have the USDA organic certification label, it has to be produced and processed without using any of the prohibited materials that are listed in the USDA organic standards rule.[4] It also means that the farmer used organic seeds or seedlings that were produced with organic methods, unless they were unavailable. Inspectors who are authorized by the USDA to certify organic farms also make sure that proper crop rotations are being followed and that on-farm composting of animal manure is done correctly. They monitor soil tests for nutrient availability to make sure that the farmer is not adding any unnecessary ingredients to the soil.[5] When you purchase a food product with the organic label, you can be assured that the farmer or processor did not use substances prohibited by the USDA, including synthetic pesticides or fertilizers, fumigants, solid waste from sewage disposal, and genetically modified seeds. It is the best assurance we have, short of growing our own food (or trusting the farmer who did), that there's no pesticide residue or that the products are not genetically modified.

What we can't be sure of is that our purchase is supporting fair treatment of farmworkers or that the price premium you pay for organic foods is making its way back down the supply chain and being distributed equitably. This is especially the case with organic foods grown in places such as China or Chile, where there may be even less control and less transparency about production practices. I buy organic produce at times, usually when it is grown closer to home, and I think doing so is a good idea for anyone who wants to minimize the risk of pesticide residue on their food or who wants to support organic farmers. We just need to realize that the organic label alone can't provide all of the information we need if our intention is to support a fair food system with our food purchases.

There are other certification systems that are more informative about the practices used to produce the food, and they hold some promise in helping consumers "vote with their food dollars." One of the longest-standing and most effective is the label from the Food Alliance, a nonprofit organization that started with a Kellogg Foundation grant in 1994. Since then, it has developed a certification program and a Food Alliance seal that can be placed on products approved by its program. The organization asks growers about their practices related to fertilizer and pesticide use, soil and water conservation, humane treatment of animals, and just and fair treatment of workers. When shoppers see the Food Alliance label (now found primarily in the Pacific Northwest, but slowly spreading to other parts of the country), they can be assured the product was produced in a system that embodies many of the principles I advocate for a redesigned food system.[6]

Free-Range and Grass-Fed

I'm aware that many conscious consumers these days look for and buy "sustainably produced" livestock products—chickens and eggs that are raised free-range or meat that is grass-fed. When chickens are raised in confined operations, they are given about fifty square inches each, about the same amount of space that a placemat takes up on a table. Their feet never touch the ground and the eggs they lay go down conveyor belts to be collected. These chickens are egg-producing machines. Fed by automated feeders, they spend their whole lives in climate-controlled sheds with the lights kept on. That's how most of our eggs are produced.

Free-range doesn't necessarily mean pasture-raised. The USDA's only requirement is that "free-range" chickens must have access to the outside—and that's only for chickens raised for meat.[7] There are absolutely no regulations regarding how long they should be outside or how much room they are to be given. According to some reports, many free-range chickens spend most of their lives in cages and are fed antibiotics and animal byproducts. One report concludes, "Unless you are confident that you know the conditions under which the chickens you are eating were raised, free-range birds may not be what you thought they were."[8]

If you choose to buy free-range eggs and your intention is to support a system where the birds are treated more humanely, or if you believe that free-range birds produce healthier eggs, then by all means, look for free-range eggs, but try to find out as much as you can about where those eggs or chickens came from by asking questions. Does the store manager know anything about the farm and its practices? What assurance does he have that the eggs were really produced under free-range conditions? I can go to several stores in my area and find Grazing Fields eggs, produced by dozens of chicken growers and marketed cooperatively under this label. Because I trust Jane Bush, the woman who started this brand with her own chickens, I know that I am getting a "real" free-range egg. If you want to find a similar source in your community, check out the directory in Chapter 10.

The situation is a bit different for grass-fed beef. The Agricultural Marketing Service (AMS) of the USDA is establishing a voluntary standard for claims that livestock are grass- (or forage-) fed. Now livestock producers can request that the USDA verify such a claim, which is accomplished through an audit of the production process in accordance with procedures that have been codified by the USDA,[9] and the meat sold from these approved programs can be labeled as such. Meat produced under this standard comes from animals that are fed only grass and forage for their entire life.[10]

However, meat labeled as "grass-fed" may or may not have been labeled according to these voluntary practices. You may want to purchase grass-fed beef because the animals are treated more humanely, or because it is a more environmentally friendly way of raising livestock, or due to the health claims that are made for grass-fed versus grain-fed meat. Whatever the reason, you need to be aware that there are not strict federal standards for grass-fed as there are for organic. You are buying based on the trust you have in that farmer's or rancher's practices.

Wild or Farm Raised?

Fish is one of the fastest-growing sources of protein in our diet, and for many years the medical community has been touting the benefits of eating it. At the same time, we are warned that fish may be less healthy due to toxins that can accumulate in the animal or about fish that are caught in unsustainable ways, including overfishing. If you want to enjoy eating fish while contributing to your own health and the health of our oceans, you need to be careful about your choices at restaurants and at the grocery store. The Monterey Bay Aquarium has a program called Seafood Watch that provides great research-based information on many popular species. They publish a small card that provides easy-to-understand information about which fish should be consumed and which should not, and why.[11] For a more complete explanation of the pluses and minuses of eating wild-caught and farm-raised fish, I recommend Paul Greenberg's new book, *Four Fish*.[12]

Beyond the Kitchen

If you are ready to participate in creating a fair food future beyond your own kitchen, one place to start is in your community. Instead of using just your personal purchasing power to support the kind of food system you want, you can help create a community buying club so that your friends and others in the community can combine their food purchasing efforts. Instead of only growing a vegetable garden in your backyard, consider participating in or supporting a community garden so more people in the community have access to land, water, and shared information. And instead of only focusing on how you can directly access great food at farmers' markets, consider supporting efforts to help those in historically underserved communities get greater access to fresh fruits and vegetables.

Buying Clubs

Simply put, a buying club is an organized group of people who purchase in bulk directly from the producer, thereby taking advantage of more favorable pricing (fewer middlemen) and shipping fees due to the higher volume, and then sharing those savings among the members of the club. It is the easiest (and most fun) community organizing I have ever done.

The Ann Arbor Wild Salmon Minyan (AAWSM for short) was born in the summer of 2003. Because I knew I would be spending a week that July conducting site visits in the Pacific Northwest, my wife, Lucinda, and I decided that she would join me when my work was done and we would find a nice, remote bed-and-breakfast for a long weekend. I asked around and found out about Lummi Island, a small gem situated in the northern part of Puget Sound, near Canada, which we reached by ferry from Bellingham, Washington.

The island is very rural in nature—there are only some small farms or gardens and a few homes. After we settled into our room at the Willows Inn, we decided a pre-dinner walk was in order. Two miles out, we came across a cluster of homes in what looked to be the center of "town." This area was at sea level, not up on a bluff like the Willows Inn. As we walked by the homes, the first thing I noticed was what appeared to be small railroad tracks across the asphalt roads coming from the front yards of several homes and continuing onto the beach and into the water. Upon closer examination, I noticed the tracks also contained large raftlike structures with small metal wheels.

When I asked about the strange structures I had seen on our walk, Riley Starks, the innkeeper, told us about reef netting salmon, a traditional method of catching the fish during their spawning run to the Frazier River on Orcas Island. The method, which had been developed by the native people who had inhabited the island before any whites came, is allowed to be practiced only by a few modern-day fishermen. They are required to keep a very close watch on their catch and provide the state Department of Natural Resources with information about the health of the salmon each year.

When the sockeye are running, the big rafts are rolled from the front yards down into the water, where they are towed to the middle of the channel and anchored in a line, fifty to one hundred yards apart. Large nets are strung between each of the rafts and twelve-feet-tall lifeguard chairs are erected on each raft. The nets are then lowered into the water and the "lifeguards" wait until they literally see the school of salmon swimming over the nets. The nets are then raised and the fish are immediately bled and put on ice. As Starks told me the story, all I could think about was the raging debates I had encountered regarding the virtues of wild-caught salmon versus the evils of farm-raised. We had decided in our own kitchen that, until there was documentation that farm-raised salmon did not compromise the ocean ecology and did not use artificial dyes to make the fish pink, we would stick with wild-caught.

The challenge for us living in Michigan is that wild-caught salmon tends to be one of the more expensive protein sources, costing $15 to $20 per pound, depending on the year and season. I asked Starks how much he could charge for his Lummi Island wild salmon, and I was stunned by his answer: $1 to $2 per pound wholesale at the docks in Seattle. At that price, he told me, they could not come close to making a living from fishing. He and his fishermen colleagues had developed a way to quick-freeze the sockeye fillets and shrink-wrap them for shipping, but so far had not had much success with retail sales.

We spent a lovely weekend on the island, walking, eating delicious meals from the inn's kitchen, and touring the small farm that Starks had established on the island to grow most of the vegetables and eggs that he served his guests. But all weekend I could not stop thinking: "$2 wholesale and $20 retail—there must be an opportunity here somewhere!"

On Monday morning, as we were about to leave for the long journey home, I said to Starks, "There ought to be a way that you can get more than $2 per pound for your salmon and that we can get wild-caught salmon in Ann Arbor for less than $20 per pound. We should start a buying club." He told me that his fishermen's cooperative had discussed the idea of buying clubs several times but had not yet found a way to implement the idea. He did, however, stick a frozen sockeye fillet in my backpack as a parting gift. He asked me to try it and let him know what I thought. As we were waiting for our flight home at the Seattle airport, I called several friends in Ann Arbor to see if they could come over for dinner the following night.

The next evening, eight of our friends gathered at our home, and I grilled the Lummi Island sockeye fillet. I waited to tell the story until dinner was finished, but I couldn't help but notice the expressions on our guests' faces as they took their first bites of fish. The almost universal exclamation was, "This is the *best* salmon I have ever tasted." After dinner I told them the story of Starks, Lummi Island, reef netting, and the wholesale-retail price spread for wild salmon. And so began the AAWSM.

Nine years later, we are still shipping in wild salmon (as well as wild black cod and halibut) from our fishermen on Lummi Island.

Some of their fish are still reef netted off of Lummi Island and some are caught in Alaska, where they take their boats each season. We now have more than one hundred families on our e-mail list. Twice a year, almost a ton of our AAWSM frozen fish is loaded onto a truck filled with seafood being delivered to locations across the country. Our AAWSM order is driven from Lummi Island's cold-storage facility directly to a loading dock in Ann Arbor, where each family comes to pick up their boxes of fish and take them home to their freezers. We pay only 50 to 60 percent of what it would cost to purchase wild-caught salmon from a local retailer, including shipping. And the fishermen at Lummi Island get three times the wholesale price for their product. We were the first buying club to connect with Lummi Island Wild, but now they have several buying clubs, of which AAWSM is one of the largest. Buying clubs now represent more than 20 percent of their total catch, and a much larger percentage of their net profit.

Anyone with a passion for good food and an ability to "connect the dots" can do the same with a variety of products. It means spending the effort to find the source of the item and then sharing with friends, colleagues, and others in your community the idea of creating this buying club. Several resource directories are listed in Chapter 10 to help you get started. You might also find someone selling locally raised meat or eggs at the farmers' market who is willing to be a source for your buying club. In our case, family by family, the wild-salmon buying club grew (and continues to grow with each order). We are now considering branching out to locally raised chicken and other meats.

I am aware that wild-salmon (or any other) buying clubs alone will not cause a redesign of the food system. But it is a step that can take us from focusing solely on our own refrigerator to connecting with like-minded individuals in our community so that more people gain access to good food while supporting those who are producing it. Even after all these years, every time our group gets together to share a meal of Lummi Island salmon, the first bite is often followed by a smile and the words, "This fish is awesome!"

Buy Local

The trend toward local food has caught on with a vengeance. Farmers' markets have increased more than threefold since 1994, and just in the past five years, direct farm-to-consumer sales have more than doubled.[13] Many in the food retail industry would say that this is the most significant current trend in food. Grocery stores large and small proudly display signs that tell us "locally grown by farmers in this area." Sometimes pictures of the farmers even hang over the produce section. And many restaurants now feature meals made from ingredients grown by farmers in the area. Local food has not always been this trendy. Capturing this trend as an opportunity to redesign the food system is challenging, but there are communities across the country doing just that. And it started with a single initiative almost twenty years ago.

In 1993, one of the first projects we funded in our Integrated Farming Systems program at the Kellogg Foundation was known as CISA (Community Involved in Sustaining Agriculture) in western Massachusetts. The project's major institutional collaborators were Hampshire College, the University of Massachusetts, and the Pioneer Valley Growers Association. Over time, many other organizations, businesses, and individuals became involved. The goal of this project was to organize and implement community-wide efforts that could sustain small-scale agriculture as a viable enterprise in an area where the pressure to sell farmland for development was intense. (Due to its topography, the area is not well suited for larger-scale agriculture, so consolidating farm operations as a strategy for financial survival was not an option.)

One of the ideas of the project team was to create focused communications that would feature local farmers and encourage shoppers in the Amherst-Northampton area to buy as much of their groceries as possible from them. The budget originally submitted to and approved by the Kellogg Foundation did not contain sufficient funding to conduct a sophisticated communications campaign. I suggested that Kellogg fund this effort, but only if the group was willing to work in a more professional manner than having staff dressed in apple and carrot costumes at the county fair. We funded focus groups to determine the most effective messaging and to explore the values that people in that community held that could be related to local food. We then connected CISA with top-notch communications professionals who knew how to poll and had a track record in creating mailings, radio, and print communications for successful political campaigns, and we asked them to create the campaign.

The "Be a Local Hero, Buy Locally Grown" effort was a resounding success. More than 60 percent of the residents in the target communities were aware of the campaign and had heard about it in the media, and the local farmers who were involved were reporting sales increases of more than 10 percent. Even more telling was what happened with such food retailers as Stop & Shop, the largest grocer in the area. Before the campaign began, CISA staff met with produce buyers from Stop & Shop and other local grocers to ask if they would like to be part of the program. CISA was turned down by most of the large food retailers, who did not see the importance of supporting an effort to get more local fruits and vegetables into their stores. By the end of the first week of the communications campaign—with bus signs, radio ads, newspaper coverage, and direct mailing to customers—Stop & Shop and other stores were calling the CISA office asking how they could participate. They had so many customers coming into their stores requesting local produce that they realized both the benefit of joining the campaign and the risk of sitting on the sidelines.

"Be a Local Hero, Buy Locally Grown" is now widely recognized as the first modern-era communications campaign to encourage local purchasing as a way to support local farming. On the heels of this successful campaign, another Kellogg Foundation grantee, FoodRoutes Network, collaborated with CISA to create communications templates and guides so other communities could create and implement successful "buy local" campaigns. There are currently more than eighty Buy Fresh, Buy Local campaigns, or chapters, in communities across the United States, helping farmers collectively brand their produce as locally grown and encouraging shoppers to buy locally. Supported by FoodRoutes (www.foodroutes.org), all of these projects are now locally funded and run. And it all started with a single communications campaign nearly twenty years ago in western Massachusetts. The FoodRoutes website has all the contact information you need to either join an existing chapter of Buy Fresh, Buy Local or to start one in your own community. This is one way to start the shift from conscious consumer in your own home to engaged food citizen in your community.

Community Gardens

Another way to engage as a food citizen is to expand your gardening chops from your home to the community. Community gardens are sprouting in almost every city in the country. Sometimes these are spontaneous expressions of the desire to grow better food and spend time with neighbors, and have very little structure apart from what the gardeners themselves decide about protocols for watering, fencing, and the like. But often there is an organization helping the garden and gardeners.

One of the largest such organizations in the United States is Greening of Detroit. Detroit has become known as a center for urban gardening and small-scale urban agriculture and has quite a long history of urban gardens, including the mayor's Farm-A-Lot program, which started in 1970. Through this program, city gardeners could access seeds, transplants, and rototilling for their garden plots. The Detroit Agricultural Network started in 1996 as a way to get gardeners to share knowledge and resources. Due to the dwindling tax base in Detroit, in 2000 the Farm-A-Lot program ceased, and Detroit's urban gardeners, many of whom are seniors, needed help. Greening of Detroit—a nonprofit organization that had been established several years earlier to guide and inspire the reforestation and creation of a "greener" Detroit through planting trees and conducting educational programs, environmental leadership, and advocacy—took on the job of getting this garden resource network funded. Ashley Atkinson, a young woman who had learned her gardening and leadership skills growing up in Flint, wrote the grants that were funded through the USDA Community Food Projects program. She then created the Garden Resource Program at Greening of Detroit. In 2010, the Greening of Detroit program supported 1,221 community, backyard, and school gardens all over the city. They are helping to grow food on more than three hundred acres of land overall, have a staff of thirty, and calculated that in 2010, their gardeners produced 160 tons of fresh food. And it's not only seniors who are growing the vegetables. They have touched the lives of 10,000 young people, ages fourteen through seventeen, through garden- and school-based nutrition education programs.

Maria, for example, is sixteen years old and has grown to love the taste of broccoli. Children like her, who are living at or below the poverty level, are eating new fruits and vegetables and beginning to redefine the concept of health for themselves and their families. According to Atkinson, "Though we don't yet have quantitative evidence, the more frequent the contact, the higher impact it has on youth's ability to try new fruits and vegetables, as well as on overall preferences and daily consumption."

Though the idea of a garden is readily associated with food, these gardens offer Maria and the youth in her community much more than the experience of harvesting a ripe, red tomato. They reap a positive group identity and valuable tools for creating community. Each garden is associated with a color, and each gardening group designs its own T-shirt logo. When asked whether she sees the program as mainly a youth enrichment or a food systems program, Atkinson replies, "I see the program more as a community development program with youth enrichment and food systems as strategies to build community."

The program has a constructive relationship with the public school system and is upheld citywide as an example of how schools can partner with nonprofit community enterprises to provide support to youth. Sixty of the community gardens in Detroit are situated at either public or charter schools. In addition to the focus on youth development, professional development of the teachers in the community is highly regarded. A series of classes has been developed for science teachers for continuing education credits, and staff have a say in the school science curriculum.

Ten percent of the gardens supported by Greening of Detroit sell produce at farmers' markets in the city, and garden groups take home up to $500 per month, representing a sustainable model for keeping youth enrichment programs within the neighborhoods. The organization is now preparing for its biggest year ever in 2011, with 1,600 gardens. Its leaders estimate that the value of food grown in these gardens surpasses $1 million.[14]

If you are interested in finding out about community gardening opportunities in your area, you can check with your local extension office or ask at a local gardening store. A national organization, the American Community Gardening Association (www.community garden.org), provides assistance in starting community gardens across the country and would welcome your interest.

Most of what you have read so far in this chapter relates to either what you can do to get yourself and your family better food while also helping to shift the food system, or what you can do to help your neighbors and friends access better food. One of the shortcomings of the "food movement" to date has been its almost sole focus on creating better access to healthy, fresh, and sustainably grown foods for those of us who can afford it or who live in communities in which access is relatively easy to create. And, rightfully so, this movement has been accused of focusing only on the elite members of our society. The big challenge for those of us working to redesign the food system is to create greater access in communities that have historically been underserved or excluded from accessing healthier, sustainably grown food.

There are many urban myths about how low-income families living in inner-city neighborhoods view food and the food system. From research that we have done at Fair Food Network, we know that in general, low-income consumers in inner-city neighborhoods, just like their suburban and higher-income urban counterparts, know what good food is and what it isn't. They understand the difference between fresh fruits and vegetables and those that come to them in cans and packages, many of them out of date and overpriced. They appreciate the difference between purchasing groceries at the only store they can access if they don't have a car (often a liquor store or gas station convenience store) and the big-box grocer in the suburbs. They perceive the inequity of a $1 price tag for a single, withered apple in a neighborhood party store. And, just like soccer moms in the suburbs, moms in the inner city would prefer to cook their families good, wholesome meals made from high-quality ingredients.[15]

Many of these inner-city residents view the disparities in the food environment between where they live and the higher-income suburbs as another example of race and class inequity in our society. A generation ago, residents of these communities were faced with a practice known in the housing industry as "redlining," a process by which mortgage lending was unavailable in certain neighborhoods, so home ownership was nearly impossible for residents in low-income areas, primarily communities of color. Redlining in the housing sector is no longer legal and its practice is now frowned upon by society. Yet, what many of these same families now face is "nutritional redlining." They understand that they are being systematically denied access to healthy, fresh, and sustainably grown food, resulting in significant health concerns in their communities compared to other more affluent neighborhoods.

As engaged food citizens, there is a lot we can do to address these disparities. In the next two chapters, I will discuss how you can be-

come active in helping shift institutional and public policy to rec-
tify these inequities and set the stage for a redesigned food system
that works for us all. Here I will consider several innovations that
began as pilot projects and that are just starting to be implemented
on a scale that can be replicated in other communities.

From Green Carts to Community Kitchens

There are programs in the food system occurring on a much smaller
scale than a state-level Fresh Food Financing Initiative (described in
Chapter 3) or new national chain supermarkets, but that are no less
significant for those involved in these endeavors. One example is
the New York City Green Carts project, envisioned as a public/pri-
vate partnership with the Mayor's Fund to Advance New York City.
In 2008, the Laurie M. Tisch Illumination Fund, a philanthropic
foundation, provided a $1.5 million grant to help entrepreneurs go
into business selling fresh produce in underserved New York City
neighborhoods. The project's goals are to provide microloans and
business development assistance for 1,000 NYC Green Cart vendors, as well as communications and outreach campaigns to encourage residents to purchase fresh fruits and vegetables from the
carts. These mobile food carts can sell only fresh fruits and vegetables and operate in designated areas. Five hundred carts were on the
streets by the spring of 2011, creating new jobs and providing thousands of households with better access to healthier food choices.
There are now more than 2,000 NYC Green Cart vending permit
applications in process.[16]

Recently I had the opportunity to visit one of the vendors, Bar-
donio Sanchez-Vivar. His cart at 163rd Street and Walton Avenue in
the Bronx was full of ripe fruits and healthy-looking vegetables. They
were certainly not all locally grown (but delicious papayas and man-
goes, nonetheless). Sanchez-Vivar not only sells at his Green Cart
with his wife, but he now has a second small business using a newly
acquired truck to distribute produce from Hunts Point market in

the Bronx to other Green Cart vendors, his uncle's bodega, and a Mexican restaurant.

The Green Carts project seems to be working and is a model that can certainly be replicated elsewhere. One of the driving forces behind this effort is Karen Karp, who is very knowledgeable about the food system and is quite adept at navigating bureaucratic hurdles. Anyone who is interested in helping to create this kind of project elsewhere should contact Karp to learn from her success.[17]

Another resource for making healthy, fresh food available in underserved communities is a community kitchen or kitchen incubator. A commercial kitchen, built to local health department standards, is made available to community members either for free or at a nominal hourly rate. A community kitchen provides the opportunity for an individual entrepreneur with a recipe and motivation to develop a food product that can be sold at local farmers' markets or at food stores. Some kitchen incubators are being developed to help aspiring food entrepreneurs access business planning expertise, affordable product liability insurance, packaging and marketing resources, and distribution channels.

The Starting Block (www.startingblock.biz) in western Michigan is one example of a successful community kitchen that is also a business incubator for food entrepreneurs. The Starting Block provides budding entrepreneurs with a commercial kitchen, low office rent that includes computers, Internet access, and phone and office support, and expert resources through Michigan State University. The commercial kitchen is available to producers and packagers of specialty and gourmet food, caterers, and church, school, and civic groups. See Chapter 10 for a resource list of incubator kitchens in many areas throughout the country.

Community Food Assessments

Before changes can take place in a community, the status of the food environment as experienced by its residents has to be determined.

This information can be elicited by undertaking what is known as a community food assessment. The city of Oakland, California, recently conducted such an assessment as part of the HOPE Collaborative, a project funded by the Kellogg Foundation and including many partners and organizations, such as the Alameda County Public Health Department, who were all concerned about creating a healthier food environment in the community.

With the help of volunteers over a three-month period, the project held listening sessions in six vulnerable neighborhoods. Residents were asked questions about where they accessed their food and what they would like to see changed in their food environment. The project also assessed inventories at corner stores to determine what was currently available to residents who did not have access to transportation to shop elsewhere. The volunteers also walked through the neighborhoods to assess the availability of open land for potential community gardens or small farms.

Here are some of the findings:

- Existing food sources are insufficient and there is little healthy or fresh food available—virtually no fresh fruits or vegetables.
- People want to cook healthy and affordable food, and most of the participants cook meals at home on a regular basis.
- There is not enough available land in Oakland (other than backyard gardens) to make a significant dent in the food needs, so any local farming would have to occur outside of the city limits.
- In the most vulnerable neighborhoods in Oakland, the spending power of the community can actually accommodate four times the grocery store square footage that currently exists, which means that residents spend 75 percent of their food dollars outside of the community, simply due to a lack of full-service stores. This translates into a $375 million "leakage" of economic activity and spending out of the community each year. That amount of spending, they calculated, would translate into 1,500 well-paying jobs, if it were to stay in the community.[18]

Oakland's community food assessment has led to several new projects related to reinventing its food system, including development of a new grocery store, a CSA specifically geared to low-income households (where they can purchase a twenty-five-pound box of fruit and vegetables each week for $20), and a partnership with the Alameda County Deputy Sheriffs' Activities League to put unemployed youth to work growing food for the CSA on available county land. The league considers it a crime-prevention strategy.

To get a community food assessment started in your community, enlist the help of one or two others and contact your local public health or wellness office. You can check out the methodology used in Oakland or access other community food assessment efforts in the reference list in Chapter 10.

How Can You Play a Role?

All of these projects can be replicated in your community, and some of them are probably already happening around you. As a first step, connect with one of these innovative projects. Or, if you see an opportunity to start something new, let your inspiration lead you to action! I can assure you that you will not be acting in isolation. Refer to the final chapter of this book for contact information, or visit www.fairfoodnetwork.org/list to find an updated listing of organizations all over the country engaged in these kinds of projects. Connect with them, ask how you can get involved, volunteer your time, and donate your money. There are also important institutional and public policies you can support to help programs like these expand and succeed. That is the topic of the following two chapters.

www.fairfoodnetwork.org/list

CHAPTER 8

Institutional Change

Making changes in our homes, neighborhoods, and communities is a great start for bringing more balance back into our food system, as these are the places where we engage with it most of the time. But currently nearly one-half of the dollars flowing through the system is for food eaten outside of the home. Some of those purchases occur in restaurants, and we have as much of a say about what we order there as we do about what we purchase at grocery stores. And residents in low-income communities face the same kinds of issues in restaurants as they do in grocery stores. Often the only restaurants in their areas are fast food chains offering primarily high-calorie, high-fat foods. Changes are coming here too (albeit slowly), with some local governments, like in New York City, starting to demand that restaurant chains remove trans fats from their menus and list the caloric content of every item. It remains to be seen how effective these measures will be in shifting food environments in low-income neighborhoods. My suspicion is "not very."

But if we look at some of the major institutions that serve us food, such as public schools, college cafeterias, and hospitals, we can start to see the outline of food-system redesign emerge. In each case, this is happening because a group of organizations in the non-profit sector is taking the lead to engage with the institutions, partner with change agents within the existing structure, and work with them to build models of change that are ready to move to a larger scale. But we don't have to leave it to these leaders alone to get the job done. If you are passionate about the issue, you can find a way to work with any institution with which you are affiliated to focus on what it can do to help.

When I first started working with the Kellogg Foundation in the early 1990s, my responsibilities included drafting funding documents for the Kellogg board to review, but we were not allowed to use the words "sustainable," "environment," or "policy." Though I was never sure why these words were prohibited, it signaled to me that the board was not ready to support sustainable approaches, environmentalism, or public policy change. I took it upon myself, over time and with good colleagues, to help the board learn how important it was to support sustainable food and agriculture projects, and how the only way to effect change in the system ultimately was to support those organizations trying to shift institutional and government policy. But to do this, I also needed to shift institutional policy within the Kellogg Foundation.

It was a slow process that took a lot of patience and required a willingness on my part to welcome conversations even with those board members who may not have agreed with me. Gradually the institution's perspective started to shift as individual board members altered their views. And then, at a 2006 board meeting when we were debating the merits of a request for funds for a project focused on land preservation, I recall the chair of the board saying, "I am not sure if a land preservation project really falls within our mission as a foundation. But I also see in this project that the land being preserved will be transitioned into small farms using sustainable agriculture practices. I think we should support this project because sustainable agriculture is at the core of our mission as a foundation." Success!

Since the first projects funded in the early 1990s, the Kellogg Foundation has financed more than $300 million of sustainable food and agriculture projects in every part of the country. Almost all of the organizations active in the fair food movement have some connection to Kellogg, and the entire field of philanthropy has started to embrace sustainable food and agriculture as an important focus. When we first started the Kellogg Integrated Farming Systems program in 1992, there were only five or six foundations that had any interest in this area. The few of us then involved created what is known in the foundation world as an "affinity" group—a loosely knit set of foundations all of which are interested in a similar topic. By 2012, the affinity group that we had named Sustainable Agriculture & Food Systems Funders boasted an active membership of sixty-three foundations, all of which are funding the activities of the group. Approximately ten additional funders are considering joining, and each year additional foundations are entering this field. The organizations working on food systems change, both with institutions and public policy, are able to look to a group of supporters more diverse than ever before.

As my own experience illustrates, when it comes to institutional change, we can each start where we are. Every institution, no matter how large or seemingly entrenched, has institutional practices that were created by people who worked there. So the people who work there now have every chance to shift the policies and culture. Once the change process started at the Kellogg Foundation, I was surprised at how many like-minded souls I found to work with. I bet you will be, too.

Making School Food Good Food

Clearly, if we are interested in harnessing the purchasing power of institutions to shift the food system while also providing healthier food for our children, there is no more important institution on which to focus than the public schools. While hard to come by, estimates of the amount of public funds spent on school food run into the billions of dollars (I have been given estimates of between $10 billion and $16 billion).[1] The USDA reports that in 2009, about

$6.3 billion of federal funds were spent on food to prepare school breakfasts and lunches nationwide.[2] By shifting a significant percentage of those dollars to purchasing healthier food, we can start to have an impact on the well-being of our children. And by ensuring that regional farmers grow some portion of that healthy food, we can also use the purchasing power of the school food system as a driver of local economic development—specifically, supporting local farmers. According to the School Nutrition Association, in 2011, 48 percent of school districts nationwide were offering locally sourced fruits and vegetables.[3]

While there are now thousands of school food reform efforts in individual schools and districts, none stands out quite as clearly as the Healthy Schools Campaign in Chicago. Started more than a decade ago by a parent activist, Rochelle Davis, this project now boasts one of the most comprehensive reform efforts to date. Davis and her cadre of concerned parents have worked together with the school administrators, food service directors, and teachers to help create new, sweeping, district-wide policies and practices in the Chicago public schools. There are new nutrition standards and menus, all created with parent input, including using only hormone-free milk and free-range eggs, and in 2011 they committed $2.5 million to purchasing fruits and vegetables from local farmers in Illinois and western Michigan and $1 million to purchasing chicken from Indiana's Miller Amish Country Poultry. Davis and her team are aware that institutional purchasing power can create big ripple effects throughout the entire system.[4]

The Chicago school system is not acting in isolation. In addition to many individual efforts in schools and districts, there are two national organizations that have been paying close attention to school food and how to shift food purchasing and menus from a food systems perspective. The powerhouse behind one of these organizations, School Food Focus: Transforming Food Options for Children in Urban Schools, is Toni Liquori, a longtime faculty member of Teachers College at Columbia University. Her intentional approach to transforming the New York City school system, the nation's largest, can be a model for all of us hoping to have an impact on our own school systems. This national initiative, created in consultation with public health experts, educators, foundations, and a variety of large educational institutions, helps urban school districts transform the quality of their food service. The organization works with thirty of the largest school districts (those with more than 40,000 students) that are ready to shift to healthier and more sustainable food options. It helps identify all the necessary partners in the community—such as farmers, food enterprises, government organizations, school districts and universities, and parents—and brings them together in a learning laboratory that educates and inspires while promoting a strong coalition of organizations and individuals committed to creating change in the school food system.

The organization also helps school districts source healthier sustainably and locally produced food. For example, they have created the Real Food Showcase, designed to introduce food service directors to companies that are ready to supply them with healthy and sustainably produced food. Liquori emphasizes how long the process takes (sometimes eighteen months from conception of an idea to initial implementation) and that at times you need to accept small steps as victories. In the St. Paul, Minnesota, district, for example, a major victory for School Food Focus in the past year was developing a formal bidding process to increase the percentage of locally grown produce. In just a three-month period, the school district purchased nearly $130,000 worth of fruits and vegetables from six farmers within one hundred miles of the city. This represented about 40 percent of all produce purchased by the school district during that time period. They have also been successful in getting suppliers to reduce the sugar content of flavored milk by 30 percent. Now that this has been accomplished, they are going to try to get flavored milk off the school food menu altogether.[5]

Another effort under way is a national network known as Farm to School, which connects educational institutions with local farms and has captured the imagination of tens of thousands of educators, parents, students, volunteers, community leaders, and farmers across the country. The organization focuses on three activities: sourcing school food from local farmers and processors; creating and maintaining school gardens; and having farmers and student groups visit each other. The objectives of the program are in line with what we want for all our children: healthier food in cafeterias for improved child nutrition; access to fresh, sustainably grown food from local farms and ongoing relationships with regional farmers; and health, agriculture, and nutrition education opportunities that expand students' understanding of the source of their food and its quality.

Anupama Joshi, one of the longtime leaders of the Farm to School Network, told me recently, "Ten years back, I would have had to explain what Farm to School was. . . . Now I just mention [the name] and people understand what I am talking about." There are now Farm to School programs in all fifty states, with almost 10,000 schools involved in more than 2,300 school districts. Clearly this is a program whose time has come. There are even state-funded Farm to School coordinators in twenty-eight state governments. And daily, more and more school districts are getting involved. Joshi proudly tells me, "Farm to School is part of changing the overall food and health environment in schools. This is happening more and more in low-income communities; not only in Santa Monica and Berkeley, but in Central Los Angeles and Chicago as well." Unlike many of the innovations in our food system that have benefited only the elite in our society, Farm to School is finding ways to span class boundaries.

Farm to School is more than simply a new food procurement system for local foods in cafeterias. It is creating a new paradigm for the relationship between children, food, farmers, and the community and offers innovative ideas about waste management, such as composting, as well as hands-on projects like planting a school garden and cooking a hot meal using those freshly harvested vegetables. This experiential model provides youngsters with a different appreciation of the earth's bounty and can foster a lifelong preference for a sweet carrot or juicy tomato.

You can check to see if your child's school is involved in the Farm to School Network by going to their website (www.farmtoschool.org). It is listed in Chapter 10, along with several other groups active in the school food reform effort, including Edible Schoolyard in Berkeley, California, s'Cool Food in Santa Barbara, California, and Slow Food USA, a national organization. In addition, federal funds are now available to upgrade school kitchens and make the farm-to-school connection even more possible. Over the next eight years, $40 million in grants will also be available for farms and schools to help make local purchasing financially sustainable over the long term.[6]

If you are interested in working with your local school or district, the experts suggest finding other parents or community members who share your interest in getting higher-quality food into school cafeterias. It always works better if eight or ten parents or community members work together. Then, once you have identified a few interested people, connect with school administrators, school food service staff, and teachers with the intention of learning how the current system works. When school food projects have been successful, it is because the leaders of the effort took time to understand how decisions are made and by whom. The school food service director is key; here are some questions to ask her or him:

- What are you now serving on the menu?
- What kinds of fruits and vegetables are available?
- Do you have the food preparation and processing equipment you need to consider using locally sourced fresh food?
- Do you have any current contacts with local farmers, or would you like us to help make those connections?

After this initial fact-finding, decide on a small change that you can work on together with those you have met at the schools. In the

words of Anupama Joshi, "Dream big—and take small steps." It is
more important initially to work on one small project that gets
everyone on the same page and builds trust. Projects that try to do
too much too soon or that are adversarial tend not to succeed.
"Even if it is just getting a local chef to visit the classroom to
demonstrate cooking with a local and healthy ingredient, that's a
good start," according to Joshi. Another small step could be raising
funds from a local business to sponsor a field trip to an area farm.

Some additional suggestions from the experts include:

- Parents: if your school has a salad bar, volunteer to staff it once
  a month. Students are more likely to try healthy foods offered
  to them directly, and elementary schools especially need help
  with salad bar service.
- Teachers: take your students on a field trip to a local garden,
  urban farm, or farmers' market.
- Teachers and parents: food education can happen in many
  ways. Give students reading assignments about healthy eating,
  cover nutrition topics in science class, and use food labels in
  math lessons. Set a good example by celebrating birthdays with
  healthy foods and active games. Share your knowledge of
  school food with parents and others to get them involved in
  improvements in your school. Submit an article to the school
  newsletter or ask the principal to create a space on the school
  website about school food.[7]

There are lots of resources to help you get started in your community. Every state has a lead coordinator identified with the Farm
to School Network (not all of them funded by state governments),
and these people are there to assist you. The Farm to School Network also has information on existing projects in your area. Another
great resource is a project called FoodCorps, a part of the Ameri-
Corps program, which recruits young adults for a yearlong term of
public service in school food systems. Once they are assigned to a

location, the FoodCorps members help connect farmers to school food buyers, expand food system and nutrition education programs, and build and tend school food gardens. FoodCorps operates in ten states across the country with an initial fifty service members. The project is due to double this number in 2012 and expand to twelve states. The longer term goal is an annual class of 1,000 service members working across all fifty states by 2020. If you or somebody you know is interested in learning more about FoodCorps or applying to become a service member, refer to the FoodCorps entry in Chapter 10 for more information.[8]

Engaging College Students and University Campuses

As a foundation program director, one of my favorite parts of the job was to conduct site visits, which were generally done either before a funding decision was made, as part of the due diligence process, or once a project was funded, to see the work in action. Only on rare occasions was I able to convince a member of the Kellogg Board of Trustees to accompany me, but when I was planning a visit to one of our projects at Washington State University, one of our trustees agreed to come. In this venture, funded as one of our original Integrated Farming Systems projects, the university was working with the American Indian communities and some of the more conventional farmers and ranchers in the eastern part of the state.

We had spent the day visiting with the dean of the College of Agriculture and others on campus, hearing about some of the sustainable practices they were instituting. They were very proud of the campuswide composting system that had been developed and that was now being implemented to recycle all the organic waste from dining facilities and grounds maintenance. We met with several faculty and staff at the university and some of the leaders of the nonprofit organizations that were also involved. As my trustee and I were driving back to our hotel for the night, I recall him asking me, "Oran, where are the students in this project and with this movement?" I did not have a good response, especially when he added, "I can't think of a single successful social movement in my lifetime that did not have some leadership and involvement from college students. Until you figure out a way to engage students in this sustainable food and agriculture movement, I am not sure that it is really going to get much traction."

There are some conversations we can't recall the next day. Others stay with us for a long time. This was one of those conversations. But only recently have I felt that this movement was making any progress at all on this front. At a recent symposium on nutrition security at Tufts University, I met with a group of students in the agriculture, food, and environment program. They are tired of focusing on the problems with the food system. They are now calling themselves "food system solutionaries." I have joined their ranks as another solutionary. There are also thousands of college students and dozens of campuses joining the Real Food Challenge. This relatively new organization—part campaign, part network—is working to shift at least $1 billion of food purchases in college cafeterias to local and sustainable cuisine, with the intention of changing the food system.

It is largely due to the passion and hard work of Anim Steel, a young leader of this movement, along with a colleague of his, David Schwartz, that the Real Food Challenge is a reality. Its mission is to increase the percentage of all food purchases by universities and colleges that are "real food," which this ever-growing cadre of young activists defines as food that truly nourishes people, communities, and the earth and that is produced in a manner that provides good working conditions and fair wages.

The creative leadership team of Steel and Schwartz is effectively laying the foundation of a nationwide network through techniques such as local and regional summits, leadership development and training, shared media resources, and web-based information access. Steel and Schwartz were recently awarded the Echoing Green Fellowship, a seed fund for emerging social entrepreneurs, in recognition of their dynamic leadership and innovative strategies in the good-food arena.

Of the 5,000 students currently involved across the country, about 2,400 of them are participating in regional summits or teaching events. The goal is to shift 20 percent of the roughly $5 billion now spent on food in institutions of higher learning by 2020.[9] In 2011, the Real Food Challenge had twenty-three commitments from schools that translated into $45 million of purchasing power. Twenty-five additional schools have completed assessments to determine the actual amount of current food purchases that are defined as "real food." The group's intermediate goal is $500 million by 2015. In addition to the eighty most active schools (where there is regular contact with campus organizers, a campaign under way, or a Calculator assessment completed or in the works), RFC has built a network of 360 schools where students have held an event on campus, attended a conference, or expressed interest.[10] They are now clustering institutions by location and by common food service providers to maximize efficiency.

The "Real Food Calculator" is comprised of four measures. Is the food that is purchased: local and community based, fair, ecologically sound, and humane? In this way, it is able to measure each institution's food purchases against a specific model developed by the organization and used nationwide. For colleges and universities to participate in this campaign, they need to make two commitments: at least 20 percent of their food purchases need to be real food by 2020, and they must create a tracking system to stay accountable to this commitment. Now a part of the Real Food Challenge, the University of California has put into place a system-wide policy that requires using this calculator in its food purchasing decisions.

While key staff positions and overhead at the Real Food Challenge are funded largely through individual donors and foundation grants, 95 percent of all programs are supported by the fund-raising efforts of students, a true testimony to the grassroots character of this movement.

How can you get involved in the Real Food Challenge? First, find out what is already happening on your campus. Steel suggests that you begin by contacting the following people:

- The director of food services. The person's title may vary (e.g., the executive chef, food service manager, director of dining services), but you're looking for the person who calls the shots for all cafeteria operations.
- University administrator. The sustainability director/officer or a VP of operations—the person who oversees the food service director or who manages contracts for the schools (if dining services are contracted out).
- Upperclassman student activists. Ask them whether there's been any student action around this issue in the past five to seven years.

If nothing is happening yet on your campus, initiate an independent study or an internship focusing on aspects of the food system at your school. Start a food assessment of the kinds of foods purchased and where the products are sourced. A good resource to help you get started can be found at www.realfoodchallenge.org/calculator. Alternatively, call the regional field organizer at the Real Food Challenge and ask for his or her help in getting connected. Don't reinvent the wheel. There may be other campuses in your area that already have a Real Food Challenge project in place, so you can follow some of the policies and practices that have already been developed to help you be effective more quickly. Finally, get to know other food system organizations in your area. Students can help facilitate relationships and connections between farmers, food organizations, and college campuses. Farmers, in particular, could use your help in making connections to a wider array of local institutions, such as public schools.

As the interest of college students in the fair food movement strengthens, there are now at least three hundred institutions that have college farms, fair trade initiatives, or farm-to-cafeteria programs, and the number is growing rapidly. According to Anim Steel, 100 percent of the students who had been actively involved during their college years are now engaged in redesigning their community's food systems in a variety of ways. This is one of his organization's goals. With the combination of market-based initiative and social action, the organization aims to train the next generation of leaders in the fair food movement while simultaneously creating a major shift in demand for real food.

Sometimes the initiative for change comes from inside the institution. This is what is happening at Luther College in Decorah, Iowa. In 2007, the president of the school took his lead from concerned faculty and students and established a goal: by 2012, 35 percent of the $2 million spent on food purchases by the college should come from local sources. From August 2010 to May 2011, Luther spent $371,041 on local food, which represents 20 percent of the total food services budget.[11] What's even more impressive is that Luther College is doing this in partnership with its food service management company, Sodexo, the largest provider for institutional cafeterias in the United States. Luther College may be small by many standards, with only 2,500 students, but with 600 employees it is also the largest employer in a six-county rural area of Iowa.

One of the challenges faced by Luther College in fulfilling its commitment to sourcing locally grown food was food safety. In the past, any farmer could sell individually to the college. Once Sodexo took over the management of the school cafeterias in June 2009, all food vendors selling to the college had to be approved Sodexo vendors. This meant that they needed to follow food safety standards that Sodexo demanded from all of its vendors, including employee training, food handling practices, audits, proper hand washing, and adequate break or lunch rooms. The smaller local farmers did not have the food safety handling procedures that would meet these standards, nor did it make sense for them to follow these same protocols that were developed for much larger operations.

The local farmers who provide produce and eggs to Luther College worked with Sodexo, representatives from the college, and Iowa State University Extension to create a small farmers' cooperative, a new legal entity, that would collectively aggregate and sell to Sodexo.

Grown Locally is now a fully functioning cooperative of seventeen farmers, each of whom grow, harvest, wash, and pack their products separately. They take their products to a central facility that the farmers built as a transfer point. With coolers, storage, and loading equipment, it is now the distribution site for all of their eggs and produce going to the college or other customers. Grown Locally worked with Sodexo and a third-party food safety certifier to make sure that their transfer station was approved for safe food handling; in addition, the cooperative is auditing each of the farmers for safe food handling practices. What appeared to be a roadblock ended up as a demonstration of how small farmers and a very large food service company can work together for the benefit of the farmers and the company's customers who are demanding more locally grown food.[12]

When I asked Ann Mansfield, one of the coordinators of food systems change at Luther College, how this happened in the middle of Iowa, of all places, she told me, "I have been working in the health care field for twenty-two years, and I am now waking up to this connection between healthy food systems and improved health impacts. I really see how local food is less processed, whole, fresher, and much healthier for our students and community." Mansfield started her work at the college but is now reaching out to the community, making sure that the institution not only takes care of the diet and health needs of its own students and staff, but uses its resources to help local farmers transition to meet the demands for locally grown food. In addition, the college is hosting AmeriCorps workers, who are now creating farm-to-school programs in the local public schools.[13]

Can Health Care Institutions Make a Difference?

If hospitals are supposed to make us well, why does so much of the food found there seem so unhealthy? By one estimate, hospitals account for approximately $12 billion of annual purchasing power for food.[14] This includes meals for patients, visitors in cafeterias, and health care workers. Though this figure represents only a small fraction of our total food system, it offers a huge opportunity to demonstrate the connection between personal health, healthy eating, and a healthy food system. By shifting how health care institutions and workers source food, we can make an immediate difference while demonstrating a more integrated approach to health in the long run.

Consider the efforts of Dr. Preston Maring, who works in California at Kaiser Permanente, one of the largest health care institutions in the country. I have long respected his leadership efforts to provide healthier, local food through the creation of farmers' markets on hospital property, as well as his tireless work to use more locally and regionally produced organic foods in hospital meals. Hospital parking lots are convenient spaces for health care workers and visitors to purchase fresh, seasonal fruits and vegetables. Starting with a single farmers' market at Kaiser Permanente's facility in Oakland in 2003, the program has now grown to include forty farmers' markets in six states, either at Kaiser Permanente hospitals or at locations they sponsor. For example, the Learning and Counseling Center at the Ted Watkins Park in Watts (Los Angeles) sponsored by Kaiser Permanente's Community Benefits Group, now has a farmers' market with twenty vendors—in the middle of what most of us would consider a food desert.

A few of the health care institutions that have followed Kaiser Permanente's example in promoting farmers' markets at their facilities include Vanderbilt Hospital, Johns Hopkins Nursing School, Yale Medical School, Cincinnati Children's Hospital, and St. Joseph Hospital in Ann Arbor. Set up in the lobby of the hospital, the St. Joseph farmers' market is patronized primarily by hospital employees and features produce grown on the hospital's six-acre organic farm. Dan Bair, the farmer hired by the hospital to farm part of its campus, which still includes thirty acres of mowed lawn, is selling out of produce on market days. When I asked Bair what it takes for a hospital like St. Joseph to make this kind of commitment to local, sustainable food grown on its own property, he said, "You need someone with clout . . . who supports the idea and project." It helps that the farmer has recruited "people with lab coats on" to help stand behind the farmers' market tables selling the produce. The ultimate goal is to bring some of the farm-raised food to patient meals. In many of the cases in which farmers' markets are succeeding at hospitals, it is because a medical doctor and top administrator have given vocal support. The top management at St. Joseph Hospital is completely behind its farm and market, according to Bair.

Kaiser Permanente now spends approximately 15 percent of its overall food budget on sustainable food, nearly twice as much as most other hospital systems of its size. By the end of 2015, that number is expected to grow to 20 percent.[15] This means that locally grown fruits and vegetables are now being served in patient meals at more than thirty hospitals and medical facilities. In 2011, this translated into more than 190 tons of produce! Much of this sourcing is happening through a partnership with a nonprofit organization, California Alliance with Family Farmers, which supports small and mid-size farms and agriculture. Kathleen Reed, Kaiser Permanente's sustainable food program manager, has worked to develop in-depth standards for how the company defines sustainable food, which differ for different kinds of food. For example, the sustainable food purchasing criteria for dairy call for hormone-free milk produced within two hundred miles of its health care facilities on farms that are certified as treating their animals in a humane way (with the confidence of third-party certification). For vegetables and fruit, the institution's goal is to have products grown within two hundred miles on farms that are certified as using organic or sustainable practices (like those that would qualify for Food Alliance certification).[16]

Maring suggests that it is difficult to increase the amount of locally grown and sustainable foods served to hospital patients primarily due to their specialized dietary needs. However, what can shift the system is how the money spent on food for cafeterias and catering is used. In 2009 alone, at a single Kaiser Permanente facility in Oakland, the company spent $900,000 on food for meetings and events. From the number of times that Maring has attended meetings with pizza as the sole lunch choice, he sees lots of room for using some of those catering funds to bring healthier choices to hospital personnel while supporting a healthier food system in the community. Currently 45 percent of Kaiser Permanente members (as their patients are called) eat only three servings of fruits and vegetables per day; even fewer consume the recommended number of five or more. This is where the health care system can have a positive influence on its patients. By encouraging them to eat a healthier diet, demand can be created for a shift in the distribution system toward an increase in fresh, sustainable food. This underscores the power of health care to change people's lives through preventative medicine.

Maring and others in the field have raised the issue of supply: will there be enough local and sustainable food to fill this growing demand? When the desire for local and sustainably produced food is perceived by farmers as stable and credible, we will see them shift their production to meet this demand. The current centralized and consolidated distribution system does not make it easy for small and mid-size farmers to get their products to these types of institutions. Thus, we need to create opportunities for these farmers to aggregate their products in local and regional food hubs to increase the flow of produce from farms to institutions. This is one reason why institutional purchasing decisions are so important as signals in the system. As more health care, educational, and other institutions shift their procurement policies, farmers will get the message to shift their production practices to meet this market. (When you or I go to the grocery store or farmers' market, we "buy" our food. When a public agency or institution spends our tax dollars on food, it is called "sourcing" or "procurement.")

Another health care group working in this arena is Health Care Without Harm, an international network of more than 450 public health, nursing, environmental, labor, and health care organizations. It was started by health care workers and activists who were concerned about the lack of healthy food choices in health care institutions as well as the life-threatening and environmentally dangerous unintended consequences of current health care practices, such as incinerating medical waste or using mercury in hospital instruments.[17] The members of this network support efforts to implement healthy and environmentally safe alternatives to health care practices that currently create pollution and contribute to disease. This is not a dues-paying organization, but a committed collection of groups and individuals who meet on a biannual basis to discuss best practices and how to move toward their vision of promoting the health of people and the environment in the health care sector (rather than focusing solely on treating illness).

Jamie Harvie, the former executive director of Health Care Without Harm, points to their program Healthy Food in Health Care, which seeks to transform the way food is sourced in the entire system to promote sustainable agricultural practices. The focus is to encourage health care leaders and medical professionals to change institutional and public policy and move toward a healthier food system. Close to four hundred hospitals in the United States and Canada, including over half of Michigan's one hundred fifty hospitals, have already signed the program's "Food Pledge" to purchase foods that both are grown in an ecological manner and also follow principles of social justice. Most of the larger health care systems have signed the pledge, but now the issue is how to properly measure progress using third-party certification, such as that of the Food Alliance. Harvie and his colleagues are creating model contracts for hospitals so they can actually accomplish this proposed shift in purchasing priorities.

Even though progress is slow, Harvie reminds me, "We have been spending only five years trying to undo fifty years of thinking and practice." He is convinced that future collaborations between health care providers and health insurers could have great potential for food systems change.[18]

Knowing that there is a nascent movement in the health care arena to participate in shifting the food system, how can you get involved? First, you can advocate for better food from food service directors in health care institutions, taking a bottom-up approach. If you are a health care worker, which is a large and growing field of employment, you can make a difference by choosing healthier and more sustainable foods when you buy or cater meals for meetings and maybe even create a farmers' market at your local health care facility—and then patronize it and encourage your colleagues to do the same.

How can you have a broader impact on this complex and expansive area of health care? You can write to your local paper and galvanize your community into collective action around this issue. You can urge your local health care facility to purchase local, sustainable food and increase the types of healthy choices available in their facilities. Physicians can band together to encourage hospitals to sign the Food Pledge. Patients and families can write letters praising positive food choices and suggesting changes in food options that do not support this healthy approach to eating. Finally, Harvie suggests that health care administrators and hospital leaders need to call for a national leadership conference focused on changes to the food system, encompassing both institutional procurement and advocating for changes in public policy.

Health care centers are not the only institutions where we are seeing shifts toward healthier eating and sustainable food procurement. It is also happening in corporate workplaces. For example, Dow Chemical, based in Midland, Michigan, with 43,000 employees around the globe, has a goal of reducing health risks to its employee population by 10 percent by the year 2014. As part of this initiative, the company is providing healthy foods in cafeterias and vending machines.[19]

And then there's Bon Appétit Management Company, which oversees food service in more than four hundred cafeterias in thirty-one states for colleges and universities, corporations, and cultural centers, with revenues of approximately $600 million annually, and serving more than 120 million meals each year. According to Maisie Greenawalt, vice president at Bon Appétit, they were the first food service company in the United States "to look at where our food comes from and the effect on our environment, communities and well being. We've been focused on local purchasing since 1999 and have since taken on sustainable seafood, cage-free eggs, antibiotics in animal husbandry, trans fats, climate change and farm workers' rights."

The current company-wide goal is to have 20 percent of food purchases come from "Farm to Fork" vendors (within 150 miles of the cafeteria, small, owner-operated farms, or artisans) annually. A few of the venues served by Bon Appétit include Abercrombie & Fitch Corporate Headquarters in Columbus, Ohio (1,700 people served per day; four vendors); Amazon Corporate Headquarters, Seattle (1,400 people served per day; fourteen vendors); eBay Corporate Headquarters, San Jose, California (2,900 people served per day; seventeen vendors); and Medtronic Corporate Headquarters, Minneapolis, Minnesota (4,700 people per day; twenty-six vendors). In September 2010, the amount of food being sourced from these vendors averaged between 13 percent and 58 percent of total food expenditures, depending on the cafeteria. Greenawalt explains, "As you can see some locations are well over twenty percent and some are under but the goal is to make 20 percent annually knowing there will be ups and downs depending on seasonality."[20]

If you dine in a corporate cafeteria or are involved in decisions about food service in your company, take the lead from some of the businesses that have already started their move toward a fair food future. Just like the students in the Real Food Challenge, each of us can have an impact in our workplace and on the larger system by sending the message that we want food sourced from farms that are close by and that practice more sustainable methods.

Encouraging our food service companies to source better food is one way for us to make the shift from conscious consumer to engaged citizen. Another is to support public policies that can create even more momentum for change—the subject of the next chapter.

CHAPTER 9

Shifting Public Policy

Being more aware of where our own food comes from is an important step that each of us can take to create a fair food future, especially when we use that information to start shopping and eating differently. Moving from conscious consumers in our own homes to engaged citizens in our communities is the next step, but as I've emphasized throughout this book, no matter how many of us decide to do this, the changes necessary to bring balance back into our food system will not happen without changes in public policy. The food system we have in place is one that was shaped by decades of public policy. We now need policies that will drive the system in a different direction. There are many opportunities for advocating for policy change in our own communities, in our states, and with Congress. By connecting with the policy organizations listed in Chapter 10, you can learn as much as you wish about the details of food and agriculture policy. In this chapter, rather than provide an exhaustive list of all the policies that need to be changed, I will focus on a few key policies at each of the governmental levels (local, state, federal) that, if altered or enacted, would give us an excellent start to a redesigned food system. And I'll provide information on additional resources and how to connect with others who are on the front lines of policy advocacy in these arenas.

Food Policy Councils

Food policy councils exist to improve the food system and coordinate the efforts of diverse entities throughout a city or region. You might ask why we need food policy councils. The answer is simple. In most cities, counties, or states, we have government entities to deal with transportation, housing, education, public health, and myriad other critical areas of concern to the community. We have economic development authorities and informal advisory groups on youth development and crime prevention. Something that most communities *don't* have is an advisory group of informed citizens to help local and state governments think about food policy in a more comprehensive way. This is the niche that food policy councils fill.

The first food policy council was created more than twenty-five years ago in Knoxville, Tennessee. In the past decade, the number of such groups has exploded with the increasing interest in local food and food environments. At the beginning of 2010, there were eighty-three food policy councils in operation across thirty-four states, according to Drake University Agricultural Law Center in Iowa; another source, the Community Food Security Coalition, puts the count at closer to one hundred thirty, with more than forty states having at least one functioning council within their borders. Some of the stated purposes of food policy councils are:

- Gathering diverse food system stakeholders, such as hunger advocates and rural farm organizations, to create linkages that can bring about innovative solutions for both, such as greater use of SNAP (Supplemental Nutrition Assistance Program) benefits at farmers' markets.
- Sharing information among those working on food systems issues, who might not otherwise have opportunities to learn about one another's efforts and perspectives.
- Inviting citizen participation in food system decision-making, such as rules and regulations around food sourcing by govern-

ment agencies. The idea here is to engage those who are most impacted by an issue in proposing solutions.

- Providing specific advice from members of the policy councils to decision makers about needed policy change, such as zoning that restricts urban agriculture.
- Examining the operation of a local food system and providing ideas and recommendations for improvement through public policy changes.

Most of the food policy councils currently functioning in the United States were sanctioned through government action, such as an executive order, public act, or joint resolution. There are other councils that formed through grassroots efforts of citizens and non-profit organizations and operate without an "official" convening document. Food policy councils are seen as innovative collaborations between citizens and government officials that can give voice to the concerns and interests of residents, many of whom have long been underserved or underrepresented by agricultural institutions.

What exactly is a food policy? It is any decision made by a government agency, business, or organization that affects how food is produced, processed, distributed, purchased, or protected,[1] including the types of foods to which consumers have access, information available pertaining to place of origin, and the rules and regulations that influence many aspects of farming. Though this definition would include policies in both public and private institutions, here I am primarily talking about public policies, those decisions made and put into place by government entities.

At times, food policy councils deal with issues that don't have an obvious "home" in a single government agency. For example, councils bring together individuals and government agencies that do not typically work directly with each other, to voice their perspectives when farm and agricultural policy is discussed. They look at issues that often go unexamined, such as the effectiveness of food assistance programs and the causes of hunger in a community. In addition, they analyze food system issues from a more comprehensive perspective, recognizing the inner workings between different parts of the food system and the need for coordination and integration of action if policy goals are to be achieved.

In essence, food policy councils become the specialists in food system issues in a community when policy makers need help with understanding a specific challenge and how to deal with it. Typical representatives on a food policy council might include farmers, consumers, antihunger advocates, food bank managers, labor representatives, members of the faith community, food processors, food wholesalers and distributors, food retailers and grocers, chefs and restaurant owners, officials from farm organizations, community gardeners, and academics involved in food policy and the law. Many food policy councils have governmental officials involved as special advisers or ex officio nonvoting members who represent departments of agriculture, economic development, inspections, education, human services, public health, cultural affairs, and transportation.

Food policy councils can be administered either as an official part of the state government or through a nonprofit or educational institution as an advisory body. In Michigan, I have had experience with both types of food policy councils. About seven years ago I wondered why, in my home state, where food issues are as important as anywhere, we did not have a state food policy council. In fact, I had not even heard any conversation about starting one. I had been invited to give a talk on our Kellogg Foundation food systems projects at a statewide conference called "Seeds of Prosperity," an event meant to kick off a new project of the Michigan Land Use Institute with what they were calling "entrepreneurial agriculture." During a break, I found myself visiting with Christine White, who at that time was Governor Jennifer Granholm's agriculture adviser. I asked her whether the governor had given any thought to creating a state food policy council. After explaining to her what such a council could accomplish and how these kinds of bodies were being created all across the country, I asked her, "If the Kellogg Foundation would consider funding the start of a food policy council in Michigan, do you think the governor would be interested, and would you be willing to take the lead to get it done?"

A few conversations later, we had a proposal at the Kellogg Foundation for the Michigan Department of Agriculture to collaborate with the Michigan Food Bank Council and Michigan State University to create the Michigan Food Policy Council. We made sure that this group would be broadly representative of the food system's interests in the state and that it would be created by a governor's executive order to legitimize the effort. The Michigan Food Policy Council was born in June 2005. Since that time, it has met regularly, has issued a detailed list of policy recommendations for the state, and has been successful in implementing some of those policies. One of its achievements has been to significantly increase the number of farmers' markets in the state that accept electronic benefits transfer as a way for low-income shoppers to more readily access locally grown products while supporting local farmers.

Another successful project of the Michigan Food Policy Council, in partnership with Michigan State University, is the creation of the Michigan Good Food Charter, which presents a vision for Michigan's food and agriculture system to advance its current contribution to the economy, protect the state's natural resource base, improve the health of the state's residents, and help generations of Michigan youth to thrive. The charter is based on the assumption that there are steps that can be taken, especially with state policy, that can expand the portion of the food system in the state that comes from local and sustainable sources—food that, according to a definition recently offered by the Kellogg Foundation, is "healthy, green, fair, and affordable." This charter is careful not to define a future food system as only local and small scale, but it also recognizes that Michigan needs a future food system in which local, regional, national, and global connections are all in place for the benefit of the state's economy and residents.

The Good Food Charter starts with a simple question: with any decision about purchasing a food product, whether you are a mom or a hospital food service director, could that product be supplied from a Michigan farmer or food processor? Assuming the answer is yes, the next question is: what needs to change in policy and practice so that Michigan farms and food businesses supply that product?

The charter outlines the steps that can be taken to adjust food policy and suggests twenty-five specific policies that could move the state's food system in the direction the charter's creators envision. The specific goals that the creators of the Good Food Charter aim to achieve by the year 2020 are:

- Michigan institutions will source 20 percent of their food products from Michigan growers, producers, and processors.
- Michigan farmers will profitably supply 20 percent of all Michigan institutional, retailer, and consumer food purchases and be able to pay fair wages to their workers.
- Michigan will generate new agrifood businesses at a rate that enables 20 percent of food purchased in Michigan to come from Michigan.
- Eighty percent of Michigan residents (twice the current level) will have easy access to affordable, fresh, healthy food, 20 percent of which is from Michigan sources.
- Michigan nutrition standards will be met by 100 percent of school meals and 75 percent of schools selling food outside of school meal programs.
- Michigan schools will incorporate food and agriculture into the pre-K through twelfth-grade curriculum for all Michigan students and provide access to food and agriculture entrepreneurial opportunities.

Another food policy council that has recently been created is in Detroit. This council developed in a much different way from the state council. A small group of Detroiters, led by Malik Yakini and the Detroit Black Community Food Security Network, studied the approach of food policy councils in several other urban areas and places with a population that was similar to theirs. They developed a written purpose, mission statement, vision, and goals, now stated in official documents as:

> The Detroit Food Policy Council affirms the City of Detroit's commitment to nurturing the development of a food-secure city in which all of its citizens are hunger-free, healthy and benefit from the food systems that impact their lives. It also affirms the City of Detroit's commitment to supporting sustainable food systems that provide people with high quality food, employment, and that also contribute to the long-term well being of the environment.

Those who started the Detroit Food Policy Council envision the city of Detroit with a:

> healthy, vibrant, hunger-free populace that has easy access to fresh produce and other healthy food choices; a city in which the residents are educated about healthy food choices, and understand their relationship to the food system; a city in which urban agriculture, composting and other sustainable practices contribute to its economic vitality; and a city in which all of its residents, workers, guests and visitors are treated with respect, justice and dignity by those from whom they obtain food.

The council's goals include producing and disseminating an annual City of Detroit Food System Report that assesses the state of the city's food system, including activities in production, distribution, consumption, waste generation and composting, nutrition and food assistance program participation, and innovative food system programs. They also intend to recommend new food-related policy as the need arises.

After holding citywide listening sessions to refine their ideas, the Detroit Black Community Food Security Network presented the idea of the Detroit Food Policy Council to the Detroit City Council, which unanimously adopted the charter. Of its twenty-one members, one represents the City Council, one the mayor, and one the city Department of Health and Wellness Promotion. The other eighteen, simply residents who decided to become engaged food citizens, come from a variety of backgrounds and organizations. In the ensuing years, we will see the results of the Detroit Food Policy Council. One of the initial efforts is to create policies that make it easier for urban farmers to get access to land and water to start farming some of the thousands of acres of vacant land within the city limits.

In areas in which food policy councils have been in place for a while, examples of public policy changes being catalyzed through those groups include:

- Mapping and publicizing local food resources
- Implementing EBT (electronic benefits transfer) equipment at farmers' markets
- Conducting an "agricultural inventory" of city-owned property, directing appropriate bureaus to identify city-owned land that may be available for community gardens or other agricultural uses
- Changing procurement rules and directing correctional facilities to purchase locally grown food rather than requiring them to make purchases based solely on the lowest bid
- Creating new forms of insurance for small producers
- Developing a simplified application for food stamp benefits
- Implementing farm-to-school programs
- Creating new transit routes to connect neighborhoods underserved by retail groceries with full-service grocery stores
- Organizing community gardens and farmers' markets

One reason food policy councils are attractive to state and local governments is that they can be created without a budgetary line item. Most food policy councils have been started with minimal funding from sources including grants from local community or private foundations. The largest "cost" of implementing a food policy council is the volunteer time provided by council organizers and members. If you live in a community that already has an active food policy council, start getting to know the members and the issues they are working on. They will welcome your involvement. You can find a list of current active food policy councils at the Community Food Security Coalition website, www.foodsecurity.org/FPC. The coalition has a national program designed to support the development and operation of food policy councils. The person who staffs this project, Mark Winne, is a national expert on this topic and is someone you should get to know if you want to create a food policy council in your community. There is a good document on the coalition's website on "lessons learned" from food policy councils. Another good resource is Food First (www.foodfirst.org/en/foodpolicycouncils-lessons), a research organization in Oakland, California, that has produced a report on the successes and challenges of food policy councils in various communities.

The experts in this policy arena suggest you focus on a concrete issue or problem as you get started, something like zoning for urban agriculture or improving food assistance programs. This provides both a specific purpose for organizing and a focus for action in the community. It's important that you educate yourself about the current food system, too. Because these councils are often volunteer-driven, sustaining energy and staff long term are challenges, although funding from local foundations can help. It is also important to pay attention to the role that politics might play in terms of who is appointed to the council, how leadership roles are determined, and who is most invested in the actions of the council and why. Since these organizations deal with policy, politics are always involved and may affect who controls the agenda. At the same time, if you actually want to accomplish policy change, you need to have people on board who understand how government and policy work in the real world. Often food system issues that are considered by food policy councils are not partisan issues; they can gain the support of both Republicans and Democrats. So consider having as members of the council people who have experience across the political spectrum with creating laws, and make sure you have buy-in from government officials. As one longtime participant in a state food policy council told me, "If you don't have that, you just have another place to complain about the man."

Farmland Preservation

Some of the more successful and important policies that have taken shape in local communities are those that protect farmland from residential and commercial development. Protection of our farmland is as important to creating a fair food future as any other policy arena I can imagine. And the good news is that it is an area of policy that can be acted on locally. There are structures and resources in place to assist any community that has a desire (and the citizen leadership) to preserve this valuable resource for the future.

Why is it so important to protect farmland? Three reasons:

- Economy: with our food system contributing more than $1 trillion to our economy and employing an estimated 17 percent of our workforce, it is an important economic engine to nurture. Without the resource of good farmland, our ability to produce for our own needs locally and for the global market will be hampered.
- Ecology: farmland and ranchland can be some of the most important areas providing wildlife habitat, protecting biodiversity, and helping to maintain clean air and water. And the aesthetic benefits we get from protecting more open space surrounding our urban centers can't be dismissed.
- Health: more than 90 percent of our fruit and almost 80 percent of our vegetables are being produced close to our urban

centers and, according to research from American Farmland Trust, are directly in the path of residential or commercial development.

The only way to have a sustainable and equitable future is to make sure we have the resources, including land, to produce food close to our population centers. This becomes even more critical as we imagine a future with much more scarce and expensive fossil fuel. The ability to transport fruits and vegetables long distances and keep them affordable will be a much greater challenge.

At the same time that our understanding of the importance of farmland preservation is increasing, the actual loss of farmland continues nearly unabated. American Farmland Trust tells us that we are losing farm- and ranchland to development at a rate of two acres per minute. That translates into more than a million acres of land each year. Luckily, the federal government has found some ways to help. In the past two Farm Bills (discussed in detail later in this chapter), farm-and ranchland protection has been funded at increasing levels. It is still a relatively small amount, and the federal funds need to be matched by local sources—which is where engaged food citizens can play an important role. For farmland protection to become a reality in a local community, two conditions need to be met. First, there needs to be a policy that allows landowners to sell their development rights either to a nonprofit land trust or a local unit of government, while maintaining ownership of the property (this takes the help of a knowledgeable attorney). Then there needs to be a local source of funds to match federal funding to purchase those development rights and protect the land from development in perpetuity.

I have had the opportunity to see such a program initiated in my own community and have participated in its implementation. Leading up to local elections in November 2003, a few passionate souls in Ann Arbor worked to place a millage issue on the ballot. The millage, which ended up being passed by nearly a two-thirds majority, slightly increased the amount of every property tax bill for the next thirty years to raise funds to help protect farmland and open space. Prior to the election, these same folks had worked with the Ann Arbor city and township governments to create a "greenbelt" area surrounding the city—an area that would be targeted for farmland and open space preservation should the ballot issue be successful. What is extraordinary about the millage in Ann Arbor is that the purpose of raising the funds through taxing property *within* the city is to protect open space and farmland *outside* of the city. Our local community recognizes that there is a value to the city of having open space and farmland available for food production in the areas surrounding it. So far, more than 8,500 acres of farmland have been preserved, much of it due to the investment of local funds matched by federal dollars.[2]

This land will never be sold for development and will be available for future generations of farmers to grow food for the local communities. The Farmland Preservation Board in Ann Arbor also recently adopted a small farm initiative to make some of this preserved farmland available for farmers (many of whom are younger and just getting into the farming profession) to start producing crops for the local market on small acreages. This is one response to urban and suburban sprawl on a local level that can be accomplished in many more communities. And we now have federal legislation that provides matching funds for these development-rights purchases, so we need to raise only half the funds locally, and the federal government will pay for the rest. The local unit of government applies for the funds, which are then paid to the landowner.

If you are interested in finding out more about the program in Ann Arbor, log on to the Ann Arbor City Government website (www.a2gov.org/greenbelt). Organizations like American Farmland Trust (AFT; www.farmland.org) can assist local communities in creating similar programs. On the trust's website, you will find information about farmland protection programs happening all across the country. You can get engaged with an ongoing program in your community (if there is one) by checking in with the local planning agency or contacting AFT to get one started.

I found it easy to get involved with farmland protection in my own community. For the past six years, I have served on the Farmland Preservation Board for Ann Arbor Township. The way I got started was to e-mail the two folks who were primarily responsible for getting the initial millage passed in the 2003 election to tell them I was ready to volunteer. Sometimes just letting the right person know that you are ready to invest your energy is all it takes.

Innovative Economic Policies

When I log on to one of the websites for Woodbury County, Iowa (www.woodburyorganics.com), I am greeted with "Welcome to Our Organic & Local Food Friendly Community." Have I misspelled something in my Google search? Such good wishes would make sense for a community like Berkeley or San Francisco or even Ann Arbor, but for one located in the middle of corn, soy, and hog country? Largely rural, Woodbury is a county with a population of just over 100,000. Its county seat and only urban area is Sioux City. How did this west-central area of the state become a center for innovation in local food and farm policy? As is so often the case, the credit goes to one extraordinary citizen. Here, it is because of Rob Marqusee, the county director for rural economic development.

When Marqusee was hired in 2005, he was up against community leaders who had very standard views of economic development, which meant attracting some manufacturing or processing firm that would be willing to relocate to the county. He had different ideas. He told me recently, "The possibility of landing an outside company in this county is about like winning the lottery. We are competing with every other economic development agency trying to do the same thing." He saw the challenges of recruiting companies from outside the region as "beyond belief." If he looked at what the Federal Reserve Bank considered the holy grail of economic development, it was, in his words, "to produce exports—so according to them we just needed to grow more corn and soybeans for export." Marqusee did not want to rely on the traditional mind-set of commodity subsidies and expanding on-farm technology to improve the economic well-being of those in the area. He even fought having his county embrace ethanol production as the next economic development wave when it was all the rage. He took a lot of heat for his position then, but now that the bottom has fallen out of the ethanol market and some ethanol plants in Iowa and elsewhere have gone bankrupt, lots of folks are glad he stood his ground.[3]

Instead, Marqusee decided it made more sense to create a more robust local food economy. He told me, "I became convinced that local food was the way to go." This made sense, especially since the Iowa Department of Economic Development did not consider agricultural production a focus of economic development. He realized that the only readily available tool was local tax policy. So, using his background as a lawyer with a specialty in taxation, he worked with other county officials to create one of the most innovative property tax policies that this good-food movement has ever seen.

Any landowner who signs an affidavit that he or she is transitioning to organic production will get a 100 percent tax refund on the property tax due on that land for five years. Marqusee did this not because he is necessarily a believer in organic food but because he saw an opportunity for local economic development based on resources that were already in his and neighboring counties: rich farmland, farmers who know how to grow soybeans, and a nearby soy processing plant already in operation. So far, farmers working a total of six hundred acres of land have signed on to the program in Woodbury County and, processing organic soybeans for a rapidly expanding market, the plant increased its capacity by 300 percent in three years. While six hundred acres may sound like a lot, it is less than 1 percent of the total farm acreage in Woodbury County.

Marqusee sees the impact of this policy not only in his own county, but in surrounding counties as well, where organic acreage is increasing because of the demand generated by the processing plant. He thinks that there are even greater opportunities than the organic conversion policy, so he recently helped the county to enact another local policy innovation. Marqusee observed, "The greatest challenge for local procurement was the lack of supply due to lack of farmers producing for local markets." In Woodbury County, as in many places, most of the locally grown products sold in the area were being bought at farmers' markets and a few restaurants. He became curious about the purchasing power of his own county government and learned that it spent about $300,000 on food purchases each year. He figured that about 40 percent of that could come from local sources, creating a new revenue stream of $120,000 for local farmers. It's not a lot, but it's a start. Marqusee helped Woodbury County pass a law that requires all food purchased with county funds to be produced within one hundred miles of the county seat, unless it is unavailable. Then it is okay to spend money on food produced in other places. He is convinced that as this program receives more attention, it will spread to other regions. Imagine if every county in every state created similar policies.

But Marqusee is not one just to sit and wait. Instead, he is introducing legislation known as the Iowa Local Farmer and Food Security Act (LFFSA). In the introduction to this new legislation, Marqusee has written, "The Sections in the LFFSA establish specified tax credits issued to grocers who source local food, under contract with local producers who grow fruits, vegetables, and meats, for sale in local markets. The tax credits are enacted as a means to reduce existing artificial barriers in the marketplace faced by local food producers. Establishing reliable markets for local food producers will facilitate agricultural diversity, encourage the availability of loans to farmers seeking to make a living through food production, will promote economic opportunities to our rural communities, and will provide a local source of food as security for our citizens."

One additional benefit of the county's innovative policies is that it is beginning to attract young farmers to start farm businesses there. With the average age of farmers in the county at sixty-two, Marqusee realizes the importance of acting now.

If this kind of local policy speaks to you, gather others in your community who have similar interests, share the stories here with your local policy makers, and use Marqusee as the example to get things moving. When I asked him recently how people might proceed if they don't have a Rob Marqusee in charge of their community, here was his response:

Clearly, someone (or [a] group of people) has to be interested in pursuing local policies that favor small farming as an economic activity. The tools needed are exactly those tools available to any local governmental body that wants to attract business: tax refunds, low interest loans, forgivable loans, cash incentives, etc. The only thing that a person (or group) needs to do is convince the local authorities that food production is a valuable target for economic development.

A person (or group) would need to get support from key people: example—if there is an old building that is just standing there with nobody using it—it could be used for storage of farm products. So a landowner may contribute land, building, etc. That would show the local authorities that there is community support.

If a plan would be presented that would increase the number of people [moving] into the rural or blighted urban area that should itself be impetus for local government going out of its way to use the standard economic development tools to encourage that economic activity.

There is only so much one can do at the local level—local governments could not offer tax credits as such. But, the locality could declare an area to be blighted, and offer local incentives for making it productive.

We are now, in Woodbury County, offering 2 percent loans—
unsecured for small farming type businesses. I would work with
the local or state economic development groups to review existing
tools and see how they could apply to increasing the local food
supply.[4]

Sourcing Food with Public Funds

In Chapter 8 I discussed food procurement, primarily from the perspective of institutions such as universities, schools, and hospitals.
Here I will explore how governments can use their powers to direct
public resources spent on food to support a redesigned food system.
One obvious way is to target the food purchases of public sources to
support more local, regional, and sustainable farms and food businesses, like Rob Marqusee is doing in Woodbury County, but on a
larger scale.

Would it make a difference if more public funds were spent on
food coming from farms, processors, and distributors that were
locally/regionally based, with a commitment to sustainable practices?
Absolutely. It is not easy to come by numbers for public procurement of food, either overall or by food category. But a couple of statistics lead me to believe that food procurement policy could be a
huge lever. One study recently conducted in New Mexico estimated
that 10 percent of all food purchased in the state was acquired with
public funds, under the control of one state agency or another.[5]
When you think about the fact that in our country's current food
system overall, less than 3 percent of purchasing is directed to local
food, then 10 percent starts to look like a big number.

In Michigan, we looked at food procurement numbers for the
university and college food services, the total K–12 public schools,
and the state Department of Corrections. The total dollar amount of
expenditures on food from these public entities was very close to
$300 million in 2009. By shifting even 20 percent of these funds
to more local/regional production and processing, we would be

infusing $60 million back into the local economy, supporting the kind of food system that would sustain us well into the future. And this change does not need lots of legislative wrangling. One enlightened government official (such as a governor) could start to reinvent the state's food and agriculture economy with a single executive order. I am looking forward to the day when a gubernatorial candidate will include the following as part of his or her campaign platform: *If I am elected, I will mandate that all state expenditures on food, whether in schools, colleges, prisons, or state office cafeterias, be directed to support our state's farmers and food companies. Our goal as a state will be to have a full 20 percent of all food eaten in these facilities come from local farmers, processors, and distributors.*

In fact, Michigan's Good Food Charter includes a recommendation for the state to set targets for state-funded institutions to procure Michigan-grown, sustainably produced products. In order for farmers to shift their production to foods that more closely serve the needs and diets of nearby residents, they need credible, accessible, and stable markets. Schools, correctional facilities, hospitals, and other publicly funded institutions that serve meals represent exactly those kinds of markets.

In the past five years, several states, such as Illinois, Washington, Wisconsin, and Vermont, have created policies to improve their economic climates through initiatives for institutional procurement of local food. The writers of the Michigan Good Food Charter realize that, while public institutions can offer contracts that translate into stable, steady markets, they may also provide smaller profit margins to farmers than would other markets. So as another policy recommendation, the Good Food Charter suggests creating temporary financial incentives to encourage farmer participation in institutional markets and increase both the supply and infrastructure available to institutions. This could be done through tax incentives for developing local food-storage, processing, packing, and distribution facilities, or through a grant and loan program that helps farmers transition from production of commodity crops to production of specialty crops (fruits, vegetables, nuts, herbs, and ornamental plants) for sale to institutions.

Now let's take a look at what's occurring on the federal level. According to the USDA Economic Research Service, governments spent close to $112 billion on food in 2010. Total U.S. food expenditures in 2010 were $1.24 trillion.[6] This means that of the entire amount the country spent on food, governments' procurement amounted to about 9 percent. Shifting a portion of this government spending to food that is produced locally/regionally and grown using more sustainable practices (with our food system redesign principles intact) could contribute significantly to the food systems change I am suggesting.

So what can you do? Most of us interact with one or more agencies that use our public funds to procure food, from our local school district to county government to day care centers. Call, write, or e-mail anyone you know at one of these institutions to ask if the agency has any stated targets for procuring food from local and sustainable sources. If the answer is yes, ask what you can do to help the agency reach its target. If the answer is no, then see what you can do to get such a target in place. Maybe it's calling your state representative or getting in touch with someone in the governor's office and suggesting this idea. Or maybe it's writing a letter to the editor of the local paper in your state capital. In reality, each of us is only a few degrees of separation from somebody who is making decisions about food procurement. If you just start asking around, I bet that you will soon find someone in a position of authority who is ready to listen to your point of view.

We are at an exciting moment in the public discourse about food and food systems. Discussions about the local food movement have captured enough attention that your inquiries along these lines will not be heard as "fringe." You may even find yourself being asked for more information to help the policy makers in your state think this through. And if that happens, you are well prepared with the link to the Michigan Good Food Charter (www.michiganfood.org), along with the information on the other policy advocacy organizations listed in Chapter 10.

The Farm Bill

Action at the community level is critical for us to create a fair food future. Focusing on local and state policy change and food procurement shifts will also help get us there. But even with all of these efforts in our homes, in our neighborhoods, and with public food procurement, we will not be able to alter this broken system until we shift the rules by which the game is played—and many of the rules that set the stage for the current system are written into the Farm Bill.

What Is the Farm Bill?

The Farm Bill is an omnibus piece of legislation that includes a wide spectrum of programs and reflects Congress's priorities for America's food and agricultural system. Farm Bills must be reconsidered about every five years because many of the programs they govern are authorized and funded only for this limited time. The bill reauthorized in 2008 covers everything from direct payments to producers of "commodity" crops (including corn, soybeans, wheat, rice, cotton, and others), often referred to as crop subsidies; to rural development grants and loans; to research and extension funding for land-grant universities; to SNAP benefits. Because of its long history as a cornerstone of federal agriculture and rural policy, its many proponents (in Congress and interest groups) have had decades to become entrenched.

The Farm Bill is important because it establishes national goals and priorities for farming, conservation, nutrition, and rural development. It offers an ongoing opportunity for Americans to look at the domestic food system, assess whether it is achieving the goals we have for it, and, through our members of Congress, negotiate ways to make it serve the country better. It is also important because it represents significant government expenditures, about $300 billion over the five-year life of the bill. Where and into which sectors of the economy these dollars go make an immediate difference to those communities and businesses. In the 1930s, the Farm Bill protected farmers from volatility in prices of crop commodities, those crops that were considered nonperishable. The purpose of these policies was to provide farmers with a basic level of income security while protecting such resources as soil and water for the future. These early bills created what we refer to today as commodity programs. The original commodity programs maintained prices by controlling the supply of nonperishable crops in the marketplace. Over the years U.S. agriculture policy has, for the most part, moved away from attempting to control supply or establish price but has maintained a commitment to protecting the income of farmers who grow tradable, nonperishable crops.

Starting in the Depression, the USDA also assumed a responsibility to meet the food needs of low-income Americans. In the 1930s Congress gave the secretary of agriculture authority to purchase surplus foods and donate them, usually to school meal programs. The National School Lunch Act of 1946 codified the system's dual purposes "to safeguard the health and well-being of the Nation's children and to encourage the domestic consumption of nutritious agricultural commodities and other food."[7] The USDA conducted a temporary food stamp program in these years and permanent authority came with the Food Stamp Act of 1964, referred to since the 2008 Farm Bill as SNAP.[8] In addition to commodity and nutrition programs, today's Farm Bills also include farm credit, conservation, trade policies, and more.

The 2008 Farm Bill, officially known as the Food, Conservation, and Energy Act of 2008, includes fifteen parts, known as titles, eight of which bear directly on the work of developing just, sustainable, regional food systems.

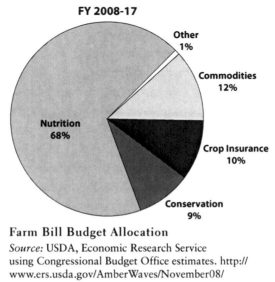

Farm Bill Budget Allocation
Source: USDA, Economic Research Service
using Congressional Budget Office estimates. http://
www.ers.usda.gov/AmberWaves/November08/
DataFeature/

Commodities: This piece of the Farm Bill provides price and income support for farmers choosing to produce corn, peanuts, sugar, wheat, rice, cotton, soy, dairy, and oilseeds (such as sunflower, rapeseed, canola, and safflower). The mechanisms for compensating farmers have been refined through the years, but currently direct payments and marketing loan assistance programs are the predominant forms of commodity farm subsidies.[9]

Conservation: Originally created to address concerns about severe soil erosion, more recent conservation programs have expanded their scope to include protection and restoration of wildlife habitat, watershed restoration, renewable energy, greenhouse gas mitigation, preservation of open spaces, and improvement of water and air quality. In the 2008 Farm Bill, the conservation title received a net funding increase of $5.3 billion over a ten-year period to expand working lands programs and conservation easement programs (such as federal cost-sharing for the purchase of development rights). The

2008 Farm Bill also expanded opportunities for specialty crop producers (those growing fruits, vegetables, nuts, herbs, and ornamental plants) and farmers transitioning to organic systems to access funding from conservation programs.

Crop Insurance and Disaster Assistance Programs: This title provides crop insurance at a variety of coverage levels, mainly for commodity crops. Insurance premiums are federally subsidized and the actual crop insurance is sold and serviced through private insurance companies. Crop insurance and disaster programs are important to the future of organic, sustainable, and diversified agricultural production because farmers will be willing to transition to these different production models only if they can manage the risk that the change will involve. Organic producers and direct marketers of high-value perishable crops are at a disadvantage purchasing crop insurance because they cannot yet buy coverage commensurate with their potential losses. Farmers have no incentive to move away from their current production practices if there is not an adequate safety net for them during the transition.

Nutrition: Although many associate the Farm Bill with agriculture, in fact, nutrition programs now receive almost three-fourths of all Farm Bill spending, the majority of which funds the SNAP (or food stamp) program. Expenditures for SNAP have increased dramatically (up 38 percent since 2008) due to the higher levels of unemployment and poverty in the past several years.[10]

The four titles above will spend 99 percent of federal funding on food and agriculture over the ten-year period 2008–2017, unless this legislation is altered when the Farm Bill is next considered (in 2012 or 2013). The titles below are all included in the smallest slice of the pie in the chart above and share the remaining 1 percent of funding.

Credit: This title authorizes loans for conservation, farm ownership and operation, and a few broader rural development endeavors. The

2008 Farm Bill expanded the scope of federal lending, creating additional loan opportunities for beginning, socially disadvantaged, and resource-limited farmers and ranchers, and authorized the Beginning Farmer and Rancher Individual Development Account pilot program.

Rural Development: The Farm Bill authorizes loan and grant programs for rural development (including broadband Internet access, water systems, housing, and energy efficiency). Because the current administration has been encouraging development of local and regional food systems, many rural development programs are also being used to promote regional food systems that increase farmers' share of food and agricultural profits while also improving consumer access to healthy food grown by producers in their region.

Horticulture/Organic: The 2008 Farm Bill provided expanded assistance for organic producers and those who would like to transition to this type of production. The bill increased funding for the Specialty Crop Block Grant program that funnels funds to state agriculture departments for investment in specialty crop research, infrastructure, marketing, and promotion, and requires the USDA to collect and report data on specialty crops in the Census of Agriculture. The title also includes the Farmers' Market Promotion Program and assistance for organic farmers to pay for organic certification.

Livestock: This title regulates market competition, interstate trade, meat inspection, food safety concerns, and livestock welfare issues. While these issues may seem more arcane, they are crucial to the basic structure of U.S. agriculture, including fair competition, decentralization, and the viability of small and mid-sized businesses.

Shifting Farm Bill Priorities

In the past, the Farm Bill has often been debated and reauthorized in Congress and signed by the president out of the public spotlight.

Luckily, that is starting to change. In this section of the book, I will discuss what I learned in supporting policy change in previous Farm Bills, the opportunities I see ahead for the next rounds of Farm Bill debates (and how we can use them to move us closer to a redesigned food system), and how you can get involved.

Traditionally the Farm Bill sets policy regarding agricultural production, trying to manage supply and demand while creating some measure of income protection for farmers of commodity crops. It also has authorized the flow of federal dollars for rural infrastructure (electrification, sanitation, and broadband, to name just three) and economic development. More recently, conservation and environmental stewardship on farms and ranches have become a big part of Farm Bill policy. Traditional interest groups that lined up to influence Congress on the outcomes of this legislation, which has directed hundreds of billions of federal dollars to farms and rural communities, included farm commodity organizations such as the corn, soybean, and wheat growers (for obvious reasons), more general farm organizations like the Farm Bureau, rural advocates, and environmentalists.

One of the biggest changes in the Farm Bill occurred when food stamps (known as SNAP since 2008) were included in the 1960s. This change expanded the Farm Bill's constituencies and advocates to include antihunger and food security advocates. The Farm Bill previously had been legislation primarily in the purview of rural legislators, which means it has been guided by representatives from rural congressional districts and senators from primarily rural or agricultural states. As SNAP becomes a greater part of the USDA budget (as part of the nutrition title), and a greater and greater percentage of SNAP recipients reside in urban communities, urban legislators are showing more interest in the Farm Bill as legislation that impacts their constituents.

There has been a lot of discussion and debate among sustainable agriculture and food system advocates about what it would take to "reform" the Farm Bill, and many times this debate centers on a restructuring of the commodity title—or Title I of the bill. In 2008,

large commercial farms (those with annual sales greater than
$250,000) composed 12.4 percent of all U.S. farms, yet received
62.4 percent of government payments. This is a direct result of programs targeting certain types of commodities, which are often
grown on large farms and in large volumes.[11] Even with all the ar-
guments that can be made about the need to diversify our agriculture and cease these incentives for largely monoculture production
(for both economic and ecological reasons; remember, a more diverse system is more resilient long term), the political practicality of
eliminating this title was low until very recently. Because of the increased focus on reducing the federal deficit, it is likely that the next
reauthorization of the Farm Bill will eliminate direct payments in
favor of an expanded crop insurance program. There is pressure on
Congress to limit payments of federal dollars to wealthy farmers. It
also makes more sense to provide fair income support to foster a
greater diversity of crop and livestock production.

During the 1980s and early 1990s, as an agronomist at Michigan State University, I viewed the Farm Bill as something important
in the realm of agricultural economics and public policy. I understood that it was Congress that authorized and appropriated funds
for agricultural research and extension, and that without federal
funds much of the research of my colleagues would be underfunded
(if funded at all). I even participated in some federally funded research projects that were ultimately authorized through the Farm
Bill. As I worked with farmers around Michigan, trying to help them
diversify their crop rotations and create more integrated systems, I
slowly realized that one of the significant barriers to many of them
taking my advice and putting it into practice in their fields was their
reliance on federal farm payments through the Farm Bill. If they
stopped growing so much corn on their acreage, they would risk losing government payments if prices went down, and they were not in
a position to take that risk. But it was not until shortly after the passage of the 1995 Farm Bill that I understood what was really at
stake. At that point I was working as a program director in food sys-

tems and rural development at the Kellogg Foundation, where we had just completed funding for our first Integrated Farming Systems projects. My colleagues and I were hearing from many of our project partners on the ground that no matter what changes they were trying to make in their communities, without supportive policy at the federal level, these changes would be short lived. For example, small farm-to-school or school garden projects are often funded initially from philanthropic dollars, as are experiments with new and innovative crop rotations or small-scale livestock processing. When foundation funding runs out, however, these projects have nowhere to turn and it is back to business as usual. At that same time, I was receiving proposals from organizations that wanted to weigh in on the next Farm Bill, which would probably pass sometime in 2001 or 2002. So the foundation decided to proactively fund projects that intended to inform policy change, specifically focused on the Farm Bill.

From 1999 to 2002, the Kellogg Foundation awarded eight organizations grants totaling more than $2 million. These grants supported efforts to provide public education and outreach on the 2002 Farm Bill. We funded these organizations assuming that no single organization had nearly enough clout to effect much change. Creating successful collaborations with organizations that had not previously worked together would be critical for success, and catalyzing working relationships among organizations focused on "sustainable agriculture" and those focused on "environment and conservation" was the strongest route to building the collaboration that over the long run could inform the Farm Bill in ways that were consistent with Kellogg's view of a desired future food system. The Joyce Foundation was the only other major national funder at that time to support federal policy efforts of nonprofits focused on sustainable agriculture and food systems.

While we cannot clearly attribute specific policy changes to specific grantees, it is clear that the efforts of the Kellogg- and Joyce-funded grantees contributed to some significant policy changes in the 2002 Farm Bill, including 75 percent more funds authorized for conservation purposes than in the previous Farm Bill and the creation of the Farmers' Market Promotion Program to establish, expand, and promote farmers' markets, community-supported agriculture programs, and other direct producer-to-consumer efforts.

My biggest revelation from funding the 2002 Farm Bill effort was that nonprofit organizations couldn't be expected to behave in mutually supportive ways unless it was clearly in their interest to do so. Because the grantees working on the 2002 Farm Bill were never funded as a coalition or collaboration, and no such expectations were articulated upfront, when one organization with a strong connection to Congress decided to leave the coalition at the last minute because it had been offered a deal, the support for a major reform bill fell short of what was needed to pass. Clearly a much stronger coalition structure was necessary if the funding was going to have a more tangible impact. We decided that in the next round of Farm Bill funding all the organizations would be funded at the same time and under the same expectations (one of which was that they would all work on similar policy goals and stay accountable to one another up until final passage of the bill). We also realized that a secretariat was needed, someone trusted by both the foundation and the nonprofit community who could assist in managing the coalition process.

2008 Farm Bill

After spending some time evaluating the events surrounding the 2002 bill, the Kellogg Foundation decided to create another round of funding for the 2008 Farm Bill. We were able to budget up to $6 million over a four-year period for this effort, and attempted to use our experiences with the previous bill to inform how we proceeded. We ended up funding five core organizations that together created the Food and Farm Policy Project.

Out of the thirty-eight policy priorities of this project, twenty-three ended up as part of the final bill. Significant accomplishments that provided a good start in creating a blueprint for a fair food future included: more focus on electronic benefit transfer in the Farmers' Market Promotion Program; completing a USDA study on food deserts; geographic preference for food procurement, especially for public schools, which meant that the institutions could favor local farmers; funding for specialty crop block grants to states; and the Healthy Urban Food Enterprise Development Program, which provides grants to organizations and businesses working to create greater access to healthy, fresh, and regionally produced food in historically underserved communities.

Looking Ahead

There are significant opportunities for change in Farm Bill policy with the upcoming reauthorization in 2012/2013 and beyond, and more favorable conditions for those of us dedicated to food justice and sustainability:

- The Obama administration has voiced its dislike of commodity programs, a sign that it understands the connection between misguided farm policy and the broader symptoms of our broken food system. The administration has pledged to end childhood hunger by 2015, recommended increased funding for child nutrition programs, campaigned on supporting family farms and sustainable agricultural producers, and provided a strong symbolic gesture with the First Lady's White House garden. The president's appointees at the USDA are accessible and regularly consult with sustainable agriculture organizations in developing the USDA's initiative called "Know Your Farmer, Know Your Food," which supports more regional food and agriculture. Sustainable agriculture advocacy groups will most likely be able to continue to influence the administration's farm policy agenda. Importantly, the First Lady has identified childhood obesity as *the* issue on which she intends to focus, and it is clear that effectively addressing childhood obesity requires shifting the food system (which the

Farm Bill shapes). It is also important to emphasize that the issues I am raising in this book are not partisan issues. There are both Democrats and Republicans who care about food and agriculture policy; this is an issue on which bipartisan cooperation is both possible and necessary.

- The food movement. Popular interest in local foods, farmers' markets, gardening, farming, food preparation, and concern about food safety is increasing. For example, Michael Pollan's book, *The Omnivore's Dilemma*, was on the *New York Times* best-seller list for more than 130 weeks, more than three times as long as Rachel Carson's book, *Silent Spring*, which many believe spurred the environmental movement. There are significant new groups with stated intentions to focus on policy change with the Farm Bill, such as Slow Food USA, which has a dedicated following of more than 200,000 people and more than 150 local chapters.

- Specialty crop groups. Growers of "specialty crops," such as fruits and vegetables, long considered outsiders to farm policy, received new funding in the 2008 Farm Bill to promote the specialty crop industry locally, for federal research funds, and for a new Fresh Fruit and Vegetable Snack Program for low-income students. The Specialty Crop Farm Bill Alliance has supporters on the House and Senate Agriculture Committees positioned to defend and expand their recent gains. These associations are important allies for helping to redesign our food system to provide greater access to regionally grown fruits and vegetables, especially in historically underserved communities.

- Public health and health care organizations. These groups started to show an active interest in food and farm policy with the 2008 Farm Bill. They have an even stronger interest now and are positioned to play a more significant role and become even more involved with future Farm Bills.

- Foundation collaborations. In the first twenty years of my experience with organized philanthropy, only a handful of foundations, most of them small regional funders, had any interest in supporting work to impact the Farm Bill. Now even many national foundations are interested in influencing food and farm policy.

In addition to the above factors, there are other significant considerations, including:

- The urban-rural divide and rural "defensiveness." The Food, Conservation, and Energy Act of 2008 was the first Farm Bill not to include the words "farm" or "agriculture" in its title, indicating the extent to which the Agriculture Committees (both in the House of Representatives and Senate) felt pushed by urban interests to make concessions. The Agriculture Committees are viewed by most of their members as the "rural" committees. Reallocating funds originally earmarked for agriculture, rural development, land retirement programs, and now biofuel renewable energy provokes a politically persuasive and effective rhetoric that rural policy is being set by outsiders "not understanding the needs of rural America." Urban and suburban advocates need to understand this dynamic and make sure to find support for their interests from rural advocates and organizations. While many urban-based organizations have an interest in remedying hunger and diet-related illness, these conditions are also widespread in rural areas. Whether urban or rural, the solutions are the same: a food system that is equitable, more geographically dispersed, diversified in production, and economically viable will help rural and urban America.
- Urban members vote for the Farm Bill. Because more than 60 percent of the funding in the Farm Bill is for nutrition and anti-hunger programs, representatives and senators from urban districts and states generally vote for the bill. These votes are necessary to pass the House and Senate floor votes, which must happen once the bill comes out of the respective committees.

These urban votes were significant enough to override vetoes by President George W. Bush, and with the public conversation about local foods and rising rates of obesity and diet-related illness in urban food deserts, it will be easier than ever to gain the support of urban legislators and advocates for Farm Bill reform.

- 2012 is a presidential election year. Agriculture has not yet become a presidential priority, and representatives generally are reluctant to finalize a large, controversial reauthorization bill in the second session of their two-year term. The uncertainty surrounding the next presidential election and the very slow economic recovery makes it difficult to predict the timing of Farm Bill reauthorization. This will challenge advocates and organizations that do not have a constant presence in Washington, D.C.

- In fall 2011, House and Senate Agriculture Committee leaders developed a bipartisan Farm Bill policy framework for the Joint Select Committee on Deficit Reduction. This framework included elimination of direct payments, an expanded crop insurance program, consolidation of conservation programs (with funding reductions), a small reduction in total SNAP spending, and modest support for farmers' markets, local/regional food systems, and healthy food incentives for SNAP recipients. Because the Deficit Reduction Committee failed to come to overall agreement, this Farm Bill policy framework did not become law in 2011. The framework will be the starting point for a more normal Farm Bill reauthorization process in 2012.

Specific Policy Suggestions

For the last several Farm Bills, debates have raged within the advocacy community about whether to lobby for incremental change or total reform. By total reform, many people mean eliminating farm subsidies, or the Title I commodity payments. I believe that this is likely to happen as part of the next Farm Bill reauthorization, with the so-called "safety net" for farmers being replaced by an expanded crop insurance program. As a society, our position over the past sixty years has been that agriculture and farming are important enough to our rural areas and our national economy that we need to transfer public dollars to keep that sector financially solvent. I agree. In late 2008 and into mid-2009, when the United States was faced with its worst economic downturn since the Great Depression, we heard both Presidents George W. Bush and Barack Obama tell us about companies that were "too big to fail." Congress agreed, and the federal government provided bailout funds—subsidies to keep these companies and industries afloat.

Rather than "too big to fail," I view food and agriculture as "too important to fail." We cannot allow the bounty of our food system to be exported somewhere else and we cannot let it wither away. Nor can we allow the system to shortchange our most vulnerable citizens. Our food policies have done a good job thus far of providing most of us with ample food at relatively low cost. We need to retain these aspects of the system and develop other areas required to create greater access to healthy, fresh, and sustainably grown food, especially in our historically underserved urban and rural communities.

In my view, the way to do this is *not* to eliminate financial safety-net programs, but to distribute them differently. We need more farmers producing specialty crops to increase the supply of locally and regionally produced healthy food for our inner-city and rural food deserts. We need support for more small and mid-size farms and ranches, not only the large commodity farms. We need to promote more diverse crop rotations and a greater diversity of farmers so that as the current farmer population ages, we have young people from a variety of backgrounds ready to step in and take over these farms and food-related businesses. One way to ensure that all of this will happen is to provide federal support, most likely in the form of credit and some kind of safety net that helps mitigate the risk of crop failure or market fluctuations.

Here are several specific policy targets for upcoming Farm Bill discussions that, if put into place, could start the shift to a fair food future:

- Specialty crops. Funding for fruit and vegetable producers has been in the form of block grants to state departments of agriculture, who then decide how to use these monies. In general, letting those closest to the issues decide how to use federal funds works well, but in-state farmer lobbies can be so strong that some of the urban requirements regarding availability and accessibility go unrecognized. We need more equitably distributed additional specialty crop funds and some portion of funds targeted to address each state's food desert issues.

- Healthy food incentives. These could be in the form of vouchers, valid only for fruits and vegetables, or a program in which food assistance recipients stretch their purchasing power by getting additional matching funds for purchasing locally grown produce (similar to the Double Up Food Bucks program). This will improve diets, increase the ability to support local farmers, and lead to changes in the types of foods offered by retailers in low-income communities. According to USDA studies, there is no evidence that a small increase in income (like with SNAP increases overall) will translate into additional fruit and vegetable expenditures for low-income families.[12] General increases in SNAP funding do not necessarily lead to increased purchases of fresh fruits and vegetables; instead, dedicated allocations are necessary to increase these kinds of purchases.[13] If this policy option cannot be implemented on a national basis immediately, then a more successful scenario likely would be to implement it as a pilot project in a few communities or states to keep the costs down. Or it could be instituted at grocery stores and corner stores as a way to link farmers with the kind of retailers found in urban and rural food deserts, and at farmers' markets to more directly support local farmers while also promoting better access to healthy food.

- Linking conservation to healthy food access. To date, there has been little overlap between advocates interested in improving the environmental performance of agriculture and those interested in healthy food access. One way to bring these two constituencies together would be to expand the advantage to farmers applying for conservation funds if they directly market healthy food to low-income communities.
- Urban food systems. As mentioned, many have viewed the Farm Bill as a piece of rural legislation. With more than two-thirds of USDA Farm Bill funding directed to nutrition assistance and the vast majority of SNAP clients living in urban areas, the bill is already the most important federal urban food systems policy. It is in the long-term interests of both urban and rural stakeholders to find a way for the Farm Bill to create cooperative urban-rural links. Having Congress give the USDA broader authority to fund urban food systems programs would be a step in the right direction.
- Healthy Food Finance. This initiative would increase the number of outlets offering produce in low-income communities, upgrade existing stores to stock healthy foods, and increase the supply and reduce the costs of healthy, fresh, and local foods by investing in more cost-effective and energy-efficient distribution systems. Providing financing for wholesale and retail distribution of healthy food will increase consumers' access to these kinds of foods. This policy idea was already included in President Obama's 2011 budget and is getting support from Congress. The Healthy Food Financing Initiative is patterned after Pennsylvania's successful Fresh Food Financing Initiative.
- Regional food system infrastructure investment. The demand for locally and regionally produced food is growing rapidly, but farmers and ranchers need better ways to get their healthy food to markets. Credit and entrepreneurial training to build regional aggregation, processing, and transportation networks would enable producers to meet the new market demand efficiently.

Investing in this type of regional infrastructure will link urban consumers with rural producers and create new job opportunities in both communities.

We are at a unique moment with food and farm policy. Public nonfarm and nonrural interest in the Farm Bill has never been higher, and indications are that it will only intensify. We have an administration that is more sympathetic to the issues of healthy food access and local/regional food systems than at any point in the past thirty-five years. We have many foundations now offering support of efforts to inform the next Farm Bill—a much different scenario than in the past.

Now is the time to have your voice heard by letting your congressional representatives know that you want them actively engaged in the Farm Bill debate. Many urban and suburban legislators still act as if the Farm Bill concerns only rural interests, and they let their rural colleagues in Congress have their way. But whether you live in a rural, suburban, or urban setting, the Farm Bill has a profound impact on how our food system functions, and we need more suburban and urban legislators weighing in with their constituents' concerns. Contact your elected representatives and let them know you want policies that incentivize local production of healthy fruits and vegetables while assisting low-income consumers to gain access to these products. This will do a lot to help a fair food system become reality. You can also join forces with one of the many organizations working to shift Farm Bill policy. Key organizations and interest groups that will likely weigh in on the types of proposals suggested here include:

- Sustainable agriculture organizations champion food produced in a healthy and safe manner, support competitive markets for all agricultural products and local/regional food production, and ally themselves with social justice groups. The National Sustainable Agriculture Coalition is the most prominent of these organizations.

- The antihunger community is the key gatekeeper on health and nutrition issues in the Farm Bill, yet so far has been involved in health and food quality issues only at the state and local levels. While the leadership of these organizations is publicly against any restrictions on what kinds of foods can be purchased with SNAP benefits, they could be strong allies in the arena of healthy food incentives, under the right conditions.

- The produce lobby actively encourages the consumption of fruits and vegetables in nutrition programs and should support policies that benefit these programs. Produce growers have critical access to the Agriculture Committees.

- The consumer lobby has traditionally had limited involvement with the Farm Bill; however, with the heightened concern about food safety issues, its interest in the Farm Bill will likely increase.

- Public health and health care organizations are critical new allies in Farm Bill policy and politics. As a top executive of the largest health insurer in the United States said in a recent presentation, "Our projections show that by 2018, the health care costs related to obesity will be $345 billion per year. If we don't do something about this now, it will bankrupt our company and the entire health care system. We now understand that your issue [food systems redesign] is our issue."[14] We need to encourage representatives of public health and health care organizations to support the kinds of Farm Bill policy proposals suggested here.

- Diverse faith-based communities have been engaged in food and farm policy at the local and national levels for a number of years and their influence can be considerable. Bread for the World and Heifer International are two of the best known, but denominations of all kinds regularly support increased funding for nutrition programs and protection of natural resources in agricultural systems. For example, more than two dozen national faith organizations signed a letter encouraging the House of Representatives to pass a child-nutrition bill in the waning days of the 111th Congress, and it was ecumenical groups that brought advocates together and organized the final lobbying push for the legislation.

How you can get involved:

- Through groups with which you are already working. Since the Farm Bill touches so many aspects of the food system, almost all organizations should have an interest in at least some of its provisions. More advocacy groups than ever before are preparing to be involved in deliberations for the next Farm Bill, including PTAs, public health groups, environmental groups, inner-city and rural economic development organizations, and green jobs councils.
- Speak with your food dollars. Legislation responds to the market, and the greater the demand for local and regional sustainably grown food, the more Congress and the USDA will pay attention and invest resources in making the system work.
- Get educated about the process through local groups and national organizations, including the Community Food Security Coalition, National Sustainable Agriculture Coalition, regional Sustainable Agriculture Working Groups and organic farming organizations, food justice groups including Slow Food USA, and local and statewide food policy councils. Fair Food Network will also keep you informed about the status of food and farm policy—sign up to receive our updates at www.fairfoodnetwork.org.

- Never underestimate your power as an individual. Call your representative or senator and let him or her know what you think. Congressional offices do listen. Even if you don't share the political perspective of your representative, don't assume that he or she won't agree with you on these issues. Food and agriculture policy is a bipartisan concern.

If those of us without a lot of positional power want to have an impact on this piece of legislation, the only way we're going to make a difference is by working together. If you want to add your voice to the growing chorus of support for food systems change, you need to do it through and with an organization that has values consistent with yours and that is active in attempting to change Farm Bill policy. The more individuals that speak out, the more powerful this coalition becomes. Remember, we are up against very strong forces that have been entrenched for decades. As I have tried to point out, a lot of progress has been made in the past ten years on the Farm Bill, especially in opening up this legislation to interests other than the traditional agriculture voices and rural interests. This is a moment when you can make a difference if you harness your voice, beliefs, passion, and resources to promote a fair and healthy food system. We can each stay isolated in our own kitchens, living with the illusion that we are changing the world by eating a more organic, local, and sustainable diet. I encourage you to use the energy and vitality that result from this good diet and healthy lifestyle to make the transformation to an engaged citizen. By working with others who are similarly engaged, a redesigned food system will become a reality.

CHAPTER 10

Resources

In this final chapter, you will find lists of organizations that are involved in one or more aspects of redesigning our food system. I chose only a fraction of the literally hundreds of organizations that are now working in the food systems world: some organizations were picked because in my experience they are the leading efforts in their category; others I selected as great examples of what is occurring in a single location but could easily be replicated elsewhere, if the desire to do so were there. One challenge with this kind of exercise for a field that is rapidly evolving is that within a few months, there will be yet more organizations and the list will continue to look different. To meet that challenge, we have dedicated a portion of our website at Fair Food Network to duplicating the list here, but with the ability to expand this admittedly partial list as new organizations emerge or as other organizations wish to be added. This chapter of the book will be a good place to start, but visit www .fairfoodnetwork.org for the most updated information.

The categories listed here include:

1. Resources for conscious consumers
2. Urban agriculture and food systems
3. Business incubators and related resources
4. Hunger, food security, and food access

5. Youth development and food systems
6. Education/research centers and programs
7. Farmer training, networks, and resources
8. Institutional purchasing
9. Environment and conservation
10. Activist networks
11. Policy advocacy networks

Many of the organizations listed in one category could just as easily have been listed in others. I used my best judgment in deciding to list each one only once. I also attempted to have the categories roughly follow the progression of Part Three in the book, starting with organizations primarily of interest to conscious consumers in their homes and ending with organizations that interest engaged citizens focused on policy change.

For each organization, the basic format is to list:

- Name
- Website
- Address
- Phone
    Where there is no phone, I have included an e-mail
        address if provided.
    Where there is no phone or e-mail, I have noted
        "contact form on site" if there is one.

My primary interest in putting this list together is to give you resources so you can learn more about the issues that interest you most and so you can contact organizations that fit your interest and offer them your energy, your volunteer time, and your charitable donations. If you are ready to make the shift from conscious consumer to engaged citizen, here are dozens of organizations ready to help you in that transition!

1. RESOURCES FOR CONSCIOUS CONSUMERS

Appalachian Sustainable Agriculture Project
www.buyappalachian.org
306 W. Haywood St.
Asheville, NC 28801
(828) 236–1282

> Helps create and expand local food markets to preserve agricul-
> tural heritage, give everyone access to fresh, healthy food, and keep
> farmers farming. Projects include a local food guide to Appalachian
> Grown certified products, a farm-to-school program, a list of local
> farmers' markets, workshops, and online resources for producers,
> consumers, purchasing departments, and retailers. Even though
> ASAP (as it is called) is local to the Asheville area, it is a great
> model of a nonprofit organization linking local sustainable farmers
> with individual and institutional customers. You can learn a lot
> about how to do this in your community by becoming familiar with
> models like this.

Basis
www.basisfoods.com
420 W. 14th St., Suite 2NE
New York, NY 10014
(212) 334–5544

> Partners with New York City–area producers and communities to
> sell good food at affordable prices. Basis delivers local produce,
> fruit, dairy, and eggs to homes, offices, restaurants, and institutions
> and is about to launch a chain of small-format retail stores to sell
> good food sourced directly from family farms. There are similar
> businesses in other cities, but not yet a good directory of them. I
> expect many more businesses like this to emerge over the next few
> years as the demand for local and sustainable food increases. Check
> them out if you live in the New York area or if you have an inter-
> est in a business like this where you live.

Civil Eats

www.civileats.com

Contact form on site.

Blog/online publication that promotes critical thought about sustainable agriculture and food systems as part of building economically and socially just communities. Supports the development of a dialogue among local and national leaders about the American food system and its effects abroad. Civil Eats can be humorous, serious, academic, philosophical, conversational—its style of conversation is as diverse as its forty-plus contributors—but it is always thought-provoking and innovative. This is a good place to learn about up-to-date thinking and action about practice and politics of fair food.

CSA Farming

www.csafarming.com

Contact form on site.

Offers a brief introduction to the concept of community-supported agriculture and has a national directory of CSAs by state. If you are interested in joining a CSA, this is one of several directories you can use to find one in your area.

Eat Well Guide

www.eatwellguide.org

215 Lexington Ave., Suite 1001

New York, NY 10016

(212) 991–1858

Free online directory of fresh, locally grown, and sustainably produced food in the United States and Canada. Listings include family farms, restaurants, farmers' markets, grocery stores, community-supported agriculture programs, U-pick orchards, and more. You can search by location, keyword, category, or product to find good food, download customized guides, or plan a trip with the innovative mapping tool, Eat Well Everywhere.

Eat Wild
www.eatwild.com
PO Box 7321
Tacoma, WA 98417
(866) 453–8489

Supports farmers who raise their livestock on pasture from birth to market and who actively promote the welfare of their animals and the health of the land. Provides comprehensive, accurate information about the benefits of raising animals on pasture and links to local farms (listed by state) that sell grass-fed products: beef, lamb, goats, bison, poultry, pork, dairy, and other wild edibles. This is a website to use if you want to find grass-fed meat raised close to home.

Edible Communities Publications
www.ediblecommunities.com
369 Montezuma Ave., Suite 577
Santa Fe, NM 87501
(505) 989–8822

Creates editorially rich, community-based, local-foods publications in distinct culinary regions throughout the United States, Canada, and Europe. Connects consumers with family farmers, growers, chefs, and food artisans through publications, websites, and events. Individuals who own publications are local-foods advocates and residents of the communities in which they publish—a business model that preserves the integrity of member publications and the communities they serve. Subscribe to and read the publication pertinent to your region for great articles about what is happening in the local food scene and also for the ads that can help you find local/regional and sustainably produced food products.

FamilyFarmed.org
www.familyfarmed.org
7115 W. North Ave.
Oak Park, IL 60302
(708) 763–9920

Works directly with family farmers as well as with local and national organizations that serve farmers and are working to build local food systems. Works through website, annual FamilyFarmed EXPO (a great combination of informational sessions and great local food connections), and Chicagoland CSA Guide to educate the public about eating locally grown food, supporting farm families, and becoming members of local CSAs. Programs include: Farm to School, CSA Promotion, Food Safety, and the FamilyFarmed EXPO. For anyone living in the Chicago region, getting to know this organization is a must. It was founded and is run by Jim Slama, one of the true pioneers of the good-food movement.

Farmers Market Coalition
www.farmersmarketcoalition.org
PO Box 331
Cockeysville, MD 21030
Contact form on site.

Serves the rapidly growing farmers' market movement with information and representation at state and federal levels. Builds networks, links peers, and connects farmers' markets old and new with tools and resources for the benefit of farmers, consumers, and communities. Helps you find a statewide or regional farmers' market association, if there is one where you live. You may be only interested in locating a farmers' market for your own shopping, or you may be interested in finding a way to support your local farmers' market as a volunteer or a vendor; in either case, this is the place to start.

Food Alliance
www.foodalliance.org
1829 NE Alberta, Suite 5
Portland, OR 97211
(503) 493–1066

Certifies farms, ranches, and food handlers for sustainable agriculture practices. The only major certification program for food produced with good environmental practices, humane treatment of animals, and fair working conditions for farmworkers. Certified products include meats, eggs, dairy, mushrooms, grains, legumes, a wide variety of fruits and vegetables, and prepared products made with these certified ingredients. Offers a practical, credible, and effective way for farmers, ranchers, and food companies to demonstrate their commitment to sustainability in agricultural practices and facilities management. Their geographical presence is primarily in the Pacific Northwest, but they are working to expand to other parts of the country. This is a label you can trust if you want to use your food dollars to support sustainable *and* equitable practices on the farm.

Food Routes
www.foodroutes.org
RR 1 Box 25
Troy, PA 16947
(570) 673–3398

National nonprofit organization providing communications tools, technical support, networking, and information resources to organizations working to rebuild local, community-based food systems. Dedicated to reintroducing Americans to their food—the seeds it grows from, the farmers who produce it, and the routes that carry it from the fields to their tables. This is the national hub for more than eighty Buy Fresh, Buy Local campaigns across the country. If you have an interest in joining or starting such a campaign in your community, check with Food Routes.

Homegrown (a project of Farm Aid)
www.homegrown.org

Online community of people interested in all things homegrown: growing, cooking, crafting, brewing, preserving, building, making, and creating. Homegrown.org is a place to learn from each other, share questions, and show off how to dig in the dirt, grow your own food, work with your hands, and cook and share your meals.

Local Harvest
www.localharvest.org
PO Box 1292
Santa Cruz, CA 95061
(831) 515–5602

Maintains a nationwide directory of small farms, farmers' markets, and other local food sources. Search engine provides information on products from family farms and local sources of sustainably grown food, encouraging consumers to establish direct contact with small farms in their area. Online store helps small farms develop markets for some of their products beyond their local area.

Local Orbit
www.localorb.it
(734) 418–0680

Web-based marketplace combining the best features of farmers' markets and full-service grocery stores. Consumers choose and buy their groceries weekly from multiple sellers in a single shopping cart, somewhat like shopping on Amazon. Orders are delivered to a single drop-off point. They are currently testing their model in Brooklyn and Detroit. Several online businesses have tried (and some have failed) to break into this sector of local food—Local Orbit may become the first big success in this area. If you want to help test this idea, try them out and provide feedback.

Locavorious
www.locavorious.com
4260 Shetland Dr.
Ann Arbor, MI 48105
(734) 276–5945

Provides locally grown, delicious, and healthy frozen fruits and vegetables, enabling people to eat locally in the winter months in southeast Michigan. A frozen CSA model: "fresh-picked flavor year round." The business buys large quantities of in-season produce from local farmers, freezes it, then distributes monthly shares to members over the winter. This particular business serves only the Ann Arbor area but is a great innovation on the CSA theme that can be done in other areas—a great opportunity for small-business development in the local/sustainable food arena.

Lummi Island Wild
www.lummiislandwild.com
PO Box 256
Lummi Island, WA 98262
info@lummiislandwild.com

Cooperative of local fishermen in northern Washington State who fish in Puget Sound and in Alaska. They catch fish only in fisheries that are designated sustainably managed and are a great source of wild-caught salmon, cod, halibut, and other species. This is the cooperative we connected with for our Ann Arbor wild salmon buying club.

Michigan Land Use Institute
www.mlui.org
148 E. Front St., Suite 301
Traverse City, MI 49684
(231) 941–6584

Works with citizens, officials, and other organizations to build a prosperous new economy in Michigan, one that expands opportunity by improving personal and environmental health and focuses on local businesses, including local food and agriculture. Hosts the Taste the Local Difference Local Food Exchange, a model for local food distribution using online classified advertisements (www.localdifference.org). The institute has established a strong model for promoting local food producers and vendors to both year-round residents and the thousands of tourists who come to this beautiful area of northern Michigan in the summer. Worth checking out if you are ever in the area or are interested in developing a similar local food guide in your area.

Monterey Bay Aquarium's Seafood Watch
www.montereybayaquarium.org/cr/seafoodwatch.aspx
886 Cannery Row
Monterey, CA 93940
(831) 648–4800

Use this website to learn more about the kinds of fish and seafood to select if you want to support sustainable fisheries and avoid eating species that are being overfished or raised in ways that are environmentally harmful. Offers regional guides and even an iPhone app to help you with these decisions about consuming seafood.

Organic Trade Association
www.ota.com
60 Wells St.
Greenfield, MA 01301

Promotes and protects organic trade to benefit the environment, farmers, the public, and the economy. Envisions organic products becoming a significant part of everyday life, enhancing people's lives and the environment. This is a good resource if you want to learn more about what it means for food to be labeled "organic" and if you are seeking information about the organic food industry.

Peaches and Greens
www.centraldetroitchristian.org/Peaches_and_Greens_Market.htm
8838 3rd St.
Detroit, MI 48202
(313) 870–9210

Produce market opened in the fall of 2008, providing community residents the opportunity to have a safe, culturally acceptable, nutritionally adequate diet through a sustainable food system that maximizes community self-reliance. In 2009 the market launched a mobile food truck that operates five days a week, bringing produce to neighborhoods without other sources. This is a "green grocer" in the middle of Detroit's food desert, run by a nonprofit organization. The mobile market is an innovation that has been tried (not always with success) in other food desert areas. The Peaches and Greens store and mobile market are succeeding due to great leadership and focus from the parent organization. Anyone considering such a venture in their community needs to become familiar with this model.

Red Tomato
www.redtomato.org
1033 Turnpike St.
Canton, MA 02021
(781) 575–8911

Connects farmers and consumers through marketing, trade, and education, and through a passionate belief that a family-farm, locally based, ecological, fair-trade food system is the way to a better tomato. Broker deals with eco-friendly family farmers in the New England area and finds retail and wholesale outlets for the farmers. A "hybrid" organization, raising funds through grants while also generating revenue through their brokerage function. There are farmers in that region still farming because of the help Red Tomato has provided. Anyone thinking of creating a business of distributing food from local farms to stores needs to learn about this organization and benefit from its decade of experience in the field.

Sustainable Table
www.sustainabletable.org
215 Lexington Ave., Suite 1001
New York, NY 10016
(212) 991–1930
Celebrates local, sustainable food, educates consumers on food-related issues, and works to build community through food. This online resource, which includes the Eat Well Guide (above), the Meatrix, and several other projects, provides information on how to eat responsibly and where to find sustainably produced products.

USDA National Agricultural Library CSA List
www.nal.usda.gov/afsic/pubs/csa/csa.shtml
Alternative Farming Systems Information Center
National Agricultural Library
10301 Baltimore Ave., Room 132
Beltsville, MD 20705
(301) 504–6559
An online CSA farms directory maintained by the USDA.

Walking Fish
www.walking-fish.org
PO Box 2357
Beaufort, NC 28516
info@walking-fish.org
Community-supported fishery (CSF) that links small-scale fishermen on the North Carolina coast to consumers in Raleigh, Durham, and Chapel Hill. As in a CSA, members purchase shares and receive

deliveries of fresh-caught fish. A model for sustainable seafood distribution.

2. URBAN AGRICULTURE AND FOOD SYSTEMS

American Community Gardening Association
www.communitygarden.org
1777 E. Broad St.
Columbus, OH 43203–2040
(877) 275–2242

Supports community gardening by facilitating the formation and expansion of state and regional community gardening networks, developing resources in support of community gardening, encouraging research and conducting educational programs, and networking. Creates publications and training and holds an annual conference in a different part of the country each year.

Center for Urban Education about Sustainable Agriculture
www.cuesa.org
1 Ferry Building, Suite 50
San Francisco, CA 94114
(415) 291–3276

Promotes a sustainable food system through the operation of the Ferry Plaza Farmers' Market in San Francisco. Offers varied educational programs, such as market-to-table and cooking classes in Spanish. There are many farmers' market organizations involved in community education—I consider CUESA a model project in this regard. Any farmers' market interested in more fully connecting with its community needs to learn from this experience.

Clean Plate Projects, LLC
www.cleanplateprojects.com
806 Foucher St.
New Orleans, LA 70115
(504) 410–7076

Supports organizations and individuals to develop local food projects. Provides a range of support customized to meet the needs of each client. Specializes in innovative food education initiatives and home or school gardens. An example of an emerging opportunity for small for-profit businesses that are urban agriculture service providers.

Detroit Black Community Food Security Network
www.detroitblackfoodsecurity.org
3800 Puritan St.
Detroit, MI 48221
(313) 345–3663

Works as a coalition of organizations and individuals to build food security in Detroit's black community by influencing public policy, promoting urban agriculture, encouraging cooperative buying, promoting healthy eating habits, facilitating mutual support and collective action among members, and encouraging young people to pursue careers in agriculture, aquaculture, animal husbandry, beekeeping, and other food-related fields. The network operates Detroit's largest urban farm and focuses on engaging youth from the community. This organization's strong leadership is emerging as a group of powerful spokespeople for the urban agriculture movement.

Eastern Market Corporation
www.detroiteasternmarket.com
2934 Russell St.
Detroit, MI 48207
(313) 833–9300

Mobilizes leadership and resources to make the Eastern Market— the oldest and largest continuously functioning public farmers' market district in the United States—the center for fresh and nutritious food in southeast Michigan. One of the largest farmers' markets in any inner city, intending to become the hub for healthy, sustainably, and regionally produced food in Michigan. Eastern Market is the centerpiece of Fair Food Network's Double Up Food Bucks healthy food incentive program. Also a great working model of public ownership (the property is owned by the City of Detroit) with a private nonprofit organization managing and operating the market.

Fair Food Philly
www.fairfoodphilly.org
1315 Walnut St., Suite 522
Philadelphia, PA 19107
(215) 386–5211
   Dedicated to bringing locally grown food to the marketplace and
   promoting humane, sustainable agriculture for greater Philadelphia
   through consulting, leading the local Buy Fresh, Buy Local campaign, and operating the Fair Food Farmstand in the Reading Terminal Market in downtown Philly. Few nonprofit organizations in
   the good-food arena have figured out how to raise most of their
   operating funds in the good-food marketplace. This organization
   has, and its model is worth exploring.

The Food Trust
www.thefoodtrust.org
1 Penn Center, Suite 900
1617 John F. Kennedy Blvd.
Philadelphia, PA 19103
(215) 575–0444
   Works to ensure that everyone in the Philadelphia area has access to
   fresh, healthy food. Active in farm-to-school projects, supports
   inner-city farmers' markets, conducts nutrition education, and is
   well known for its healthy corner-store initiative. The Food Trust
   has also been one of the lead organizations with both the Pennsylvania Fresh Food Financing Initiative and the Federal Healthy Food
   Financing Initiative.

Garden Resource Program Collaborative
www.detroitagriculture.com
(313) 285–1249
   Provides resources (such as tools and seeds), education, and volunteer support to hundreds of home, school, and community gardens
   in Detroit, Highland Park, and Hamtramck, Michigan. A cooperative effort among the nonprofit groups Capuchin Soup Kitchen/
   Earthworks Garden, the Greening of Detroit, and the Detroit Agriculture Network, along with Michigan State University Extension.

Largely due to this collaborative, Detroit has become recognized as a hub of urban agriculture.

Growing Home
www.growinghomeinc.org
2732 North Clark St., Suite 310
Chicago, IL 60614
(773) 549-1336

Demonstrates the use of organic agriculture as a vehicle for job training, employment, and community development. Trains citizens returning from incarceration in urban organic farming and helps them regain a foothold in the community by growing healthy food for themselves and others. Runs an inner-city CSA and helps hard-to-employ men and women get training in the growing field of urban farming.

Growing Power
www.growingpower.org
5500 W. Silver Spring Dr.
Milwaukee, WI 53218
(414) 527-1546

Supports people from diverse backgrounds and the environments in which they live by helping to provide equal access to healthy, high-quality, safe, and affordable food. Implements this mission by providing hands-on training, on-the-ground demonstrations, outreach, and technical assistance through the development of community food systems that help people grow, process, market, and distribute food in a sustainable manner. They conduct workshops in Milwaukee and other cities. Will Allen, the founder of Growing Power, is known as a dynamic leader and teacher. Anyone interested in grassroots urban agriculture needs to learn more about him and about Growing Power.

Hartford Food System

www.hartfordfood.org
86 Park St., 2nd Floor
Hartford, CT 06106
(860) 296–9325

Fights hunger and improves nutrition for disadvantaged members of the community through sustainable, non-emergency strategies. Implements programs that improve access to nutritious and affordable food and help consumers make informed food choices, and advances responsible food policies at all levels of government. Many urban food systems organizations have emerged in the past two decades; Hartford Food System was one of the first. An important organization in the field in part because of its long-lasting presence in the community and the ability to shift local policy, such as routing of public transportation for residents to more easily get to grocery stores.

Just Food

www.justfood.org
1155 Avenue of the Americas, 3rd Floor
New York, NY 10036
(212) 645–9880, ext. 221

Connects local farms to NYC neighborhoods and communities. Provides city residents of all economic backgrounds with fresh, seasonal, sustainably grown food from local farms. If you are looking for a way to plug into the urban food systems scene in New York, Just Food is a good place to start.

Marketumbrella.org

www.marketumbrella.org
200 Broadway St., Suite 107
New Orleans, LA 70118
(504) 861–4485

Cultivates community markets that utilize local resources to bolster authentic local traditions. Organizes and runs a series of public markets in New Orleans that feature local produce and seafood. After Hurricane Katrina, one of the first places residents of New Orleans could find fresh food was at these markets. The leadership of Richard McCarthy is an inspiration to many people working in the urban food systems field, and he is always glad to share what he has learned.

Mvskoke Food Sovereignty Initiative
www.mvskokefood.org
100 E. 7th St., Suite 101
Okmulgee, OK 74447
(918) 756–5915

Works to enable the Mvskoke people and their neighbors to provide for their food and health needs now and in the future through sustainable agriculture, economic development, community involvement, and cultural and educational programs. They run a farmers' market program that connects youth and elders and a seed bank to ensure that important crops are preserved.

Nuestras Raíces
www.nuestras-raices.org
245 High St.
Holyoke, MA 01040
(413) 535–1789

Promotes economic, human, and community development in Holyoke, Massachusetts, through projects relating to food, agriculture, and the environment. Has organized and maintains many community gardens, as well as a thirty-acre urban farm in Holyoke. Known for its focus on local economic development, with more than forty small businesses having been spawned by this nonprofit organization.

People's Grocery
www.peoplesgrocery.org
909 7th St.
Oakland, CA 94607
(510) 652–7607

Works to build a local food system that improves the health and economy of Oakland, California. Its work involves increasing local supply of fresh foods through an urban farm, advocating for living-wage business and job opportunities, and developing strong relationships and community leadership. People's Grocery was one of the first nonprofit organizations in the country to experiment with a mobile produce market.

3. BUSINESS INCUBATORS AND RELATED RESOURCES

Intervale Center
www.intervale.org
180 Intervale Rd.
Burlington, VT 05401
(802) 660–0440

Trains aspiring farmers in organic practices, agricultural land preservation, waste management, stream bank restoration, and large-scale composting. Situated on a 350-acre farm, Intervale also manages most of the water treatment function for the city of Burlington. One of the earliest examples of integrating a working farm with a beginning farmer training program. Regularly consults with others who are establishing similar programs.

Kitchen Chicago
www.kitchenchicago.com
324 N. Leavitt St.
Chicago, IL 60612
(312) 455–0863

Rents a fully equipped, commercially licensed, shared-use kitchen, allowing food entrepreneurs to build a business with lower risk and minimal start-up costs. Provides resources for expansion into an industrial kitchen: insurance referrals, kitchen planning/design contacts, food vendor list, combined ordering service, links to continuing education, trade associations, business registration, etc. Anybody in the Chicago area interested in starting a local food-related business needs to know about this organization.

Kitchen Incubator
www.kitchenincubator.com
907 Franklin St., Suite 150
Houston, TX 77002
info@kitchenincubator.com

Rents three fully equipped and licensed kitchens to local start-up businesses. Provides a culinary business advisory, multi-chef café showcasing client products, consulting services for certification processes, referrals for business plan, financing, or website development.

Kitchen Table Consulting

www.kitchentableconsulting.com
3129 22nd St.
San Francisco, CA 94110
(415) 412–8784

Provides leadership training, strategic planning, business communications plans, and marketing materials for good-food enterprises and campaigns.

La Cocina

www.lacocinasf.org
2948 Folsom St.
San Francisco, CA 94110
(415) 824–2729

Provides affordable commercial kitchen space, shared resources, an array of services, technical assistance, and access to market opportunities. Focuses primarily on low-income women from communities of color and immigrant communities.

Mi Kitchen Es Su Kitchen

www.mikitchenessukitchen.com
Queens, NY
(718) 392–2550

Creates partnerships with nonprofit organizations that have an existing kitchen space and converts them into business incubator rental facilities, a win-win proposition that generates revenue for the nonprofits while providing inexpensive kitchen space for start-up businesses. Additional services provided include business coaching, license filing and procurement, nutritional analysis and food testing, marketing, graphic design, and website development. A very innovative idea started in Queens and poised to go nationwide—stay tuned!

Rutgers Food Innovation Center
www.foodinnovation.rutgers.edu
450 E. Broad St. (Route 49)
Bridgeton, NJ 08302
(856) 459–1900

Helps new and established food companies in the mid-Atlantic region with market research, product development, quality assurance,
and food safety compliance. One of the first business incubators at
a land-grant university. Many more are likely to follow. Check with
the land-grant university in your state.

The Starting Block
www.startingblock.biz
1535 Industrial Park Dr.
Hart, MI 49420
(231) 873–1432

Provides a shared-use, licensed commercial kitchen to new and expanding businesses in a multicounty region. Additional services include product development, ingredient sourcing, packaging and
labeling, nutritional analysis, and marketing strategies. Initiated by
a partnership between MSU Extension and Michigan Food and
Farming Systems, a statewide nonprofit organization, the Starting
Block has already spun off several successful businesses.

4. HUNGER, FOOD SECURITY, AND FOOD ACCESS

Alliance to End Hunger
www.alliancetoendhunger.org
50 F St. NW, Suite 500
Washington, DC 20001
(202) 639–9400

Fosters strategic partnerships and creates global connections to
engage diverse institutions in building the public and political will
to end hunger in the United States and globally. This alliance has
been influential in hunger and food aid policy both domestically
and internationally. Membership restricted to organizations and
institutions.

Bread for the World
www.bread.org
425 3rd St. SW, Suite 1200
Washington, DC 20024
(800) 822–7323

>   Working through churches, campuses, and other organizations, engages groups in advocacy to end hunger through nationwide letter-writing campaigns and meetings with elected representatives.

Center for Budget & Policy Priorities
www.cbpp.org
820 First St. NE, Suite 510
Washington, DC 20002
(202) 408–1080

>   Works at the federal and state levels on fiscal policy and public programs that affect low- and moderate-income individuals and families. One of the major policy forces in Washington, D.C., from the standpoint of hunger and food assistance policy, especially related to the Supplemental Nutrition Assistance Program (SNAP). Also an important informational resource for exploring how SNAP functions state by state and understanding the causes and extent of food insecurity.

Congressional Hunger Center
www.hungercenter.org
400 N. Capitol St. NW, Suite G100
Washington, DC 20001
(202) 547–7022

>   Operates Congressional Hunger Fellows Program, which trains and inspires future leaders who work to end hunger and advocate for public policies that address food insecurity. One of the major policy forces in Washington, D.C., from the standpoint of hunger and food assistance policy, especially related to the Supplemental Nutrition Assistance Program.

Feeding America
www.feedingamerica.org
One Constitution Ave. NE, Suite 200
Washington, DC 20002–5655
(202) 546–7001

> Formerly known as America's Second Harvest, feeds America's hungry through a nationwide network of more than two hundred member food banks in all fifty states and engages in the fight to end hunger. Provides food to more than 37 million low-income people in the United States annually. A leading domestic hunger-relief charity that supports approximately 61,000 local charitable agencies and 70,000 programs, providing food directly to individuals and families in need. Connect to your local food bank through their website.

Food Research and Action Center
www.frac.org
1875 Connecticut Ave. NW, Suite 540
Washington, DC 20009
(202) 986–2200

> Works to eradicate hunger and undernutrition in the United States and their root cause, poverty, through public-private partnerships that improve public policies. One of the major policy forces in Washington, D.C., from the standpoint of hunger and food assistance policy, especially related to SNAP. Provides an annual assessment of the percentage of individuals eligible for food stamp benefits who actually receive those benefits.

Forgotten Harvest
www.forgottenharvest.org
21800 Greenfield Rd.
Oak Park, MI 48237
(248) 967–1500

> Relieves hunger in the Detroit metropolitan area by rescuing prepared and perishable surplus and donating it to emergency food providers. Delivers food free of charge to individuals and families in greater Detroit. There are now many similar food rescue organizations throughout the country; Forgotten Harvest is the largest.

National Association of Farmers' Market Nutrition Programs
www.nafmnp.org
PO Box 9080
Alexandria, VA 22304
(703) 837–0451

A nonprofit corporation linking states, the District of Columbia, Indian tribal organizations, territories, and others with a stake in USDA's Farmers' Market Nutrition Programs, including local fruit and vegetable growers and low-income families and seniors.

Senior Farmers' Market Nutrition Program
www.fns.usda.gov/wic/seniorfmnp/sfmnpmenu.htm
Contact form on site.

The Senior Farmers' Market Nutrition Program (SFMNP) awards grants to states, U.S. territories, and federally recognized Indian tribal governments to provide low-income seniors with coupons that can be exchanged for eligible foods (fruits, vegetables, honey, and fresh-cut herbs) at farmers' markets, roadside stands, and community-supported agriculture programs. The majority of the grant funds must be used to support the costs of the foods provided under the SFMNP. State agencies may use up to 10 percent of their grants to support administrative costs for the program. See the above website to find contact information for the agency that administers the Senior Farmers' Market Nutrition Program in your area.

Wholesome Wave
www.wholesomewave.org
189 State St.
Bridgeport, CT 06604
(203) 226–1112

Supports increased production of and access to healthy, fresh, and affordable locally grown food. Fosters double value coupon programs in various communities. Develops healthy food hubs. Created the fruit and veggie prescription program. Founded by celebrity chef Michel Nischan in partnership with Paul Newman, Wholesome Wave is pioneering many community-based innovations that increase access to healthy food in underserved communities.

WhyHunger
www.whyhunger.org
505 Eighth Ave., Suite 2100
New York, NY 10018
(800) 548–6479

Connects people to nutritious, affordable food by supporting grass-roots solutions that inspire self-reliance and community empowerment. Projects include Food Security Learning Center, Grassroots Action Network, Artists Against Hunger and Poverty, Hungerthon, and National Hunger Clearinghouse.

5. YOUTH DEVELOPMENT AND FOOD SYSTEMS

4-H
www.4-h.org
Contact form on site.

The nation's largest youth development organization, 4-H helps young people learn the fundamentals of environmental science as well as health and nutrition, plant and animal science, citizenship, and healthy living through practical, hands-on projects on farms and in communities. A program of the 109 land-grant universities and the Cooperative Extension System, largely run on adult volunteer efforts.

Added Value/Red Hook Farm
www.added-value.org
370 Van Brunt St.
Brooklyn, NY 11231
(718) 855–5531

Promotes sustainable development through youth empowerment and urban agriculture. Creates opportunities for the youth of South Brooklyn to expand their knowledge base, develop new skills, and positively engage with their community through the operation of an urban farming enterprise. The program has formed strong relationships with the Brooklyn public schools. Youth participate in selling what they grow through a weekly farmers' market and providing organic vegetables to area restaurants.

Center for Land-Based Learning

www.landbasedlearning.org

5265 Putah Creek Rd.

Winters, CA 95694

(530) 795-1520

Provides practical, hands-on agricultural education to high school students through experiential learning done in the context of ecological stewardship. If you are looking for curriculum ideas for high school–age students, check this out.

The Edible Schoolyard

www.edibleschoolyard.org

Martin Luther King Jr. Middle School

1781 Rose St.

Berkeley, CA 94703

(510) 558-1335

A "flagship" school garden project, a program of the Chez Panisse Foundation. A one-acre organic garden and kitchen classroom for urban public school students, where students participate in all aspects of growing, harvesting, and preparing nutritious, seasonal produce. Classroom teachers and Edible Schoolyard educators integrate food systems concepts into the core curriculum. This is a program that could be emulated and replicated across the country.

FFA

www.ffa.org

6060 FFA Dr.

Indianapolis, IN 46268

Premier partnership organization in high schools across the country, helps prepare young people for careers in agriculture and food systems. Includes classroom instruction, supervised practical experience, and job/higher educational placement. Any high school student interested in a career in food or agriculture should check to see whether there is an active FFA chapter in his or her school.

The Food Project
www.thefoodproject.org
10 Lewis St.
Lincoln, MA 01773
(781) 259–8621

A stunning example of a national model that has continued to engage youth in personal and social change through sustainable agriculture. Young people and adults work together to develop models of sustainable metropolitan food systems, build interracial dialogue, address critical environmental and social issues on a local and national level, and reconnect people from all backgrounds with the land. Through agriculture and community service, teens learn about teamwork, labor, and persistence, take responsibility for their actions, and develop a sense of ownership in the future of their communities.

FoodCorps Inc.
www.foodcorps.org
281 Park Ave. South
New York, NY 10010
(212) 596-7045

Through the hands and minds of emerging leaders, FoodCorps strives to give all youth an enduring relationship with healthy food. Places motivated leaders in limited-resource communities for a year of public service. Works under the direction of local partner organizations to implement a three-ingredient recipe for healthy kids. Service members deliver hands-on nutrition education, build and tend school gardens, and bring high-quality local food into public-school cafeterias.

Greening of Detroit
www.greeningofdetroit.com
1418 Michigan Ave.
Detroit, MI 48216
(313) 237–8733

Originally created to "reforest" Detroit with trees, more recently focusing on community gardening, small-scale urban farming, and youth entrepreneurship training. Supports more than 1,200 community gardens and has influenced more than 8,000 young people, ages fourteen through seventeen, through garden- and school-based nutrition education programs. Youth education programs include school gardens, environmental stewardship, and summer camp. Of all the organizations in the country engaged in youth and food systems, none comes close to Greening of Detroit's sheer number and scale of on-the-ground garden projects.

Soil Born Farms
www.soilborn.org
PO Box 661175
Sacramento, CA 95866
(916) 363–9685

Facilitates programs focused on organic food production, healthy food education, and food access for all residents. They farm on several plots of land, each one closely connected to a middle school or high school where students are actively engaged in growing and preparing organic vegetables.

Tohono O'odham Community Action (TOCA)
www.tocaonline.org
PO Box 1790
Sells, Arizona 85634
(520) 383–4966

Creates and implements a curriculum for the Tohono O'odham youth through the school system, and is reintroducing traditional foods back into the community to combat the highest rate of diabetes in the world. Native American youth gain knowledge about their original food culture, creating a pathway to healthier lives.

6. EDUCATION/RESEARCH CENTERS AND PROGRAMS

Agroecosystems Management Program, Ohio State
www.oardc.ohio-state.edu/amp
201 Thorne Hall
1680 Madison Ave.
Wooster, OH 44691
(330) 202–3537

Provides opportunities for those involved in research, teaching, and outreach, from different disciplines and different institutions, to interact, discuss, and develop whole-systems approaches to the challenges affecting the food system. Fosters an ecological approach to agriculture, linking together social, biological, and engineering sciences to provide a foundation for innovative processes and projects. This university-based program conducts research and develops solutions through collaboration among many disciplines.

Center for Agriculture and Rural Development
www.card.iastate.edu
578 Heady Hall
Ames, IA 50011
(515) 294-1183

Conducts public policy and economic research on agricultural, environmental, and food issues. Communicates through publications, policy briefs, and presentations.

Center for Environmental Farming Systems
www.cefs.ncsu.edu
1323 Pleasant Hill Church Rd.
Siler City, NC 27344
(919) 513-0954

Serves as a center dedicated to sustainable agriculture research, extension, and education. Develops knowledge of technology for farmers so they can implement more environmentally sound systems. The premier sustainable agriculture university research center in the southeastern United States.

Center for Food & Justice — Urban and Environmental Policy Institute at Occidental College
www.departments.oxy.edu/uepi/cfi/
2106 Colorado Blvd.
Los Angeles, CA 90041
(323) 341-5099

Develops, evaluates, and institutionalizes innovative programs. Activates grassroots organizing and coalition building to empower local communities. Conducts research and policy analysis. Has been the lead institution in developing the national Farm to School Network.

Center for Integrated Agricultural Systems
www.cias.wisc.edu
1535 Observatory Dr.
Madison, WI 53706
(608) 262–5200
Sustainable agriculture research center at the University of Wisconsin produces publications, research briefs, reports, enterprise budgets, and other resources for farmers and food-related businesses. The center's goal is to develop and share knowledge about how different integrated farming systems can contribute to environmental, economic, social, and intergenerational sustainability.

Center for Sustaining Agriculture and Natural Resources at Washington State University
www.csanr.wsu.edu
2606 W. Pioneer Ave.
Puyallup, WA 98371
(253) 445–4626
Programs focus on small farms, organic agriculture, biologically intensive agriculture, and climate-friendly farming. Projects include pesticide reduction, organic production and marketing, conservation practices, sustainable agriculture policy, limited resource farmers, and farm energy. This center has been conducting research and training students for more than twenty years.

College of the Atlantic
www.coa.edu
105 Eden St.
Bar Harbor, ME 04609
(207) 288–5015
One of the most recently developed programs in sustainable agriculture and food systems. Program includes commercial and educational organic farm, complete with CSA and farm stand; an endowed professorship focused on creating a full range of curricula and research projects; and a transatlantic partnership connecting with programs in England and Germany. A big step for a small college. This will be of interest to prospective students.

Crossroads Resource Center
www.crcworks.org
7415 Humboldt Ave. S
Minneapolis, MN 55423
(612) 869–8664

A nonprofit organization that analyzes the economic impact of local food economies and helps communities fashion a food system that responds to local needs. Offers a variety of tools, including state-of-the-art technical information, consulting on business strategy, and community investment options. Ken Meter, who founded and leads Crossroads Center, is one of the first people I turn to when thinking through ways to express the economic impact of local and regional food systems.

The C. S. Mott Group for Sustainable Food Systems at Michigan State University
www.mottgroup.msu.edu
312 Natural Resources Building
East Lansing, MI 48824
(517) 432–1612

Conducts research and education on a variety of topics related to sustainable food systems, including community food assessments, ecosystem services modeling, farm-to-school programs, farmers' markets, hoop houses for season extension, community food, organic agriculture production, small farms, and sustainable food business development. Led by Dr. Mike Hamm, the C. S. Mott endowed chair of sustainable agriculture—the first such chair in the United States.

Kerr Center
www.kerrcenter.com
PO Box 588
Poteau, OK 74953
(918) 647–9123

Develops sustainable food and farming systems through programs in communications, community/local foods, horticulture and organics, and livestock management. Conducts an internship program and a professional development program, and distributes a solid newsletter with research-based results on grass-based farming.

The Land Institute
www.landinstitute.org
2440 E. Water Well Rd.
Salina, KS 67401
(785) 823–5376

Independent research institute focused on developing grain production systems for the Great Plains that mimic the perennial grasslands that existed prior to modern agriculture. Founded and led by Wes Jackson, an icon of the sustainable agriculture movement for a generation.

Leopold Center for Sustainable Agriculture
www.leopold.iastate.edu
209 Curtiss Hall
Ames, IA 50011

Highly respected research and education center associated with Iowa State University. Focused on programs in marketing and food systems, ecology, and policy that can make agriculture more profitable and keep small and mid-size farmers on the land. Conducts research into negative impacts of agricultural practices. Assists in developing alternative practices. A portion of state fees assessed on nitrogen fertilizer sales and pesticide registrations provides support for the center.

National Center for Appropriate Technology
www.ncat.org
3040 Continental Dr.
Butte, MT 59701
(406) 494–4572

Helps family farmers learn more about sustainable energy, agriculture, and community development opportunities. Serves economically disadvantaged people by providing information and access to appropriate technologies. National Sustainable Agriculture Information Service is part of NCAT (www.attra.org).

Organic Farming Research Foundation
www.ofrf.org
PO Box 440
Santa Cruz, CA 95061
(831) 426–6606

Fosters the improvement and widespread adoption of organic farming systems by sponsoring organic research, disseminating results, and educating the public. Their website and newsletter are good sources of research-based information for organic farmers.

Rodale Institute
www.rodaleinstitute.org
611 Sigfriedale Rd.
Kutztown, PA 19530
(610) 683–1400

Researches best practices of organic agriculture. Shares findings with farmers and scientists. *New Farm* magazine is one of the institute's outreach tools. Conducted some of the earliest research and demonstration projects on organic farming in the United States.

Sustainable Agriculture Research and Education
www.sare.org
1400 Independence Ave. SW
Washington, DC 20250
(202) 720–5384

Since 1988, the Sustainable Agriculture Research and Education program has helped advance farming systems that are profitable, environmentally sound, and good for communities through a nationwide research and education grants program. They also regularly disseminate results of the research projects that they support.

Sustainable Agriculture Research and Education Program—
University of California at Davis
www.sarep.ucdavis.edu
One Shields Ave.
Davis, CA 95616
(530) 752–7556

Administers competitive grants for research on sustainable agricultural practices and systems in California. Develops and distributes information through publications and on-farm demonstrations. Supports long-term research and sustainable farming systems on University of California farmlands.

7. FARMER TRAINING, NETWORKS, AND RESOURCES

American Forage and Grassland Council
www.afgc.org
PO Box 867
Berea, KY 40403
(800) 944–2342

Promotes the use of forage as a primary feed resource for animal agriculture. Represents the academic community, producers, industry, and foundations. Takes the lead in advancing economically and environmentally sound production and use of forage and grasslands through planning, conferences, leadership development, publications, and awards programs. A great organization for grass-based livestock farmers to learn techniques from one another and from the university researchers who focus on this area.

American Small Farm
www.smallfarm.com
1867 N. Galena Rd.
Sunbury, OH 43074
(740) 200–7030

A national publication focused on ideas, farming practices, and appropriate technology related to the needs of the small farmer and family farms with the goal of improving the profitability of the small farm operation.

Angelic Organics Learning Center
www.learngrowconnect.org
1547 Rockton Rd.
Caledonia, IL 61011
(815) 389-8455

Empowers people to create sustainable communities of soils, plants, animals, and people through educational, creative, and experiential programs. The learning center, a nonprofit organization, is the educational partner to Angelic Organics, a vibrant biodynamic/organic community-supported farm. Provides education to people interested in organic farming in both a farm and an urban setting. Farm tours, skills workshops, and custom learning opportunities for individuals, families, schools, and community groups. Workshops offered include beekeeping, composting, cheesemaking, and a variety of summer day camps for kids.

Appalachian Sustainable Development
www.asdevelop.org
310 Valley St. NW
Abingdon, VA 24210
(276) 623-1121

Network in Appalachia helping former tobacco farmers grow organic vegetables and eggs. A leading organization in the area of food systems social enterprise.

Beginning Farmer Center
www.extension.iastate.edu/bfc/
478E Heady Hall
Ames, IA 50011
(877) 232-1999

Coordinates education programs and services for beginning farmer efforts across Iowa. Assesses needs of beginning farmers and delivers targeted education: programs and services that develop skills and knowledge in financial management and planning, legal issues, tax laws, technical production and management, leadership, sustainable agriculture, human health, and the environment. Created by the Iowa legislature in 1994, part of Iowa State University Extension. Facilitates the matching of beginning farmers with existing farmers who want to transition their farm businesses to the next generation.

Beginning Farmers
www.beginningfarmers.org
Contact form on site.

A comprehensive and up-to-date compilation of information resources for new, experienced, and potential farmers, as well as educators, activists, and policy makers interested in the development of new farm enterprises. Through core resource pages and frequent blog postings, provides a robust and constantly growing forum for sharing information and ideas about starting new farms, as well as other content related to sustainable agriculture and food systems.

Black Farmers and Agriculturalists Association
www.bfaa-us.org
PO Box 61
Tillery, NC 27887
(252) 826–2800

Responds to the issues and concerns of black farmers in the United States and abroad. Formed in 1997, with a membership of more than 1,500 farmers nationwide and twenty-one state chapters, the organization is dedicated to seeking justice for small farmers and opposing environmental injustice confronting rural communities. Membership consists of both small-scale farms and very large-scale production operations owned and run by black farmers.

Michigan State University Student Organic Farm
www.msuorganicfarm.org
3291 College Rd.
Holt, MI 48842
(517) 230–7987

Teaches the ideas and principles of organic farming via an organic farming certificate program, and community-supported agriculture training program. An intensive training program in year-round organic farming, focusing on diversified production of vegetables, flowers, fruits, and herbs for local markets. Emphasizes student learning in hands-on farm management and decision-making as well as development of necessary farming skills and knowledge. Designed to give participants a strong background in production skills as well as the knowledge, management, and decision-making skills necessary to operate a diversified small farm. Program components include rotations in CSA, farm stand, propagation, and edible forest gardening as well as management and oversight of a production field or garden and development of a personal learning plan.

The Minnesota Food Association, Big River Farms
www.mnfoodassociation.org/default.aspx
14220-B Ostlund Trail North
Marine on St. Croix, MN 55047
(651) 433–3676

Provides education, training, and technical assistance in sustainable farming, marketing, business planning, identification, and use of resources. Builds public awareness through communication, public events, and farm visits, and by building partnerships with funding sources, government and university agencies, nonprofit organizations, businesses, and individuals. This is the only organic-certified, immigrant farmer training program in Minnesota.

National Farmers Union
www.nfu.org
20 F St. NW
Washington, DC 20001
(202) 554–1600

Founded in 1902 to protect and improve the economic health and quality of life for family farmers, ranchers, and rural communities. Now represents ranchers and farmers in every state, working in the policy arena from a grassroots structure where policy positions initiated locally are then advocated nationwide. Farmers Union policies address a wide range of issues such as federal fiscal policy, the Farm Bill, federal and state tax policies, energy policy, and the regulation of banks and credit unions.

National Immigrant Farming Initiative
www.immigrantfarming.org
524 River St.
Mattapan, MA 02126
Contact form on site.

Provides training, information sharing, networking opportunities, project funding, and other resources to support immigrant farmers. Advocates for immigrant farmers and works to build awareness about the unique challenges immigrant farmers face, while increasing the visibility of their important contributions to our communities and agriculture.

Northeast Organic Farming Association
www.nofa.org
Box 164
Stevenson, CT 06491
(203) 888–5146

An affiliation of seven state chapters, NOFA coordinates activities, organizes a well-respected annual summer conference, and acts as an umbrella organization for organic farmers throughout the northeastern United States. Publishes a quarterly newspaper, the *Natural Farmer*, which presents features on issues such as certification and organic farming techniques.

Ohio Ecological Food & Farm Association
www.oeffa.org
41 Croswell Rd.
Columbus, OH 43214
(614) 421–2022

A membership-based grassroots coalition of farmers, backyard gardeners, consumers, retailers, and educators creating a regional food system encompassing farming, processing, and distribution of sustainably produced local food. Provides its members with a membership directory, quarterly newsletter, yearly conference, hands-on workshops, apprenticeship program, organic certification services, and policy advocacy.

Pennsylvania Association for Sustainable Agriculture
www.pasafarming.org
PO Box 419
Millheim, PA 16854
(814) 349–9856

The largest statewide membership-based organization dedicated to sustainable farming in the country. Services provided include an annual Farming for the Future Conference; educational programs; regional marketing and business support, such as developing new farmers' markets, connecting restaurants and retailers to local food sources, and assisting farms and other businesses with marketing and business planning. Coordinates Buy Fresh, Buy Local chapters in Pennsylvania, helping consumers find, choose, and appreciate seasonal, local foods. The latest addition to this program is a new online social networking community called the Good Food Neighborhood, which links people to local food, farms, and one another. Monitors legislative activities on state and national levels, making recommendations for policies that promote farmland preservation, farmer retention, protection of natural resources, and increased access to healthy food.

Practical Farmers of Iowa
www.practicalfarmers.org
137 Lynn Ave., Suite 200
Ames, IA 50014
(515) 232–5661

Researches, develops, and promotes profitable, ecologically sound, and community-enhancing approaches to agriculture through a network of farmers and non-farmers who work together to promote small, local agriculture. The diverse group of 2,400 farmers and friends of farmers believes that farmers can provide multiple benefits to society, including food and fiber, clean air and water, and biodiversity on the land. Sponsors field days to showcase innovative farming practices, shares on-farm research results, and builds urban-rural understanding.

Purdue Small Farm and Sustainable Agriculture Team
www.ag.purdue.edu/smallfarms
615 W. State St.
West Lafayette, IN 47907
(765) 494–8396

Provides educational opportunities in the area of small farms and sustainable agriculture to help producers establish or expand successful, sustainable farm businesses and strengthen Indiana's rural communities. Their farmer education program focuses on forestry, fruits and vegetables, field crops, horticulture, pasture and forages, marketing and agritourism, organic practices, business planning, and budgeting resources.

Texas Organic Farmers & Gardeners Association
www.tofga.org
PO Box 48
Elgin, TX 78621
(512) 656–2456

Enhances the credibility of organic, natural, sustainable agricultural practices and production through public education. Assists in creating viable systems, approaches, and infrastructure for the successful organic, natural, sustainable production and marketing of plants, animals, and their associated products. Promotes safeguards for human and animal health by preserving the environment, including healthy topsoil, clean water, and clean air. Hosts several workshops for new farmers around the state each year. TOFGA members include ranchers, farmers, commercial plant growers, retailers, wholesalers, processors, distributors, consumers, and anyone desiring to support the organic industry in Texas.

UCSC Center for Agroecology & Sustainable Food Systems
http://casfs.ucsc.edu
1156 High St.
Santa Cruz, CA 95064
(831) 459–3240

Offers practical as well as academic training in the techniques of agroecology and organic farming and gardening through its well-respected apprenticeship program in ecological horticulture and through UCSC summer session courses (the Agroecology Practicum). The full-time apprenticeship program is held at the center's twenty-five-acre farm and three-acre Alan Chadwick Garden on the UCSC campus. Topics covered during the six-month course include soil management, composting, pest control, crop planning, irrigation, farm equipment, marketing techniques, and community-supported agriculture (CSA) practices. The center also conducts research in a variety of areas, such as community food security and consumer attitudes toward the food system, biocontrol options, and nutrient management on organic farms. The center has taken a lead role in developing curriculum resources for those teaching about sustainable agriculture at the college and university level and has helped organize the first national-level conference on postsecondary sustainable agriculture education. Staff members have produced internationally recognized instructional resources for those teaching organic farming, gardening, and marketing skills.

USDA Beginning Farmer & Rancher Development Program
www.nifa.usda.gov/fo/beginningfarmerandrancher.cfm
U.S. Department of Agriculture
National Institute of Food and Agriculture
1400 Independence Ave. SW, Stop 2201
Washington, DC 20250–2201
(202) 720–4423

In the last two Farm Bills, Congress funded and the USDA established the Beginning Farmer and Rancher Development Program. According to this legislation, a beginning farm is run by one or more operators who have ten years or less of experience operating a farm or ranch. In 2007, approximately 21 percent of family farms

met that definition. To learn about what projects have been funded
with this program, look at the directory of funded projects on the
website.

Women, Food & Agriculture Network

www.wfan.org
PO Box 611
Ames, IA 50010
(515) 460–2477

A community of women involved in sustainable agriculture. Members are farmers, landowners, researchers, students, advocates, and
mothers concerned about their families' health. Women own nearly
half the U.S. farmland today but are rarely represented on the
boards of policy-making bodies. WFAN exists for women to give
one another the information, connections, and encouragement to
be effective practitioners and supporters of sustainable agriculture
and healthy localized food systems. The network grew out of a
Women, Food and Agriculture working group formed to remedy
the absence of women's voices in food and agricultural issues in
preparation for the United Nation's Fourth World Women's Conference in Beijing, China.

8. INSTITUTIONAL PURCHASING

Bon Appétit Management Company

www.bamco.com
100 Hamilton Ave., Suite 400
Palo Alto, CA 94301
(650) 798–8000

One of the many food service companies starting to source food
from local and sustainable farms for cafeteria and food service venues. Has focused on local purchasing since 1999 and has since
taken on issues regarding sustainable seafood, cage-free eggs, antibiotics in animal husbandry, trans fats, climate change, and farmworkers' rights.

Chef Ann Cooper

www.chefann.com
PO Box 20708
Boulder, CO 80308
(631) 697–0844

The self-described "Renegade Lunch Lady" leads an organization focused on changing the way children eat at school. Tackles outdated district spending policies and commodity-based food service organizations. Includes recipes, tools, and links for anyone wanting to take on the school food issue.

Farm to College

www.farmtocollege.org
105 Bucher Hill Rd., Suite 2
Boiling Springs, PA 17007
(717) 240–1361

A project of the Community Food Security Coalition. Connects colleges to local farmers to provide food on campus. Provides information on basics of farm-to-college, searchable database to learn about existing programs, resources for starting and maintaining programs, and online survey to add your program.

Health Care Without Harm

www.noharm.org
12355 Sunrise Valley Dr., Suite 680
Reston, VA 20191
(703) 860–9790

One program is Healthy Food in Health Care, which includes the Healthy Food Pledge for health care institutions to sign. Helps hospitals and other health care institutions with identifying opportunities for sourcing more sustainably grown and locally produced food. Sponsors an annual conference on healthy food in health care.

Healthy Schools Campaign

www.healthyschoolscampaign.org

175 N. Franklin, Suite 300

Chicago, IL 60606

(312) 419–1810

An independent nonprofit organization that works with schools in Chicago and advocates for change in school environments. Works with parent networks, school food service staff, and school district policy makers to shift school food menus so children in public schools are fed healthier food.

Michigan Market Maker

www.mimarketmaker.msu.edu

Contact form on site.

Locates businesses and markets of agricultural products in a number of states via an interactive mapping system. Presents searchable database of demographic and business data that can forge important links among producers, distributors, and retailers. A vital resource for those interested in starting a food-related business in Illinois, Iowa, Georgia, Mississippi, Nebraska, Kentucky, Michigan, Indiana, Ohio, or New York.

National Farm to School Network

www.farmtoschool.org

Contact form on site.

A national program that connects schools (K–12) and local farms to serve healthy meals in school cafeterias, improve student nutrition, provide agriculture, health, and nutrition education opportunities, and support local and regional farmers. Establishes relationships between local farmers and school food service providers so that schoolchildren are fed fresh, local food in cafeterias and classrooms. Sponsors school gardens, farm tours, culinary education, and visits to farmers' markets. Provides vital links for anyone interested in a Farm to School initiative.

Real Food Challenge
www.realfoodchallenge.org
(617) 442–1322, ext. 16

Supports both a campaign and an online network. Works to increase the procurement of real food on college and university campuses, with the national goal of 20 percent real food by 2020. Includes support, training, resources, and materials for students and their allies to make connections, learn from one another, and grow the movement. Provides vital links for anyone interested in connecting college dining operations with a fair food system.

School Food FOCUS
www.schoolfoodfocus.org
40 Worth St., 5th Floor
New York, NY 10013
(646) 619–6728

National initiative that supports school districts with 40,000 or more students in their efforts to procure more healthful, sustainably produced, and regionally sourced food. Works to disseminate lessons learned and best practices to amplify the movement. Led by Toni Liquori and Kathy Lawrence, two recognized long-term activists in the fair food movement.

s'Cool Food
www.scoolfood.org
1283 Coast Village Circle
Santa Barbara, CA 93108
(805) 565–7550

Works to empower school districts in Santa Barbara County to implement and sustain nourishing cook-from-scratch food programs through education and training opportunities for school communities, intensive culinary workshops, in-service training, ongoing professional development programs, food systems education for food service staff, funding for school equipment, hands-on cooking and gardening experiences for students, and development of local food distribution networks. An important resource for other regions as well as documentation of best practices and a general

road map are provided. A very local project with strong support of
a local foundation.

9. ENVIRONMENT AND CONSERVATION

American Farmland Trust
www.farmland.org
1200 18th St. NW, Suite 800
Washington, DC 20036
(202) 331–7300

Works with federal, state, and local leaders and communities to develop legislation, implement policies, and execute programs that
keep farmers on their land and protect the environment. Supports
environmentally responsible farming practices on America's farm-
and ranchland. Works to change U.S. farm and food policy, especially in the area of farm- and ranchland protection.

Beyond Pesticides
www.beyondpesticides.org
701 E St. SE, #200
Washington, DC 20003
(202) 543–5450

Effects change through local action, helping individuals and community-based groups understand hazards of toxic pesticides
while providing information on safer alternatives. Advocates for
solutions to pesticide problems on federal, state, and local levels.

Bio-Integral Resource Center
www.birc.org
PO Box 7414
Berkeley, CA 94707
(510) 524–2567

Offers more than twenty-five years of experience in development
of least-toxic, sustainable, and environmentally sound integrated
pest management (IPM) methods. Works with local, state, and national agencies in devising programs of scientific research, policy,
project design, and implementation. Programs include integrated
pest management, IPM service providers, and IPM training.

Environmental Defense Fund
www.edf.org
1875 Connecticut Ave. NW, Suite 600
Washington, DC 20009
(800) 684–3322

Works on projects seeking practical solutions to environmental problems. Leverages power of markets and partnerships to achieve goals based on adherence to scientific principles and the law. EDF has been an active participant in conservation policy development for the Farm Bill.

Environmental Working Group
www.ewg.org
1436 U St. NW, Suite 100
Washington, DC 20009
(202) 667–6982

Works to protect the most vulnerable segments of the population from health problems attributed to a wide array of toxic contaminants, and to replace federal policies, including government subsidies that damage the environment and natural resources, with policies that invest in conservation and sustainable development. Has developed a database that tracks federal farm subsidies.

Food and Water Watch
www.foodandwaterwatch.org
1616 P St. NW, Suite 300
Washington, DC 20036
(202) 683–2500

Advocates for safe, accessible, and sustainably produced food, water, and fish. Works to protect the environmental quality of oceans. Encourages governmental protection of the environment and more stringent food safety. Educates about the importance of keeping shared resources under public control. Projects focus on food safety, factory farms, and fish farming.

Hazon
www.hazon.org
125 Maiden Lane, Suite B
New York, NY 10038
(212) 644-2332

Since 2004, Hazon's international CSA program has put more than $4 million in Jewish purchasing power behind local, sustainable farms. Recognized by the Sierra Club in 2008 and by Michelle Obama in 2010, Hazon's work for sustainable food systems now encompasses curriculum materials, tools to address food systems within Jewish institutions, an award-winning blog ("The Jew & the Carrot"), and the Jewish Food Education Network. Hazon's annual Food Conference, which began in 2006, brings together people from across the United States and beyond to explore the intersection of food, Jewish tradition, and contemporary issues. Though rooted in the Jewish world, Hazon welcomes participation and involvement from people of all religions and of none, and is especially interested in developing interfaith food initiatives and in offering resources to develop faith-based CSA systems in other denominations.

IPM Institute of North America, Inc.
www.ipminstitute.org
4510 Regent St.
Madison, WI 53705
(608) 232–1410

An independent nonprofit organization that assists agricultural firms in implementing and tracking integrated pest management (IPM) practices on farms. Services include developing crop- and region-specific best practices, guidelines for labeling IPM products, certification in IPM practices for growers, and consumer education.

Land Stewardship Project
www.landstewardshipproject.org
821 E. 35th St., Suite 200
Minneapolis, MN 55407
(612) 722–6377

One of the first statewide organizations to focus on the intersection of agriculture and the environment. Conducts on-farm research and publishes results that help farmers and policy makers create more environmentally sound practices and policies.

Maine Farmland Trust
www.mainefarmlandtrust.org
97 Main St.
Belfast, ME 04915
(207) 338-6575
info@mainefarmlandtrust.org

A statewide organization committed to preserving farmland and strengthening farming in Maine. Structured as a land trust, MFT is the state's leading force in preserving farmland, often working in partnership with local and regional land trusts. It is equally engaged in keeping farming vital through both direct assistance and innovative community projects. Since 1999, MFT has helped to preserve more than 17,000 acres of farmland and is leading the efforts of farmers, landowners, local land trusts, farm groups, towns, and state agencies collaborating to keep Maine's productive agricultural land available for farming now and in the future.

Natural Resources Defense Council
www.nrdc.org
40 W. 20th St.
New York, NY 10011
(212) 727–2700

Works on projects seeking practical solutions to environmental problems. Combines activist grassroots membership base with legal and scientific expertise to ensure a safe and healthy environment. Has been an active participant in environmental policy development for the Farm Bill.

New Mexico Acequia Association
www.lasacequias.org
805 Early St.
Building B, Suite 203
Santa Fe, NM 87505
(505) 995-9644

Acequias are the historic communal irrigation systems that support the culture and livelihood of thousands of families in New Mexico and other areas in the semi-arid southwestern United States. The association's mission is to sustain small farmers' way of life by protecting water as a community resource and strengthening the farming and ranching traditions of their families and communities. Has had tremendous policy impact by challenging state laws and successfully arguing in the New Mexico Supreme Court for the rights of local acequias to determine water transfers.

USDA Natural Resource Conservation Service
www.nrcs.usda.gov
14th and Independence Ave. SW
Washington, DC 20250
(202) 720-3210 (Public Affairs Division)

Works with landowners through conservation planning and assistance designed to benefit the soil, water, air, plants, and animals that form productive lands and healthy ecosystems. NRCS is the lead agency within the USDA that provides funding and other resources to help farmers and communities steward their natural resources for the future.

Water Keepers Alliance
www.waterkeeper.org
50 S. Buckhout, Suite 302
Irvington, NY 10533
(914) 674-0622

A global movement of on-the-water advocates in two hundred local organizations who patrol and protect more than 100,000 miles of rivers and streams in the United States and abroad. Provides support, research, and organization for policy advocacy to protect waterways. Pressures local and state policy makers to place limits on confined animal feeding operations.

10. ACTIVIST NETWORKS

Agricultural Justice Project
www.agriculturaljusticeproject.org
agjusticeproject@gmail.com

A nonprofit initiative to create fairness and equity in our food system. Addresses the needs of farmers and farmworkers in organic and sustainable agriculture. Its goal is to create social standards for sustainable and organic agriculture and to codify in concrete terms what making a legitimate claim of "social justice" means.

Alliance for Fair Food
www.allianceforfairfood.org
1107 New Market Rd.
Immokalee, FL 34142
(212) 253–1761

Works with the Coalition of Immokalee Workers (CIW) to eliminate modern-day slavery and sweatshop labor conditions from Florida agriculture. Functions as a loosely knit network of human rights, religious, student, labor, sustainable food and agriculture, environmental, and grassroots organizations. This alliance was key to creating agreements with fast food companies to pay higher wages for tomato field workers. They are a great example of student/activist collaboration.

Association of Farmworker Opportunity Programs
www.afop.org
1726 M St. NW, Suite 602
Washington, DC 20036
(202) 828–6006

Provides advocacy and educational services for member organizations that serve migrant and seasonal farmworkers and their families. The thread that binds the association is the concept that training and education can provide the launching pad to a better and more stable life for the workers who plant, tend, and harvest the crops that Americans consume at their tables.

Coalition of Immokalee Workers
www.ciw-online.org
PO Box 603
Immokalee, FL 34143
(239) 657–8311

Fights for fair wages and healthy working and living conditions for farmworkers, especially in central Florida. They were instrumental in recent negotiations with large food companies to get the tomato pickers higher wages through a cooperative agreement among workers, growers, and end users. This is a stunning example of youth-led collaborative organizing in the food system with tangible and replicable results.

Community Food Security Coalition
www.foodsecurity.org
3830 SE Division St.
Portland, OR 97202
(503) 954–2970

Dedicated to building strong, sustainable, local and regional food systems that ensure access to affordable, nutritious, and culturally appropriate food to all people at all times. Focuses on policy advocacy and organizing, including farm-to-cafeteria projects. They run an annual national conference that brings together many varied leaders and organizations. A great conference for anyone interested in quickly learning about the issues and leaders of the good-food movement.

Domestic Fair Trade Association
www.thedfta.org
PO Box 300190
Boston, MA 02130
(617) 680–9862

A membership-based collaboration of organizations representing farmers, farmworkers, food system workers, retailers, manufacturers, processors, and nongovernmental organizations. Supports family-scale farming by ensuring that member organizations are committed to principles of fairness, equity, and diversity, and by working to communicate that message to consumers who want to support these values in the food system.

Farm Aid
www.farmaid.org
501 Cambridge St., 3rd Floor
Cambridge, MA 02141
(800) FARM-AID

Promotes fair farm policies and grassroots organizing campaigns designed to defend and bolster family farm–centered agriculture. Works with local, regional, and national organizations to protest factory farms and inform farmers and eaters about issues like genetically modified food and growth hormones. They work to strengthen the voices of family farmers through annual benefit concerts, communications campaigns, and funding of family farm–centered projects.

Farm Labor Organizing Committee
www.supportfloc.org
1221 Broadway St.
Toledo, OH 43609
(419) 243–3456

Builds membership of migrant farm workers so that they have collective power to get their needs met. Current membership is in the tens of thousands. They work from the principle that farmworkers need a voice in the decisions that affect them. Allowing workers to form a union and collectively bargain with their employer is the only way to address the huge imbalance of power and provide an effective structure for self-determination. Seeks a structure where all those in the system (corporations, growers, and farmworkers) work together to solve problems.

Farmworker Justice
www.fwjustice.org
1126 16th St. NW
Washington, DC 20036
(202) 293–5420

Empowers migrant and seasonal farmworkers to improve their living and working conditions, immigration status, health, and occupational safety. Accomplished through litigation, administrative and legislative advocacy, training and technical assistance, coalition building, public education, and support for union organizing. Monitors and analyzes decisions by Congress, the White House, the courts, and administrative agencies that affect farmworkers, then works to implement decisions that create improved lives and working conditions for farmworkers.

Federation of Southern Cooperatives/Land Assistance Fund
www.federationsoutherncoop.com
2769 Church St.
East Point, GA 30344
(404) 765–0991

Assists in the development of cooperatives and credit unions as a collective strategy to create economic self-sufficiency. Assists in land retention and development for family farmers, especially African Americans. Develops self-supporting communities with programs that increase income and enhance other opportunities.

First Nations Development Institute
www.firstnations.org
351 Coffman St., Suite 200
Longmont, CO 80501
(303) 774–7836

Supports dozens of projects across the country for Native American communities to relearn and reclaim indigenous food systems. Through the leadership of Mike Roberts, the organization's president, it focuses on economic development strategies to promote economic as well as food systems self-sufficiency.

Growing Food and Justice for All Initiative
(an initiative of Growing Power)
www.growingfoodandjustice.org
Contact form on site.

A new comprehensive network hosted by Growing Power that views dismantling racism as a core principle that brings together social change agents from diverse sectors. These agents are working to bring about new, healthy, and sustainable food systems and are supporting and building multicultural leadership. One of the few organizations with an annual conference that brings together the many, varied people concerned about food justice to find ways to work together more productively.

Land Loss Prevention Project
www.landloss.org
PO Box 179
Durham, NC 27702
(800) 672–5839

Provides legal support and assistance to all financially distressed and limited-resource farmers and landowners in North Carolina. Focuses on litigation, public policy, and promotion of sustainable agriculture and environment. Works alongside state, regional, and national coalitions that support sustainable agriculture practices, development, and policy innovations.

National Family Farm Coalition
www.nffc.net
110 Maryland Ave. NE, Suite 307
Washington, DC 20002
(202) 543–5675

Strengthens the voices and actions of its diverse grassroots members to demand viable livelihoods for family farmers, safe and healthy food for everyone, and economically and environmentally sound rural communities. Represents family farms and rural groups. Chooses projects based on potential to empower family farmers by reducing the corporate control of agriculture and promoting a more socially just farm and food policy. Seeks to effectively challenge existing farm, food, trade, and rural economic policy with policy alternatives that ensure family farmers receive a fair price for what they produce and have access to the credit and land they need to remain in business.

National Good Food Network
www.ngfn.org
2121 Crystal Dr., Suite 500
Arlington, VA 22202
contact@ngfn.org

Serves the growing community of civic, business, and philanthropic organizations involved in building a new "good food" system in the United States. In particular, focuses on advancing regional, collaborative efforts to move good food—healthy, green, fair, affordable—beyond the direct-marketing realm into larger scale markets so that more producers benefit, more communities have viable economies and greater access to good food, and a greater number of acres are managed through sustainable practices. Supports projects in several regions in the United States. To get involved, contact the Wallace Center to see where your closest regional project is happening and to connect with the regional team leader there.

Restaurant Opportunities Centers United
www.rocunited.org
350 7th Ave., Suite 1504
New York, NY 10001
(212) 243–6900

Conducts restaurant workplace justice campaigns, provides job training and placement, runs cooperatively owned restaurants, and conducts research and policy work. Initially founded after September 11, 2001, to provide support to restaurant workers displaced as a result of the World Trade Center tragedy, ROC has grown to support restaurant workers in several major cities (New York, New Orleans, Detroit, Miami, and Chicago) and advocate for improved working conditions. Trains restaurant workers to find good jobs and advance within the industry, and publishes reports on the restaurant industry. For those interested in other locations, ROC United conducts fundraising to launch a ROC in a particular city and then provides intensive training and technical assistance to help develop that branch.

Roots of Change
www.rootsofchange.org
Contact form on site.

Develops and supports a collaborative network of California leaders and institutions interested in establishing a sustainable food system by the year 2030. This network involves food producers, businesses, nonprofits, communities, government agencies, and foundations that share a commitment to changing our food thinking, food markets, and food policies. The resulting system will provide healthy and affordable food, benefits, and wealth to workers and farmers, and will help restore the soil, water, species diversity, and climate upon which food production depend. Roots of Change works with California industries and communities to ensure that every aspect of our food—from the time it's grown to the time it's eaten—can be healthy, safe, profitable, and fair for those who grow it and for the state where it's grown. They focus their efforts on convening and policy making.

Rural Advancement Foundation International, USA
www.rafiusa.org
274 Pittsboro Elementary School Rd.
Pittsboro, NC 27312
(919) 542-1396

Works toward strong family farms and rural communities, close connections between producers and consumers, environmentally sound farming, and safeguarding of biological diversity. Helps create a movement among farm, environmental, and consumer groups to ensure that family farmers have the power to earn a fair and dependable income; everyone who labors in agriculture is respected, protected, and valued by society; air, water, and soil are preserved for future generations; the land yields healthy and abundant food and fiber that is accessible to all members of society; and the full diversity of seeds and breeds, the building blocks of agriculture, are reinvigorated and publicly protected. RAFI focuses on North Carolina and the southeastern United States.

Slow Food USA
www.slowfoodusa.org
20 Jay St., Suite M04
Brooklyn, NY 11201
(718) 260–8000

Seeks to create dramatic and lasting change in the food system by reconnecting Americans with the people, traditions, plants, animals, fertile soils, and waters that produce our food. Works to inspire a transformation in food policy, production practices, and market forces so that they ensure equity, sustainability, and pleasure in the food we eat. Runs a variety of programs, including U.S. Ark of Taste, Renewing America's Food Traditions, Slow Food in Schools, and Slow Food on Campus. Chapters (called convivia) exist across the country and boast a paid membership of more than 30,000. As Slow Food USA transitions from its earlier focus on celebration of good food to issues related to environment and social justice in the food system, this organization may evolve into a major policy force. Easy to join or to start a convivium in your community; contact the national office.

Student/Farmworker Alliance
www.sfalliance.org
PO Box 603
Immokalee, FL 34143
(239) 657–8311

A national network of students and youth organizing with farmworkers to eliminate sweatshop conditions and modern-day slavery in the fields. Works in alliance with the Coalition of Immokalee Workers, a Florida-based, membership-led organization of mostly Latino, Haitian, and Mayan Indian low-wage workers. These student leaders understand their work as part of a larger movement for economic and social justice. Their work with farmworkers to win higher wages and commitments to better living conditions was truly groundbreaking. Any student interested in these issues needs to check them out.

11. POLICY ADVOCACY NETWORKS

California Food and Justice Coalition
www.cafoodjustice.org
2530 San Pablo Ave., Suite F
Berkeley, CA 94702
(510) 704–0245

Promotes the basic human right to healthy food while advancing social, agricultural, environmental, and economic justice priorities. Collaborates with community-based efforts to create a sustainable food supply for California residents through advocacy, organizing, and education. Focuses on increasing access to land and resources for rebuilding local food systems. Involved in farmland preservation, land use, climate action, planning, and funding mechanisms for local food system development.

Center for Rural Affairs
www.cfra.org
145 Main St.
Lyons, NE 68038
(402) 687–2100

Works to establish strong rural communities. Advocates for federal policies supporting rural community development that reduces poverty, rewards land stewardship, and strengthens small farms and businesses. Provides loans, technical assistance, and training to small entrepreneurs through the Rural Enterprise Assistance Program. Develops new cooperatives to reach and expand markets. A nationally recognized policy analysis and advocacy organization focused on the upper Midwest and Great Plains, with a national grassroots base of nearly 30,000 individuals, including people in all fifty states.

Drake Law Food Policy Council Database
www.law.drake.edu/centers/agLaw/?pageID=fpcDataBase

A comprehensive listing of food policy councils in the United States. An important resource for anyone who is thinking about starting a food policy council in their community.

Fair Food Network
www.fairfoodnetwork.org
205 E. Washington St., Suite B
Ann Arbor, MI 48104
(734) 213-3999

Works in partnership with other organizations to design a food system that upholds the fundamental right to healthy, fresh, and sustainably grown food, especially in historically excluded communities. Major policy focus is related to increasing access to healthy foods in underserved communities. Healthy food incentives and healthy food finance are two specific policy goals that FFN seeks to impact. Informs public policy from the evaluation and data from on-the-ground efforts in Detroit and other Michigan communities.

Food First: Institute for Food and Development Policy
www.foodfirst.org
398 60th St.
Oakland, CA 94618
(510) 654-4400

Analyzes the root causes of global hunger, poverty, and ecological degradation. Develops solutions in partnership with movements working for social change. Projects focus on building local food systems and democratizing development. The purpose of the institute is to eliminate the injustices that cause hunger. They believe a world free of hunger is possible if farmers and communities take back control of the food systems currently dominated by transnational agrifoods industries. Carries out research, analysis, advocacy, and education with communities and social movements for informed citizen engagement with the institutions and policies that control production, distribution, and access to food.

Institute for Agriculture and Trade Policy
www.iatp.org
2105 First Ave. S
Minneapolis, MN 55404
(612) 870-0453

Works with organizations around the world to analyze how global trade agreements impact domestic farm and food policies, and advocates for fair trade policies that promote strong health standards, labor and human rights, the environment, and democratic institutions. Works to develop alternative economic models that include clean sources of energy, such as wind power and biofuel, and that would spur rural development, and advocates for green businesses and farms that reduce toxic runoff into the Great Lakes and Mississippi River. Works to stop the overuse of antibiotics in agriculture and aquaculture while limiting the release of mercury and other toxic pollutants that fall onto farmland and enter the food supply. A unique organization that spans the arenas of production agriculture and public health. IATP works both locally in the Minnesota area and nationally on policy initiatives related to its mission.

National Sustainable Agriculture Coalition
www.sustainableagriculture.net
110 Maryland Ave. NE
Washington, DC 20002

An alliance of grassroots organizations that advocates for federal policy reform to advance the sustainability of agriculture, food systems, natural resources, and rural communities. Focuses on policy reform and advocacy to support small and mid-size family farms, protect natural resources, promote healthy rural communities, and ensure access to healthy, nutritious foods for all. Relies on input from grassroots to develop policy and promotes citizen engagement in policy process.

New York Sustainable Agriculture Working Group
www.nysawg.org
758 South Ave.
Rochester, NY 14620
(716) 316–5839

Contributes to the building of local food systems. Focuses on food justice and food access for low-income communities and communities of color in urban and rural settings. Programs focus on Buy Fresh, Buy Local, small-scale food processing, policy development, training, and technical assistance.

Northeast Sustainable Agriculture Working Group
www.nefood.org
PO Box 11
Belchertown, MA 01007

A regional network of member organizations and individuals that works toward a more sustainable, safe, and secure regional food system, one that is economically viable, environmentally sound, and socially just. Programs focus on public policy, food systems development, and public and member education.

Organic Consumers Association
www.organicconsumers.org
6771 S. Silver Hill Dr.
Finland, MN 55603

Focused on promoting the interests of the nation's estimated 50 million organic and socially responsible consumers. Represents more than 850,000 members, subscribers, and volunteers, including several thousand businesses in the natural foods and organic marketplace. An online and grassroots nonprofit public interest organization campaigning for health, justice, and sustainability. Deals with issues of food safety, industrial agriculture, genetic engineering, children's health, corporate accountability, fair trade, and environmental sustainability.

Organization for Competitive Markets
www.competitivemarkets.com
PO Box 6486
Lincoln, NE 68506

A national, membership-based, nonprofit public policy, research, and advocacy organization that works to return the food and agricultural sector to true supply-and-demand-based competition. Focused on antitrust and trade policy in agriculture to enhance competitive markets. Supports government regulatory role as well as law of supply and demand to preserve ability of independent family farm enterprises to compete with agribusiness.

PolicyLink (Healthy Food Financing Initiative)
www.policylink.org
1438 Webster St., Suite 303
Oakland, CA 94612
(510) 663-2333

Connects the work of people on the ground to the creation of sustainable communities of opportunity that allow everyone to participate and prosper. Guided by the belief that those closest to the nation's challenges are central to finding solutions to its problems, PolicyLink relies on the wisdom, voice, and experience of local residents and organizations, focusing attention on how people are working successfully to use local, state, and federal policy to create conditions that benefit everyone, especially people in low-income communities and communities of color. Findings and analysis are shared through publications, website and online tools, convenings, national summits, and in briefings with national and local policy makers. PolicyLink has been the leading force behind the Healthy Food Financing Initiative, a federal policy that supports the creation and expansion of healthy food retail in underserved communities.

Rural Coalition
www.ruralco.org
1012 14th St. NW, Suite 1100
Washington, DC 20005
(202) 628–7160

An alliance of farmers, farmworkers, and indigenous, migrant, and working people from the United States, Mexico, Canada, and beyond seeking to build a more just and sustainable food system that brings fair returns to minority and other small farmers and rural communities, establishes just and fair working conditions for farmworkers, protects the environment, and brings safe and healthy food to all consumers. Its programs focus on policy research, Farm Bill advocacy, and grassroots activism.

QUESTIONS FOR DISCUSSION

Part I: Our Broken Food System

Chapter 1: The System and Its Dysfunctions

1) What is a system?
2) Why do we call the food system a system?
3) What other systems have an effect on your daily life?
4) How would you describe the food system? What part(s) of this system do you most interact with?
5) How do specialization and centralization affect each part of the food system, or the entire food system?
6) What are some of the unintended consequences of the current organization of the food system? How did these unintended consequences occur?
7) Which parts of the food system most affect your daily life?

Chapter 2: The Problem Is . . .

1) What are the environmental symptoms that indicate our food system is failing?
2) What are the symptoms of a broken food system in terms of physical health of our citizens?
3) What social inequalities are manifested in the failing food system?
4) Which symptoms of the current broken system are most evident in your daily life?

5) Which of the symptoms of the broken food system most sur-
prise you? Why?

Part II: Principles of a Fair Food System

Chapter 3: A Fair Food System

1) What is meant by the principle of equity in the food system?
2) How is the concept of equity applicable to each step of the
food system (production, processing, distribution, point of
sale, waste)?
3) Can you think of an organization in your region working to
make the food system more equitable?
4) What role can you imagine playing to make the food system
more equitable?

Chapter 4: Strength Through Diversity

1) What is meant by the principle of diversity in the food
system?
2) How is the principle of diversity related to crop/livestock
production?
3) To producers and consumers?
4) To business structures?
5) What organizations in your area work to make the food system more diverse?
6) What role can you imagine playing to make the food system
more diverse?

Chapter 5: Nurturing the Land That Feeds Us

1) What is meant by the principle of ecological integrity?
2) Why are organic/sustainable agricultural practices important
for the environment?

3) What are some important changes needed in the food system to ensure future ecological integrity?
4) What organizations in your area work to ensure ecological integrity in the food system?
5) What role can you imagine playing to make the food system more ecologically sound?

Chapter 6: Feeding the Green Economy

1) What is meant by the principle of economic viability?
2) Discuss how the multiplier effect works in a local economy.
3) In what ways can a business make sure that its economic value and returns are shared with the community in which it operates?
4) What are the locally owned businesses in your area that give you the option to "buy local"?
5) What national/regional chains do you know that give back locally, and in what way do they do so?
6) What role can you imagine playing to strengthen the economic viability of your local food system?

Part III: From Conscious Consumer to Engaged Citizen

Chapter 7: Becoming a Fair Food Activist

1) Do you already consider yourself a conscious consumer? If so, what inspired you to become one?
2) What do you already do in your kitchen and community to build a fair food system?
3) What are the next steps you can see yourself taking in this direction?
4) In what ways can you imagine working to help others become more conscious consumers?

Chapter 8: Institutional Change

1) Do your local schools/colleges/universities have farm-to-cafeteria programs in place? How do you know? How could you find out?

2) Do your local health care institutions have programs to source locally and sustainably produced food? How do you know? How could you find out?

3) In what ways can you imagine working to create more institutional purchasing of locally grown and sustainable food?

Chapter 9: Shifting Public Policy

1) Do you already consider yourself an engaged citizen in the area of creating a fair food system? In what ways?

2) Is there a food policy council in your area? If yes, who are its members? If no, whom would you include in one?

3) What are the most important issues in your community (or state) for a food policy council to focus on?

4) What types of farming occur in your area—urban? rural? small, medium, or large scale?

5) Is there an organization heading up farmland preservation? How successful is it?

6) Are there initiatives in your area for institutions to procure food locally, and have these initiatives improved the local economy? How would you find out?

7) Give a brief outline of the Farm Bill's history and original intent.

8) How have Farm Bill priorities changed since the legislation's inception?

9) How can the Farm Bill be altered to shift government funds to building a fair food system?

10) What key organizations and interest groups in your area have a stake in Farm Bill policy? Do they have ways to involve your participation?

11) What key organizations and interest groups in your area educate citizens about the Farm Bill process?

12) Who are your elected representatives to the U.S. House of Representatives and Senate? Are any of them directly involved in House or Senate Agriculture Committees? How can they be contacted?

Chapter 10: Resources

Spend some time searching Chapter 10 or the Fair Food List online (www.fairfoodlist.org/list) for organizations in your area.

1) Were you surprised to find so many (or so few) in your area?

2) Did you find one or more organizations with which you would like to get involved?

3) Do you know of an organization that is working to build a fair food system and should be listed online? Contact it and suggest its organizers submit an entry!

ACKNOWLEDGMENTS

As I was writing this book, I was repeatedly asked, "How long have you been working on it?" My stock answer was, "either eighteen months or thirty-five years, depending on how I look at it." I have been engaged in the work of food systems sustainability since my first days on the Santa Cruz Farm in the early '70s (in fact, having spent part of my childhood on a working cattle ranch in Northern California and part of a year on kibbutz, probably even longer than this). A person gains the perspective and knowledge of a field as I have only by relying on many others who have helped form my thinking, challenged my assumptions, and encouraged me to continue. The number of people who have been my teachers, students, colleagues, and supporters is huge, and my only concern about thanking them all is that I am sure I will miss someone. So if I have missed you, I ask your forgiveness in advance.

First and foremost, my thanks go to my wife and soulmate, Lucinda. She has never stopped believing in me, and for that I am truly grateful. My mother, Mildred Hesterman, blessed be her memory, was a source of strength and compassion in my life. She was always there to help me set direction in life, to celebrate my achievements, and soothe my sorrows. She will be missed by me and all those whose lives she touched. I thank my grandfather, who taught me to bake challah as a way to connect to my ancestral roots; my father, whose spirit and mentorship enables me to see connections where others do not; and my loving siblings, Arla, Reuel, Megan, and Evrith. I thank our three children, Sarah, Matt, and Bryce, for keeping me grounded so much of the time and for helping me see most clearly the reasons for working to create a sustainable path for future generations.

There are many who have helped build our new organization, Fair Food Network (FFN), among them, my childhood friend and current coconspirator Anthony Garrett; the FFN staff: Jean Chorazyczewski, Liza Baker, Meredith Freeman, Rachel Blair, Christy Gehringer, Alex Linkow, Kate Fitzgerald, Liz Kohn, Winona Bynum, Liz Alpern, and Jubek Yongo-Bure; and the generous Ken and Jeanne Levy-Church. I also want to express appreciation to our FFN board and advisory board members, Ismael Ahmed, Karen Aldridge-Eason, Angela Glover-Blackwell, Ray Goldberg, Eugene Kahn, James Ella James, Frederick L. Kirschenmann, Anna Lappé, Rudy Mathelier, Antonio Medina, Carlo Petrini, LaDonna Redmond, Mark Ritchie, Michael E. Roberts, Paul Saginaw, Gus Schumacher, Alan Schwartz, Nancy Snyderman, Jackie Victor, Diana Chapman Walsh, Dan Warmels, DeWayne Wells, and Malik Yakini.

Without my many years at the Kellogg Foundation, I would never have had the opportunity to learn about the work of philanthropy and the nonprofit sector, so critical for the innovation we need for the future. I also acknowledge the leadership of Kellogg Foundation board and staff in helping build the field of sustainable food and agriculture, and supporting the important communications and framing research I rely on in my own work. To my colleagues at the Kellogg Foundation (past and present), I give much appreciation—Gillian Barclay, John Burkhardt, William Buster, Nicole deBeaufort, Gail Christopher, Patti Grimes, Susan Jenkins, Val Johnson, Chris Kwak, Karen Ladley, Larraine Matusak, Russ Mawby, Jim McHale, Ricardo Millett, Dan Moore, Betty Overton, Anne Petersen, Tom Reis, Bill Richardson, Karen Roth, Craig Russon, Ricardo Salvador, Miguel Satut, Sterling Speirn, Roger Sublett, Frank Taylor, Tom Thorburn, Ali Webb, April Wilbur, Teresa Williams, Terri Wright; Gail Imig and Rick Foster, my close colleagues and co-leaders during my years at the Kellogg Foundation; and Linda Jo Doctor, a strong food systems and public health leader who has helped me stretch my thinking and practice in so many ways.

It has taken a "village of funders" to get FFN flying—we maintain the growing list of donors on our website, and my strong appreciations go out to all of them. A special thanks goes to the Woodcock Foundation (Alexandra Christy, Steve Liebowitz, and their marvelous board and their founder, Polly Guth). Without their early support, FFN would not have stood a chance of succeeding. There are several other funders who have made a huge contribution to getting this new nonprofit off the ground:

Mimi Corcoran, Elise Dellinger, Benita Melton (C. S. Mott Foundation), and their group at Open Society Foundations, David Fukuzawa, Wendy Jackson, and Laura Trudeau and Rip Rapson at Kresge Foundation, Doug Stewart and Phillip Fisher at the Fisher Family Foundation, Mariam Noland and Elizabeth Sullivan at Community Foundation for Southeast Michigan, Steve Wilson and Raquel Thueme at Ruth Mott Foundation, Shannon Polk at C.S. Mott Foundation, Walt Reid at Packard Foundation, Michel Nischan at Wholesome Wave, Amanda Musilli, Walter Robb, and David Lewis at Whole Foods Market, Jodee Raines and John Erb at Erb Family Foundation, Marty Fluharty at Americana Foundation, and my former compatriots at W. K. Kellogg Foundation.

I also have had the chance to work with so many talented thought leaders and strategists who have guided my thinking over the years and to whom I give profound thanks—Gary Appel, Carol Andersen, Marlene Arnold, Bobby Austin, Kenny Ausubel, Rabbi Chava Bahle, Dan Barber, Zenobia Barlow, Michael Bassik, Valerie Batts, Judith Bell, JoAnne Berkenkamp, John Biernbaum, Bill Bolling, George Boody, Tim Bowser, Eileen Brady, Elaine Brown, Marland Buckner, Patty Cantrell, Dan Carmody, Annie Cheatham, Susan Cheng, Margaret Christie, Susan Clark, Virginia Clark, Elliott Coleman, Craig Cox, Nancy Creamer, Jimmy Daukas, Steve Davies, Vic DeLuca, Michael Dimock, Michael Eric Dyson, Curt Ellis, Scott Exo, Andy Fisher, John Fisk, Randall Fogelman, Kim Fortunato, Miguel Garcia, Paula Garcia, Rabbi Elliot Ginsburg, Amy Gonzalez, Robert Gottlieb, Pat Gray, Tom Guthrie, Hal Hamilton, Mike Hamm, Allen Hance, Bruce Hirsch, Ferd Hoeffner, Savi Horne, Alan Hunt, Saul Hymans, Kelly Irwin, Terroll Dew Johnson, Paul Johnson, Anupama Joshi, Deborah Kane, Eric Kessler, Oliver Kim, Fred Kirschenmann, Luke Knowles, Ben Kohrman, Ari Kurtz and Moira Donnel, Karen Lehman, Yael Lehmann, Howard Lerner, Ilana Levinson, Russell Libby, Diane MacEachern, Darci McConnell, Meredith Maislin, Ed Maltby, Preston Maring, Richard McCarthy, Leslie Michelson, Joan Nathan, Marion Nestle, Larry and Lucie Nisson, Denise O'Brien, Ayn Perry, Duane Perry, Gayle Peterson, Rich Pirog, Tristan Reader, Daniel Ross, Michael Rozyne, Paul Saginaw, Ruth Schechter, Jeremy and Laura Seligman, Neelam Sharma, David Sheie, John Sherman, Shirley Sherrod, Michael Shuman, Nina Simmons, Jim Slama, Brian Snyder, Loel Solomon, Anim Steel, Marty

Teitel, Francis Thicke, Tom Tomich, Maria Van Hekken, Josh Viertel, Arlin Wasserman, Hal and Marilyn Weiner, Emily Williams, Larry Yee, Bill Zirinsky, and Kolu Zigbi.

Without the important partnerships at USDA there would be much less to write about. My appreciations for long-standing collegial relationships to Errol Bragg, Bill Buchanan, Andy Jermolowicz, Kathleen Merrigan, Doug O'Brien, Debbie Tropp, Liz Tuckermanty, Wendy Wasserman, and Dave White.

I continue to be inspired by the leadership of my own Senator Debbie Stabenow and her excellent staff (Amanda Renteria, Chris Adamo), Jacqlyn Schneider (Senior Professional Staff, Senate Committee on Agriculture, Nutrition, and Forestry), and my own Congressman John Dingell and his capable staff. I also am grateful to former Congresswoman Carolyn Cheeks Kilpatrick and her able aide Riley Grimes and current Detroit Congressman Hansen Clarke. Congressman Bobby Rush and Congresswomen Marcy Kaptur and Chellie Pingree have been stalwart supporters of a fair food system for years, and I am grateful for their support and ideas.

I am indebted to two special professors who always gave me enough rope to get myself in trouble during my graduate years, Craig Sheaffer and Larry Teuber. I am also grateful for all the education I received from those graduate students whom I had the pleasure of advising over the years—John Durling, John Fisk, Tim Griffin, Glenn Harris, Peter Jeranyama, Jeremias Rodriguez, Anil Shrestha, Eric Spandl, and Peter Tiffin.

And finally, this book would have remained only an idea and lots of notes without the able assistance of my agent, George Greenfield (with thanks to Diana Cohn for the introduction), and the entire team at PublicAffairs: Susan Weinberg, Lisa Kaufman, Jaime Leifer, Emily Lavelle, Lindsay Fradkoff, and Melissa Raymond. And a big thank-you to Mindy Werner, editor extraordinaire!

NOTES

Introduction

1. Presented by Pamela Moore, director, Detroit Workforce Development Department: A Michigan Works! Agency, at the Urban Policy Roundtable, August 18, 2011.

2. This figure comes from the Michigan Department of Human Services, the state SNAP agency, and includes the 13 percent increase in benefits authorized in the Federal Stimulus Bill of 2009.

3. Mari Gallagher Research & Consulting Group, "Examining the Impact of Food Deserts on Public Health in Detroit," 2007, Chart 2, 5.

4. "How He Did It," *Newsweek*, www.newsweek.com/2008/11/05/how-he-did-it.html, accessed October 7, 2010.

Chapter 1: The System and Its Dysfunctions

1. USDA National Agricultural Statistics Service, Economics, Statistics, and Marketing Information Systems, www.usda.mannlib.cornell.edu, accessed October 25, 2011, and www.ers.usda.gov/Data/MajorLandUses, accessed October 25, 2011.

2. USDA National Agricultural Statistics Service, Economics, Statistics, and Marketing Information Systems, www.usda.mannlib.cornell.edu, accessed October 5, 2010.

3. See www.agguide.agronomy.psu.edu/weights.cfm, accessed October 5, 2010.

4. There are many differing views on the cost versus benefit of growing genetically modified crops (or GMOs, as they are called). The technology of genetic modification may hold promise for developing future crop varieties that are more drought- or pest-resistant, for example, which could be very beneficial where needed. But we also know that widespread use of herbicide-tolerant corn and soybean varieties is now also associated with the emergence of herbicide-tolerant weeds, making the job of weed control more costly and causing farmers to use greater amounts of diverse chemicals, some of which were thought to have been replaced by the Roundup-ready technology.

5. USDA National Agricultural Statistics Service, Economics, Statistics, and Marketing Information Systems, www.usda.mannlib.cornell.edu, accessed October 25, 2011.

6. American Ag Radio Network, July 20, 2011, http://americanagnetwork.com /2011/07/livestock-feed-remains-number-one-use-of-u-s-corn, accessed October 28, 2011.

7. According to Food Marketing Institute, "Supermarket Facts," www.fmi.org/ facts_figs/?fuseaction=superfact, accessed October 25, 2011, the average supermarket in 2010 carried 38,718 different items. Both the Ontario Corn Growers Association (www.ontariocorn.org/classroom/products, accessed October 4, 2010) and Michael Pollan, in *Omnivore's Dilemma* (p. 19), agree that 25 percent of the items in a typical grocery store contain corn in some form or another.

8. U.S. Department of Agriculture Food Safety and Inspection Service, "Federal Meat Inspection Act," Regulations & Policies: Acts & Authorizing Statutes, www .fsis.usda.gov/Regulations_&_Policies/Acts_&_Authorizing_Statutes/index.asp, accessed October 8, 2010.

9. Eric Schlosser, *Fast Food Nation* (New York: Houghton Mifflin, 2001), Chapter 8, pp. 169–190.

10. Leopold Center for Sustainable Agriculture at Iowa State University, www .leopold.iastate.edu.

11. University of Michigan Center for Sustainable Systems, *U.S. Food Systems Fact Sheet.*

12. Rick Tolman, "Corn and Ethanol: Green, Getting Greener," PowerPoint presentation at 2nd Annual Iowa Renewable Fuels Summit, January 31, 2008, www .iowarfa.org/documents/Tolman.ppt, accessed October 7, 2010.

13. U.S. Census Bureau, *Population: 1790–1990*, Table 4, www.census.gov/ population/www/censusdata/files/table-4.pdf, accessed October 10, 2010.

14. See www.agweb.com/farmersfeedingtheworld, accessed October 7, 2010.

15. See www.quickstats.nass.usda.gov, accessed October 7, 2010.

16. Dr. Mary Hendrickson, University of Missouri, personal communication, October 1, 2010.

Chapter 2: The Problem Is . . .

1. G. F. Koltun, M. N. Landers, K. M. Nolan, and R. S. Parker, "Sediment Transport and Geomorphology Issues in the Water Resources Division," http://water .usgs.gov/osw/techniques/workshop/koltun.html, accessed June 19, 2009.

2. David Pimentel and Marcia Pimentel, *Food, Energy, and Society*, 3rd ed. (New York: CRC Press, 2008), 206.

3. Based on data from J. Risser, "A Renewed Threat of Soil Erosion: It's Worse than the Dust Bowl," *Smithsonian* (1981): 120–122, 124, 126–130; Gary A. Klee, *Conservation of Natural Resources* (Englewood Cliffs, NJ: Prentice Hall), 1991; and Pimentel and Pimentel, *Food, Energy, and Society.*

4. Pimentel and Pimentel, *Food, Energy, and Society.*

5. David Pimentel et al., "Environmental and Economic Costs of Soil Erosion and Conservation Benefits," *Science* (1995): 1117–1122.

6. Rattan Lal, Terry M. Sobecki, Thomas Iivari, and John M. Kimble, *Soil Degradation in the United States: Extent, Severity, and Trends* (New York: Lewis Publishers, 2004), 158.

7. Keith Wiebe and Noel Gollehon, *Agricultural Resources and Environmental Indicators* (Washington, DC: U.S. Department of Agriculture, Economic Research Service, 2006), 24.

8. Ibid., 26.

9. Ibid., 25.

10. Ibid., 25.

11. Jane Braxton Little, "The Ogallala Aquifer: Saving a Vital U.S. Water Source," *Scientific American* (2009): 32.

12. Ibid., 37.

13. The Docking Institute of Public Affairs, "The Value of Ogallala Groundwater," http://bigcat.fhsu.edu/docking/img/Archives/SW%20Groundwater-Ogallala/Part%205 .Chapter%202.pdf, accessed January 8, 2011, 15.

14. Paul Roberts, *The End of Food* (New York: Houghton Mifflin, 2008), 217.

15. Wiebe and Gollehon, *Agricultural Resources*, 36.

16. Valerie White, "Agriculture and Drinking Water Supplies: Removing Nitrates from Drinking Water in Des Moines, Iowa," *Journal of Soil and Water Conservation* (1996): 454.

17. Sierra Club, "Sick Waters: Excess Nutrients Harm the Health of our Waters," www.sierraclub.org/cleanwater/sickwaters/map.asp, accessed July 22, 2009, 6.

18. Wiebe and Gollehon, *Agricultural Resources*, 37.

19. Craig Cox, "Cleaning Up the Food System," presentation at Friedman Nutrition Symposium, Tufts University, Boston, Massachusetts, November 6, 2010.

20. Wiebe and Gollehon, *Agricultural Resources*, 35.

21. U.S. Environmental Protection Agency, "Report to Congress: Nonpoint Source Pollution in the United States," http://nepis.epa.gov/Exe/ZyNET.exe/2000RU80 .PDF?ZyActionP=PDF&Client=EPA&Index=1981%20Thru%201985&File=D%3A\ ZYFILES\INDEX%20DATA\81THRU85\TXT\00000009\2000RU80.txt&Query= %28agriculture%29%20OR%20FNAME%3D%222000RU80.txt%22%20AND %20FNAME%3D%222000RU80.txt%22&SearchMethod=1&FuzzyDegree=0& User=ANONYMOUS&Password=anonymous&QField=&UseQField=&IntQField Op=0&ExtQFieldOp=0&Docs=1984, accessed January 8, 2011, xiii.

22. Wiebe and Gollehon, *Agricultural Resources*, 33.

23. Ecological Society of America, "Hypoxia," www.esa.org/education_diversity/ pdfDocs/hypoxia.pdf, accessed January 8, 2011, 1.

24. Robert J. Diaz and Rutger Rosenberg, "Spreading Dead Zones and Consequences for Marine Ecosystems," *Science* (2008): 926–929.

25. Wiebe and Gollehon, *Agricultural Resources*, 36.

26. According to research led by Dr. Nancy Rabalais, one of the world's leading experts on hypoxia and dead zones, www.nola.com/news/gulf-oil-spill/index.ssf/ 2010/08/dead_zone_as_big_as_massachuse.html, accessed January 8, 2011.

27. U.S. Department of Agriculture, National Agricultural Statistics Service, "2007 Census of Agriculture: United States Summary and State Data" (Washington, DC, 2009a), 49.

28. American Farmland Trust, "Farmland Protection Issues," www.farmland .org/programs/protection/default.asp, accessed June 3, 2009.

29. American Farmland Trust, "Farmland Protection Issues."

30. U.S. Environmental Protection Agency, "Inventory of U.S. Greenhouse Gas Emissions and Sinks: 1990–2007 (Public Review Draft)" (Washington, DC, 2008), 250.

31. Ibid., 30.

32. World Health Organization, www.who.int/food_crisis/fact_sheet/en/, accessed January 8, 2011. This statement is not meant to imply that the U.S. food system is solely to blame for hunger worldwide. Even so, the U.S. food aid system, which constitutes a market for U.S. farmers, discourages agriculture development and sustainability in developing countries, and does contribute to hunger in those places.

33. World Health Organization, www.who.int/food_crisis/fact_sheet/en/, accessed July 23, 2009.

34. Alisha Coleman-Jensen, Mark Nord, Margaret Andrews, and Steven Carlson, "Measuring Food Security in the United States: Household Food Security in the United States, 2007," www.ers.usda.gov/publications/err66/err66.pdf, accessed January 8, 2011, 4.

35. Mari Gallagher Research & Consulting Group, "Examining the Impact of Food Deserts on Public Health in Detroit," 9.

36. Ibid., 4.

37. Mari Gallagher Research & Consulting Group, "Examining the Impact of Food Deserts in Chicago" (Chicago, 2006), 30.

38. "Food, Conservation, and Energy Act of 2008," 110th Cong., 2nd sess., www.govtrack.us/congress/bill.xpd?bill=h110–6124, accessed June 15, 2009.

39. U.S. Department of Agriculture Economic Research Service, "Access to Affordable and Nutritious Food—Measuring and Understanding Food Deserts and Their Consequences: Report to Congress," www.ers.usda.gov/Publications/AP/ AP036/AP036.pdf, accessed December 31, 2010, 15.

40. Nicole I. Larson, Mary T. Story, and Melissa C. Nelson, "Neighborhood Environments: Disparities in Access to Healthy Foods in the U.S.," *American Journal of Preventive Medicine* 36, no. 1 (2009): 75.

41. K. Morland, S. Wing, and A. Roux, "The Contextual Effect of the Local Food Environment on Residents' Diets: The Atherosclerosis Risk in Communities Study," *American Journal of Public Health* 92, no. 11 (2002): 1761–1767.

42. Larson et al., "Neighborhood Environments," 75.

43. Tara Parker-Pope, "After Steady Climb, Childhood Obesity Rates Stall," www.nytimes.com/2008/05/28/health/research/28obesity.html?_r=3&partner=rss-nyt, accessed June 9, 2009.

44. Centers for Disease Control and Prevention, National Center for Health Statistics Health Data Interactive, www.cdc.gov/nchs/hdi.htm, accessed March 8, 2009.

45. Centers for Disease Control and Prevention, National Center for Health Statistics Health Data Interactive, www.cdc.gov/nchs/pressroom/07newsreleases/obesity.htm, accessed June 10, 2009.

46. American Diabetes Association, Diabetes News, www.diabetes.org/diabetes newsarticle.jsp?storyId=15351710&filename=20070623/ADA20070623118262585 6641EDIT.xml, accessed June 12, 2009.

47. Centers for Disease Control and Prevention, National Center for Chronic Disease Prevention and Health Promotion, www.cdc.gov/diabetes/projects/diab_children .htm#1, accessed June 8, 2009.

48. David Pimentel et al., "Ecology of Increasing Diseases: Population Growth and Environmental Degradation," *Human Ecology* (2007): 653–668.

49. Andrew C. Voetsch, "FoodNet Estimate of Burden of Illness Caused by Nontyphoidal Salmonella Infections in the United States," *Clinical Infectious Diseases* (2004): 127–134.

50. Roberts, *The End of Food*, 190.

51. Chuck Jolley, "Five Minutes with Jeff Benedict, E. coli & Jack In the Box," www.cattlenetwork.com/Jolley—Five-Minutes-With-Jeff-Benedict—E—coli—-Jack -In-The-Box/2010–10–15/Article.aspx?oid=1273062&fid=CN-TOP_STORIES, accessed October 27, 2010.

52. Margaret Mellon, "Testimony Before the House Committee on Rules on the Preservation of Antibiotics for Medical Treatment Act H.R. 1549," www.ucsusa .org/assets/documents/food_and_agriculture/july-2009-pamta-testimony.pdf, accessed January 8, 2010, 3.

53. Pew Commission on Industrial Farm Animal Production, "Putting Meat on the Table: Industrial Farm Animal Production in America" (2008): 15.

54. Brad Spellberg, "The Epidemic of Antibiotic-Resistant Infections: A Call to Action for the Medical Community from the Infectious Diseases Society of America," *Clinical Infectious Diseases* (2008): 155–164.

55. Infectious Diseases Society of America, "Bad Bugs, No Drugs: As Antibiotic Discovery Stagnates . . . A Public Health Crisis Brews," www.fda.gov/ohrms/dockets/ dockets/04s0233/04s-0233-c000005–03-IDSA-vol1.pdf, accessed January 8, 2011, 4.

56. Lisa Isenhart (coordinator, Keep Antibiotics Working), personal communication, October 4, 2010.

57. William Kandel, "Profile of Hired Farmworkers, A 2008 Update," www .ers.usda.gov/Publications/ERR60/, accessed June 16, 2009, iii.

58. Ibid., 16.

59. U.S. Department of Labor, Bureau of Labor Statistics, "Union Member Summary," www.bls.gov/news.release/union2.nr0.htm, accessed January 8, 2011.

60. Kandel, "Profile of Hired Farmworkers," 28.

61. Ibid., table 13.

62. William Kandel, *Meat-Processing Firms Attract Hispanic Workers to Rural America* (Washington, DC: U.S. Department of Agriculture, Economic Research Service, 2006), 457–458.

63. Restaurant Opportunities Center of New York (ROC NY), New York City Restaurant Industry Coalition, "Behind the Kitchen Door: Pervasive Inequality in New York City's Thriving Restaurant Industry," www.urbanjustice.org/pdf/publications/ BKDFinalReport.pdf, accessed January 8, 2011.

64. Restaurant Opportunities Centers United, "Behind the Kitchen Door: A Summary of Restaurant Industry Studies in New York, Chicago, Metro Detroit, New Orleans, and Maine," www.rocunited.org/files/National_EXEC_edit0121.pdf, accessed October 11, 2010.

65. Jayachandran N. Variyam, "The Price Is Right: Economics and the Rise in Obesity," U.S. Department of Agriculture, Economic Research Service, www.ers.usda.gov/AmberWaves/February05/Features/ThePriceIsRight.htm, accessed June 11, 2009.

Chapter 3: A Fair Food System

1. Kari Wolkwitz and Joshua Leftin, "Characteristics of Food Stamp Households: Fiscal Year 2007," Report No. FSP-08-CHAR (Alexandria, VA: U.S. Department of Agriculture, Food and Nutrition Service, Office of Research and Analysis, 2008).

2. Jeremy Nowak, "The Reinvestment Fund," Congressional Black Caucus Foundation presentation, September 16, 2010.

3. Ibid.

4. Interview with Walter Robb, COO, Whole Foods Market, October 1, 2010.

5. Data from Michigan Department of Human Services.

6. See www.allianceforfairfood.org, accessed October 12, 2010.

7. Amy Bennett Williams, "Tomato Grower, Harvesters Strike Historic Accord," *Fort Myers News-Press*, October 14, 2010, www.news-press.com/article/20101014/NEWS01/10140385/1075/Tomato-grower-harvesters-strike-historic-accord.

8. Interview with Sean Sellers, Student Farmworkers Alliance, October 12, 2010.

9. U.S. Bureau of the Census, County Business Patterns, 2007, available at http://censtats.census.gov/cgi-bin/cbpnaic/cbpdetl.pl.ii. U.S. Department of Commerce, Bureau of Economic Analysis, *Gross Domestic Product by Industry Accounts*, available at www.bea.gov. ROC United, www.rocunited.org/files/National_EXEC_edit0121.pdf, accessed October 15, 2010.

10. Interview with Minsu Longiaru, ROC Detroit, October 8, 2010.

11. Interview with Paula Garcia, October 11, 2010.

12. Lloyd D. Wright, *Racial Equity in Agricultural and Rural Development Report: Preventing the Decline of Black Farmers and Black Rural Landownership*, p. 6, available from the Land Loss Prevention Project. Spencer D. Wood writes, "I would say that this is an oversimplification of the counting of black farms, farmers, and farmland. The three are conceptually distinct. Why it matters is that each paints a different picture of what has happened. In fact, there are nearly 7 million acres of black-owned farmland. Most of this is not farmed by blacks. It is generating income but becoming distant from the black family who owns it. Saying that there are 29,690 farmers is using a particular count that might include multiple farm operators per farm. This matters because the USDA has devised several enumeration changes that may produce more accurate counts but make direct comparison with earlier years more difficult." Spencer D. Wood, "A Violation of Civil Rights: Discrimination in Farm Credit, the Largest Class-Action Civil Rights Settlement in U.S. History, and the On-Going African-American Freedom Movement," unpublished manuscript.

13. Ibid., 12.

14. "The Impact of Heir Property on Black Rural Land Tenure in the Southeastern Region of the U.S.," www.federationsoutherncoop.com/landloss.htm, accessed October 31, 2010.

15. Angela Browning, *The Decline of Black Farming in America* (Washington, DC: U.S. Department of Agriculture, U.S. Commission on Civil Rights, 1982).

16. Interview with Savi Horne, October 11, 2010.

17. Federation of Southern Cooperatives/Land Assistance Fund website, www.federationsoutherncoop.com/landloss.htm, accessed October 20, 2010.

18. Land Loss Prevention Project, www.landloss.org/predatorylending.php, accessed October 27, 2010.

19. "Type-II Diabetes & Obesity: A Community Crisis," www.tocaonline.org/www.tocaonline.org/Oodham_Foods/Entries/2010/3/30_The_Health_Effects_Caused_by_the_loss_of_the_Traditional_Food_System.html, accessed October 31, 2010.

20. Ibid.

21. Tristan Reader, "The Traditional Tohono O'odham Food System: A Short History," www.tocaonline.org/www.tocaonline.org/Oodham_Foods/Entrics/2010/3/30_The_Health_Effects_Caused_by_the_loss_of_the_Traditional_Food_System.html, accessed October 31, 2010.

22. Interview with Tristan Reader, November 3, 2010.

23. See www.tocaonline.org/www.tocaonline.org/Oodham_Foods/Oodham_Foods.html, accessed October 31, 2010.

Chapter 4: Strength Through Diversity

1. Michael H. Shuman, *The Small-Mart Revolution: How Local Businesses Are Beating the Global Competition* (San Francisco: Berrett-Koehler Publishers, 2006).

2. Michael H. Shuman, "Building Prosperity, Valuing Community: Exploring Community Food Enterprise," panel presentation at the W. K. Kellogg Foundation's Food & Society Conference, San Jose, California, April 21–23, 2009.

3. Michael Shuman, personal communication, October 16, 2010.

4. See www.livingeconomies.org/aboutus, accessed October 16, 2010.

5. Michael Shuman, personal communication, November 29, 2010.

6. See www.communityfoodenterprise.org/case-studies.

7. Jackie Victor, personal communications, October 18, 2010 and October 30, 2011.

8. The Food Project, "State of the Field: Youth in Sustainable Food Systems," October 2007, 2.

9. Ibid., 5.

Chapter 5: Nurturing the Land That Feeds Us

1. Dennis Avery, *Saving the Planet with Pesticides and Plastic: The Environmental Triumph of High-Yield Farming* (Indianapolis, IN: Hudson Institute, 2000).

2. Eric Chivian and Aaron Bernstein, "Genetically Modified Foods and Organic Farming," in *Sustaining Life: How Human Health Depends on Biodiversity* (New York: Oxford University Press, 2008), 399–400, 402.

3. George Shetler, personal communication, November 1, 2011.

4. Jeff Tietz, "Boss Hog: The Rapid Rise of Industrial Swine," in *The CAFO Reader*, ed. Daniel Imhoff (Berkeley: University of California Press, 2010), 110.

5. M. S. Honeyman et al., "The United States Pork Niche Market Phenomenon," *Journal of Animal Science* 84 (2006), www.leopold.iastate.edu/research/marketing _files/NichePork_0806.pdf 2269, accessed October 15, 2010.

6. Thomas A. Green, personal communication, October 12, 2010. Interviews with Rick Schnieders, May 29, 2009, and Craig Watson, May 28, 2009.

7. USDA National Agricultural Statistics Service, "2007 Census of Agriculture," www.agcensus.usda.gov/Publications/2007/Online_Highlights/Specialty_Crops/spec crop.pdf, accessed October 19, 2010, 1.

8. 2009 Sysco Sustainable/Integrated Pest Management Initiative, accessed through Tom Green, IPM Institute, October 12, 2010.

9. Craig Watson, personal communication, October 7, 2010.

Chapter 6: Feeding the Green Economy

1. Anthony Flaccavento, personal communication, October 22, 2010.

2. Flaccavento presented at a February 11, 2010, webinar titled "Building the Supply of Healthy Foods—Experiences and Tools from the Field." It was sponsored by the National Good Food Network.

3. Eileen Brady, "New Seasons Market Case Study," *Ag-of-the-Middle Task Force Regional Case Studies* 1 (July 2004), www.agofthemiddle.org/pubs/newseasons.pdf, accessed October 14, 2010.

4. See http://newseasonsmarket.blogspot.com/2010/08/next-step.html, accessed October 20, 2010.

5. Michael Shuman, "Economic Impact of Localizing Detroit's Food System," www .fairfoodnetwork.org/resources/economic-impact-localizing-detroits-food-system.

6. Studies listed on BALLE website, www.livingeconomies.org/aboutus/research -and-studies/studies, accessed October 22, 2010.

7. Don Seville, Sustainable Food Lab, personal communication, October 24, 2010.

8. Sustainable Food Lab, www.sustainablefood.org/images/stories/pdf/hvcn%20 innovations%20master%20document%20v15.pdf, accessed June 2, 2009, 63.

Chapter 7: Becoming a Fair Food Activist

1. November 28, 2008, www.pbs.org/moyers/journal/11282008/watch2.html, accessed November 12, 2010.

2. Eliot Coleman, *Four-Season Harvest: Organic Vegetables from Your Home Garden All Year Long* (White River Junction, VT: Chelsea Green, 1999); *The New Organic Grower* (White River Junction, VT: Chelsea Green, 1995); *Winter Harvest Handbook* (White River Junction, VT: Chelsea Green, 2009).

3. The U.S. Department of Agriculture has one such list at www.nal.usda.gov/ afsic/pubs/csa/csa.shtml.

4. "Electronic Code of Federal Regulations," http://ecfr.gpoaccess.gov/cgi/t/
text/text-idx?c=ecfr&sid=baf51da897f7937de131c7ca43d710cb&rgn=div8&view
=text&node=7:3.1.1.9.32.2.354.6&idno=7, accessed October 25, 2010. Actual lists
are about twenty pages and can be found at http://ecfr.gpoaccess.gov/cgi/t/text/text
-idx?c=ecfr;sid=baf51da897f7937de131c7ca43d710cb;rgn=div5;view=text;node=
7%3A3.1.1.9.32;idno=7;cc=ecfr#7:3.1.1.9.32.7.354.

5. Ari Kurtz and Moira Donnel, organic CSA farmers, personal communication,
November 7, 2010.

6. See www.foodalliance.org.

7. J. S. Bailey and D. E. Cosby, USDA Agricultural Research Service, "Salmonella
Prevalence in Free-Range and Certified Organic Chickens," *Journal of Food Protection* 68, no. 11 (2005): 1, accessed October 20, 2010, http://ddr.nal.usda.gov/bitstream/
10113/36509/1/IND44295179.pdf.

8. Stephanie Dickison, "Eggs: Free Range, Cage Free, Organic . . . What's the Difference?" *Organic Lifestyle Magazine* 7 (February–March 2009), accessed October
20, 2010, www.organiclifestylemagazine.com/issue-7/eggs-free-range-cage-free
-organic.php.

9. Contained in Part 62 of Title 7 of the Code of Federal Regulations.

10. The codification states that "grass and forage shall be the feed source consumed for the lifetime of the ruminant animal, with the exception of milk consumed
prior to weaning. The diet shall be derived solely from forage consisting of grass (annual and perennial), forbs (e.g., legumes, *Brassica*), browse, or cereal grain crops in
the vegetative (pre-grain) state. Animals cannot be fed grain or grain byproducts and
must have continuous access to pasture during the growing season. Hay, silage, crop
residue without grain, and other roughage sources may also be included as acceptable
feed sources. Routine mineral and vitamin supplementation may also be included in
the feeding regimen. If incidental supplementation occurs due to inadvertent exposure
to non-forage feedstuffs or to ensure the animal's well being at all times during ad-
verse environmental or physical conditions, the producer must fully document (e.g.,
receipts, ingredients, and tear tags) the supplementation that occurs including the
amount, the frequency, and the supplements provided." Authority: 7 U.S.C. 1621–
1627. Effective Date: November 15, 2007.

USDA Agricultural Marketing Service, "United States Standards for Livestock and
Meat Marketing Claims, Grass (Forage) Fed Claim for Ruminant Livestock and the
Meat Products Derived from Such Livestock," *Federal Register* 72, no. 199 (October
16, 2007): 1, 7, accessed October 20, 2010, www.ams.usda.gov/AMSv1.0/getfile
?dDocName=STELPRDC5063842.

11. You can order it at www.montereybayaquarium.org/cr/cr_seafoodwatch/
sfw_recommendations.aspx.

12. Paul Greenberg, *Four Fish* (New York: Penguin, 2010).

13. USDA websites, including www.ams.usda.gov/AMSv1.0/ams.fetchTemplate
Data.do?template=TemplateC&navID=FarmersMarkets&rightNav1=Farmers
Markets&topNav=&leftNav=WholesaleandFarmersMarkets&page=WFMFarmers
MarketsHome&description=Farmers%20Markets&acct=frmrdirmkt and www.ams

.usda.gov/AMSv1.0/ams.fetchTemplateData.do?template=TemplateS&navID=Whole
saleandFarmersMarkets&leftNav=WholesaleandFarmersMarkets&page=WFM
FarmersMarketGrowth&description=Farmers%20Market%20Growth&acct=frm
rdirmkt, accessed October 7, 2010; USDA Agricultural Marketing Service, "Farmers
Markets and Local Food Marketing," www.ams.usda.gov/AMSv1.0/ams.fetchTemplate
Data.do?template=TemplateS&navID=WholesaleandFarmersMarkets&leftNav=Whole
saleandFarmersMarkets&page=WFMFarmersMarketGrowth&description=Farmers
%20Market%20Growth&acct=frmrdirmkt, accessed October 25, 2010.

14. Interview with Ashley Atkinson, October 7, 2010.

15. Fair Food Network, *Healthy Food for All,* www.fairfoodnetwork.org/resources/
healthy-food-for-all.

16. Report to the New York City Council on Green Carts FY2010, submitted by
the New York City Department of Health and Mental Hygiene, October 2010, www
.nyc.gov/html/doh/downloads/pdf/cdp/cdp-green-cart-report-cc.pdf, accessed November 2011.

17. Visit her website at www.karpresources.com.

18. Henry Herrera, Navina Khanna, and Leon Davis, "Food Systems and Public
Health: The Community Perspective," *Journal of Hunger & Environmental Nutrition* 4, no. 3 (2009): 430–445.

Chapter 8: Institutional Change

1. Anupama Joshi, Farm to School Network, personal communication, August
27, 2010; Zenobia Barlowe, Center for Ecoliteracy, personal communication, October 27, 2010.

2. Lunch and Breakfast Cost Study II (SLBCS II), www.fns.usda.gov/oane/
MENU/Published/CNP/FILES/MealCostStudy.pdf; www.fns.usda.gov/pd/slsummar
.htm; and www.fns.usda.gov/pd/sbsummar.htm, accessed October 27, 2010.

3. School Nutrition Association, *School Nutrition Operations Report 2011.* Susan
Coppess, personal communication, November 15, 2011.

4. Rochelle Davis, personal communications, August 27, 2010, and November
29, 2011.

5. Interview with Toni Liquori, September 21, 2010.

6. Anupama Joshi, personal communications, August 27, 2010, and November
19, 2011. $40 million for Farm to School was authorized in the Senate "Healthy,
Hunger Free Kids Act of 2010," the Senate base bill for Child Nutrition Reauthorization. This funding will be used for a Farm to School Competitive Grants program as suggested by Senator Leahy in the "Growing Farm to School Programs
Act" (SB 3123) and Representative Holt in the "Farm to School Improvements
Act" (HR 4710). www.farmtoschool.org/files/publications_272.pdf, accessed October 25, 2011.

7. A. Kwan, K. Mancinelli, and N. Freudenberg, *Recipes for Health: Improving
School Food in New York City,* Hunter College Healthy Public Policies Project and
City Harvest, 2010.

8. Curt Ellis, FoodCorps founder, personal communication, November 11, 2011.

9. The $5 billion figure is estimated by the USDA Economic Research Service and the National Association of College and University Food Services.

10. Anim Steel, personal communication, November 11, 2011.

11. Maren Stumme-Diers, sustainable foods educator, Luther College, personal communication, November 13, 2011.

12. Interview with Teresa Wiemerslage, Iowa State University Extension regional communications and program coordinator, November 11, 2010.

13. Interview with Ann Mansfield, August 26, 2010; Jon Jensen, director of environmental studies, Luther College, personal communication, October 20, 2010.

14. Jamie Harvie, Leslie Mikkelsen, and Linda Shak, "A New Health Care Prevention Agenda: Sustainable Food Procurement and Agricultural Policy," *Journal of Hunger and Environmental Nutrition* 4 (2009): 409–429.

15. "Kaiser Permanente Makes Great Strides in Sustainable Food for Health," November 8, 2011, http://xnet.kp.org/newscenter/aboutkp/green/stories/2011/110811 sustainablefood.html, accessed November 11, 2011.

16. Kathleen Reed, personal communication, September 4, 2010.

17. Harvie, Mikkelsen, and Shak, "A New Health Care Prevention Agenda: Sustainable Food Procurement and Agricultural Policy."

18. Interview with Jamie Harvie, September 2, 2010.

19. Stephanie Armour, "Corporate Cafeterias Go the Green, Healthy Route," *USA Today*, February 8, 2008, www.usatoday.com/money/workplace/2008-02-07-cafeteria -healthy_N.htm, accessed October 25, 2010.

20. Maisie Greenawalt, personal communication, November 4, 2010.

Chapter 9: Shifting Public Policy

1. According to Drake University Agricultural Law Center.

2. Barry Lonik, farmland preservation specialist, personal communication, December 21, 2011.

3. Rob Marqusee, personal communication, June 30, 2009.

4. Rob Marqusee, personal communication, October 8, 2010.

5. Michael Shuman, personal communication, October 11, 2010. He used data the USDA Economic Research Service last published in 2003, then adjusted it to current food consumption and the population in New Mexico to arrive at his number.

6. U.S. Department of Agriculture Economic Research Service, "Food CPI and Expenditures: Measuring the ERS Food Expenditure Series," www.ers.usda.gov /Briefing/CPIfoodandexpenditures/Data/Expenditures_tables/table5.htm, accessed December 21, 2011.

7. P.L. 396, 79th Congress, June 4, 1946, 60 Stat. 231.

8. See www.fns.usda.gov/snap/rules/Legislation/timeline.pdf#xml=http://65.216 .150.153/texis/search/pdfhi.txt?query=history+of+food+stamps&pr=FNS&prox=page &rorder=500&rprox=500&rdfreq=500&rwfreq=500&rlead=500&rdepth=0&sufs =0&order=r&cq=&id=4ca12ecd14.

9. A marketing assistance loan is a short-term loan from the government to the farmer with his/her crop as the collateral and the loan rate set by legislation. It allows

farmers to hold onto their crops so they don't all have to sell at the same time and drive prices down. It's essentially a way for the government to soften the rules of the marketplace for the farmer. If the price goes up the farmer pays back the loan with a little bit of interest and keeps the profit. If the price goes down the farmer gives his crop to the government instead of repaying the loan. These loans were established in 1933 and have gone through numerous permutations since then and gotten incredibly complicated. If you are interested in exploring them further, I recommend Scott Marlow's publication for RAFI, *A Non-Wonk Guide to Understanding Federal Commodity Payments* (www.rafiusa.org).

10. "Web Site to Promote Food Stamp Reform," http://m.upi.com/m/story/UPI-91291323835427, accessed December 23, 2011.

11. USDA Economic Research Service, "Farm and Commodity Policy: Government Payments and the Farm Sector," www.ers.usda.gov/Briefing/Farmpolicy/gov-pay .htm, accessed November 16, 2010.

12. Noel Blisard, Hayden Stewart, and Dean Jolliffe, *Low-Income Households' Expenditures on Fruits and Vegetables*, May 2004, p. 22, www.ers.usda.gov/publications/ aer833/aer833.pdf.

13. U.S. Department of Agriculture Food and Nutrition Service, *Request for Application: Supplemental Nutrition Assistance Program Healthy Incentives Pilot*, CFDA #10.580 (December 18, 2009): 7, www.fns.usda.gov/snap/hip/docs/RFA.pdf, accessed October 7, 2010.

14. Dr. Reed Tuckson, executive vice president, United Health, "Refocusing the National Food System," presented at the Sustainable Agriculture & Food Systems Funders Forum, Philadelphia, June 17, 2010.

INDEX

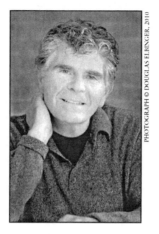

Dr. Oran B. Hesterman is the president and CEO of Fair Food Network. For fifteen years, he co-led the Integrated Farming Systems and Food and Society programs for the W.K. Kellogg Foundation, during which time the foundation seeded the local food systems movement with over $200 million. A native of Berkeley, California, and a former professor of agronomy at Michigan State University in East Lansing, he currently lives in Ann Arbor, Michigan.